REMARKS ON ARCHITECTURE

REMARKS ON ARCHITECTURE

THE VITRUVIAN TRADITION IN ENLIGHTENMENT POLAND

IGNACY POTOCKI

Edited and translated by Carolyn C. Guile

The Pennsylvania State University Press
University Park, Pennsylvania

Library of Congress Cataloging-in-Publication Data

Potocki, Ignacy, 1750–1809, author.
[Uwagi o architekturze. English]
Remarks on architecture : the Vitruvian tradition
in enlightenment Poland / Ignacy Potocki ;
edited and translated by Carolyn C. Guile.
pages   cm
Summary: "A translation of Polish politician and
architect Ignacy Potocki's unpublished treatise
Remarks on Architecture. Includes an introduction
that places Potocki and the treatise within the
political, social, and cultural context of eighteenth-
century Poland"—Provided by publisher.
Includes bibliographical references and index.
ISBN 978-0-271-06628-8 (cloth : alk. paper)
ISBN 978-0-271-06629-5 (pbk. : alk. paper)
1. Architecture—Poland—Early works to 1800.
2. Architecture—Early works to 1800.
3. Potocki, Ignacy, 1750–1809.
I. Guile, Carolyn C., editor, translator.
II. Title.

NA1455.P6P6813   2015
720.9438'09034—dc23
2014044324

The Pennsylvania State University Press is a member
of the Association of American University Presses.

FOR *my parents*

CONTENTS

———◆◆※◆◆———

LIST OF ILLUSTRATIONS

Maps

Figures

The origins of this book reside in a series of encounters with Poland's early modern architecture and a desire to understand the ideas that informed it. Absent from standard surveys of Western arts and architectures, early modern Polish architectural thought has escaped the notice of most Anglophone scholars otherwise attuned to European developments of the sixteenth through eighteenth centuries. My choice to excavate and study Ignacy Potocki's late eighteenth-century treatise on architecture emerges from my interest in architectural theory in relation to the intellectual history of early modern Poland and to both national identity and artistic geography. Studies in English of early modern architectural theory and practice have yet fully to examine developments in Eastern or East-Central Europe. The territory of the vast Polish-Lithuanian Commonwealth, comprising what is now Poland, Lithuania, Belarus, and western Ukraine, formed an important European borderland—a term that has seen broad application but that here refers to the region between the German lands of the Holy Roman Empire and the former empires of Russia and the Ottomans.[1] The invocation of the term "borderland" here acknowledges earlier scholarship, such as Oscar Halecki's project, that contributed to the introduction of East-Central Europe to a Western readership. Halecki's impetus arose in part from the imperatives of his time, a moment when the area from the Soviet Baltic countries through Hungary was isolated from the West, cut off by the Iron Curtain; he aimed to demonstrate the relationship of this area, broadly speaking, to Western traditions—to explain that these places too experienced a "renaissance," an "enlightenment," and historically and culturally did not sit apart from western continental Europe. The work sought to shed light on this "vast *terra incognita* of European historiography"[2] and focused primarily on political developments. The discipline of art

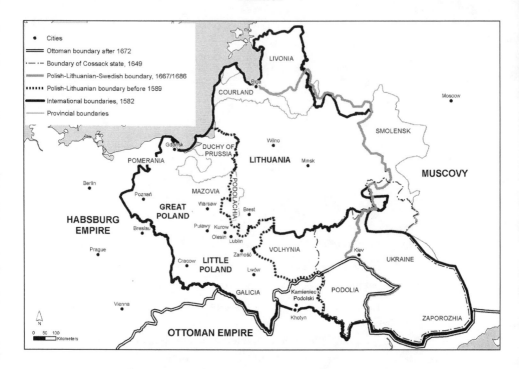

MAP 1   Poland-Lithuania at its greatest extent, in the seventeenth century.
Map by Myonsung Kong and Carolyn Guile.

history has been slow to consider this region, in part due to very real, practical
issues such as language barriers, limited or restricted access to primary and
secondary sources, and the misconception that wartime destruction left little
to study. As the situation began to change in the 1990s, the subject matter, in
the words of Katarzyna Murawska-Muthesius, "instigated . . . the vexed issue
of a kind of local European Orientalism" that grappled with the "ontological
status of the apparently indisputable border between Western and East Central, or Eastern European art, and the notoriety of teleological projections of
the Iron Curtain divide into the past."[3]

Informed by the study of cultural geography, the consideration of paradigmatic fault lines in the East European borderland has been moving away from
rigid distinctions between East and West in order to address the less tidy but
extremely interesting problem of multidirectional cultural transfer across
boundaries that were in important ways porous. In turn, strict notions of
artistic "centers" and "peripheries" have been challenged. I had become interested in this particular issue first while studying topics such as the "Orient" in

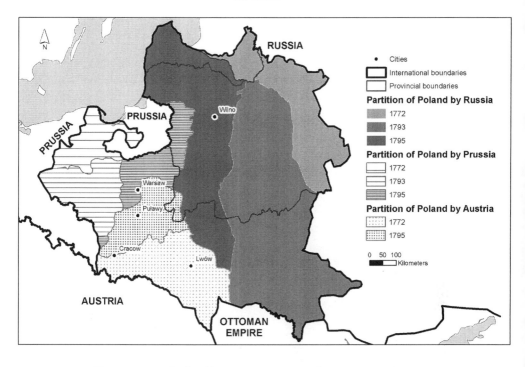

MAP 2   The partitions of Poland by Prussia, Russia, and Austria, 1772, 1793, 1795.
Map by Myonsung Kong and Carolyn Guile.

Polish-Lithuanian visual culture[4] and in vernacular architecture; I arrived at
the basic conclusion that models explaining the transmission of artistic and
architectural form across space needed to be understood not as unidirectional
but as multidirectional—that the transmission of ideas and forms in borderland areas should be understood not as diluted expressions arriving or trans-
planted strictly from a unique point of origin but as having emerged from
within a more complex environment that resulted in a truly multicultural
expression in which the notion of "origins" played an important role. The
problem of Western architecture's origins received its first articulation in
Vitruvius's late first-century B.C.E. text, *De architectura;* the rediscovery of
that text by Italian humanists in the early fifteenth century prompted early
modern architectural theoreticians to return to Vitruvius's conception of the
primitive hut in their discussions about architecture's beginnings. Turning in
part from Vitruvian exegesis to a questioning of Vitruvius's absolute authority, Enlightenment-era architectural theoreticians continuously returned to the
theme of origins in works that analyzed the concepts of beauty, proportion,

and the Vitruvian triad: *firmitàs, utilitàs,* and *venustàs,* the most persistent points of departure.[5]

The Polish art historian Jan Białostocki's conception of vernacular expression in architecture and his formulation of the relationship between borrowing and originality represent other important points of departure for the analysis of architectural theory and practice in early modern Eastern Europe. Although his goals were not dissimilar to Halecki's, Białostocki tended to focus more on the alignment of Eastern European tendencies in the arts with traditional Western ones and considered things that did not fit neatly within the scheme vernacular expressions, far removed from a center of conceptual origin.[6] While Białostocki's use of the "vernacular" to account for a "hybrid" art form in Poland that resulted from a combination of Italian, Netherlandish, Germanic, and local elements has been useful, it is insufficient for an understanding and interpretation of the regional artistic and architectural cultures of the borderlands. Attitudes expressed in other recent scholarship theorize the place of these cultures in the histories of European arts and culture more broadly, providing other in-routes for understanding its monuments and primary sources.[7] Beyond the idea of the periphery, which for Białostocki implies a diluted reception of a salient idea or form, scholars have revisited the notions of place and localization as these pertain to the relationship of geography to historical change, especially that change which constitutes the history of art.[8] Likewise, studies of East European or East-Central European arts and architectures in relation to the definitions of "peripheries" and "transidentities" have questioned whether art and geography can be separated and whether the analysis of arts and architectures ought to consider first and foremost spatial and geographical factors or historical change. What this scholarship has in common is its questioning of the division of the history of art into different periods with distinct regional boundaries according to nationalist models.[9] With specific interest in the Polish context, and akin to Białostocki's work, other studies have taken a comparative approach that attempts to frame the Polish achievement in art and architecture in relation to that of other European centers.[10] Contrasting with the preservation of strict or anachronistic boundaries between national cultures is the introduction of the metaphor of "circulation" to describe the production and use, transmission and reception, of culture in all its forms.[11]

Apart from isolated studies on patronage, English-language scholarship has addressed the arts and architecture of the Polish-Lithuanian Enlightenment only infrequently, and usually in the context of the patronage of the Commonwealth's last king, Stanisław August Poniatowski (r. 1764–95).[12] The problem besets mainland European scholarship as well. As Mario Carpo has pointed out in his study on the printed architectural treatise in the early modern period, "the absence of any discussion of the editions [of architectural treatises] in the Slavic languages [is] not the result of deliberate omissions but [is] the unfortunate consequence of the rarity of primary materials—and of their remoteness."[13] Potocki's treatise stands as one such rare example, belonging to the works of Poland-Lithuania's gentlemen architects and amateurs, statesmen and clerics who saw the arts and architecture as the vehicle for conveying social, official or national cultural values. Most studies in the Polish language are monographic, dedicated to a single architect or a specific monument. These works, as well as ongoing encyclopedic projects surveying monuments by region, prove indispensable for the scholar interested in the Polish-Lithuanian Commonwealth's built environment.[14] No study in English treats the early modern architectural treatise in the East European borderlands or early modern Polish-language architectural theory. Ignacy Potocki's treatise, the *Remarks on Architecture,* dating from around 1786 or possibly later, is here printed, translated, and contextualized for the first time. The questions raised by the treatise and its context are not confined to Polish subjects but rather are relevant to early modern Europe more broadly. Further, the *Remarks on Architecture* represents an exemplar of an emergent national tradition of architectural writing that deserves further study.

Why read a work of Polish architectural theory, a didactic treatise for the Polish nobility wishing to improve their estates and a statement of its author's aesthetic principles? The significance of Potocki's work resides in part in its interpretation of a common past, a subject raised initially by Halecki in a broad historical context and considered by Potocki more specifically within an art-historical one. The treatise illuminates the extent to which its author shared or denied that past and thought about architecture in his own land in relation to achievements elsewhere—from Vitruvius's ideas through those of authors who engaged them while formulating their own principles. Poland's relevance to a broader history of European artistic culture and value extends beyond the reaches of the Commonwealth's own historically mutable borders. This book is concerned not only with the treatise's situation within Polish architectural history but also, and more broadly, with how historical artifacts such as Potocki's treatise facilitate and contribute to an understanding of architecture and political culture within Europe's easternmost borderlands in a time of constant change, within an Enlightenment context, and in relation to similar principles explicated in the Continental literature from which Potocki drew. Here I am embracing Carpo's point that "when we speak of architecture we may mean either something built or a body of knowledge—a collection of experiences that may be transformed into models or rules and that continues to exist only if these are recorded, accumulated, and transmitted. . . . Vitruvian architectural theory did not escape either in its form or content from the conditions of use inherent in the manuscript medium."[15] Potocki's manuscript is characterized by an urgent imperative to foreground, to define, and to cultivate the ideas he found most suited to architecture for the Commonwealth as learned and derived from Greco-Roman example, Vitruvius, and early modern textual traditions that followed from these. Political instability engendered in the Polish nobility a consciousness of the need to articulate the exigencies for the reform not only of politics but of culture itself. Their aims were both reformist and preservationist in nature.

ACKNOWLEDGMENTS

Over the course of writing this book I have incurred professional and personal debts too numerous to count in the space allotted here. This book would not have been possible without the generosity and encouragement of my first Polish language teacher, Viola Próchniak at the Katolicki Uniwersytet Lubelski Jana Pawła II. I am indebted to the late Michael Baxandall for encouraging me to explore early modern East-Central European achievements in the field of art and architectural history. John Pinto and Jerome Silbergeld enthusiastically supported my interest in bringing this material to light. Jeffrey Herbst provided me with my first funding opportunity to visit Polish archives during my studies at Princeton University's Department of Art and Archaeology. I also owe my sincere gratitude to Prof. Dr. hab. Andrzej Rottermund, Prof. Dr. hab. Adam Żiółkowski, and Przemysław Wątroba, Gabinet Rycin, Biblioteka Uniwersytetu Warszawskiego, who provided indispensable advice in the project's early stages and access to the architectural drawings printed in this volume. The insights and advice of Prof. Dr. hab. Marcin Fabiański, Dr. Joanna Wolańska, and Prof. Dr. hab. Wojciech Bałus also mark these pages. I am grateful to each of them. I have been fortunate to have the assistance of the archivists at the Archiwum Główne Akt Dawnych who granted me access to Ignacy Potocki's original manuscript, and of the custodians of special collections at the Biblioteka Narodowa and the Muzeum Narodowe, Warsaw, for permission to view and reproduce architectural drawings from their collections. I thank Kenneth Belanger and the Colgate University Research Council for funding that defrayed the cost of image reproductions and permissions, as well as for research-related travel support. Robert Frost and Anna Brzyski provided me with indispensable feedback on the manuscript as well as excellent suggestions for my continued work on the subject of the intersection between architecture and political culture in early modern East-Central Europe. I am also grateful to Paweł Styrna for his assistance with matters of transcription. I thank Ania Wellisz who helped me bring Potocki to life. At the Pennsylvania State University Press, Eleanor Goodman's interest and inquisitiveness have been critical to this work at every stage. I also thank Charlee Redman and Laura Reed-Morrisson for their cheer and attention to detail, as well as Keith Monley for his editorial grace and acumen. These acknowledgments would not be complete without mention of my appreciation for the input of numerous colleagues, including Nadja Aksamija, Claire Baldwin, Clorinda Donato, Ludovico Geymonat, Nicola Knipe, Tine Meganck, Heather Hyde Minor, Vernon Minor, Olenka Pevny, Naomi Rood, Wendy Roworth, Kira Stevens, Emily Sun, Frank Sysyn, Larry Wolff, and Michael Yonan, over the course of this project. I reserve special gratitude for my teacher Thomas DaCosta Kaufmann, whose erudition and respect for primary sources have served as examples to me as a scholar. I warmly thank Val and Daisy Fitch for the friendship and hospitality they have shown me for many years. David Frick's philological and historical expertise has challenged and inspired me. Finally, I note with deep appreciation my parents, Christine and Roy Guile. Their support and particular—indeed peculiar—sense of humor continues to guide me.

A NOTE ON THE TEXT

My transcription in Polish of Ignacy Potocki's manuscript "Uwagi o architek-turze" (Remarks on architecture) is based on direct contact with the original document at the Archiwum Główne Akt Dawnych (Central Archive of Early Records) in Warsaw. Eighteenth-century Polish sentence structures are complex and highly Latinate. While I have inserted diacritics where necessary, I have preserved Potocki's orthography in the transcription so as to remain faithful to the original text in its historical moment. Potocki's spelling is inconsistent in places within the treatise itself, but I have not corrected these inconsistencies. I have preserved Polish archaisms throughout ("ia" for "ja"). In places where the handwriting in the treatise is unclear, I have stated so in the notes and used ellipses.

In translating Potocki's text and other archival sources, I have taken care to remain as faithful to the text as possible while introducing punctuation and phrasing in English that preserves the connectivity of ideas. I inserted connector words or phrases, indicated with square brackets, or reiterated referents where necessary in order to clarify Potocki's meaning. I have used syntax more friendly to the English language while maintaining Polish meaning in the translation of vocabulary. Except in instances for which English forms exist, I have preserved Polish forms for place names within the Polish-Lithuanian Commonwealth. Where convenient, I have also chosen standard spellings for names (e.g., Buonarroti).

Potocki indicates clearly that he borrowed from many sources when composing his text. He frequently paraphrased and combined sources without explicitly naming them. While my aim is not to identify every last source he may have consulted, I do wish to impart to the reader the nature of some of those sources, as well as how he employed them conceptually.

Potocki's text includes references to figures and illustrations that I am presuming he either designed himself or commissioned. Unfortunately, these images were separated from the document at an unknown point in time and to date remain lost. One hopes they will one day be reunited with the treatise.

INTRODUCTION

————◆▸✕◂◆————

Beware.
The same fate to which other fields are subject befalls architecture. All the
tomes written in this manner serve the master more than the student. And that
is why those who without a mentor who wish to have any knowledge of
architecture whatsoever are at first intimidated merely by looking at the great
tomes. And, so to speak, they lose desire to read them before they
even begin to understand the subject.
—IGNACY POTOCKI, *Remarks on Architecture*

The Manuscript and Its Author

Notable among the surviving examples of architectural theory written by Polish
authors in the early modern period is a heretofore unpublished, late eighteenth-
century treatise, *Remarks on Architecture,* by Ignacy Potocki (1750–1809).
Addressed to the nobility, or *szlachta,* and written in a conversational style,
Potocki's treatise conveyed the lessons of what might be called a Vitruvian
canon, which shaped Continental classical architectural theory and practice
throughout the early modern period. Potocki advanced the claim that patrons
and architects could significantly alleviate society's ills by raising architecture
in the country to a higher standard, comparable to that of neighboring countries and consistent with a shared Latinate orientation. Although patrons bore
responsibility for funding the construction of edifices that ennobled the Commonwealth in the private and public domains alike, he called upon authors and
architects to mentor and to lead, and to convey the received rules of architecture
in a clear, accessible manner.

1

For seventeenth- and eighteenth-century practitioners, both professional and amateur, discussions and writing about architecture and the arts in Poland took many forms, ranging from formal treatises dedicated to the king to didactic manuals, letters, private journals, and scattered notes. Polish scholars have written monographic studies of Polish architects, and general Enlightenment studies on Polish art and architecture are plentiful (in Polish), but apart from Stefan Muthesius's brief survey in *Art, Architecture, and Design in Poland, 966–1990,* no general study of eighteenth-century East European or Polish architecture exists in English, nor has there been an in-depth study of early modern East European or Polish art and architectural theory per se. In isolated instances, scholars have acknowledged the impact of Continental ideas on Polish Enlightenment projects; the treatises of Marc-Antoine Laugier (1753) and later of Jean-Nicolas-Louis Durand (1800) informed Polish writing about architecture; André Le Nôtre's work influenced the form of Polish palace and garden design.[1] Architectural theory emerging in early modern Poland-Lithuania and written both by professional architects and amateurs sometimes reached beyond the scope of technical matters and addressed the problems of beauty, stability, and progress, both domestic and national, in relation to progress in the arts, with varying and intriguing results. The *Remarks on Architecture* reveals an author aware of his perspective and of his participation in a Continental dialogue as he raised the issues of local custom and need. Significantly, a text such as Potocki's broadens our understanding of European architectural history and theory during the early modern period through its translation and absorption of primary sources known on the eastern borderlands of Europe. The last decades of the eighteenth century are revelatory of the ways in which patrons and theoreticians of architecture collaborated with practitioners to construct the Polish-Lithuanian Commonwealth's cultural relationship to classical and European visual expression and connected their political goals with their aesthetic interests and didactic agendas. Form carried social meaning.

Ignacy Potocki is best known as a figure who played a crucial role in the Commonwealth's conversation about the durability of its statehood. Notably, he coauthored the 3 May 1791 Constitution, intended to be permanent. In her exquisite pastel portrait of Potocki dating to 1783 or 1784, Anna Gault de Saint Germain, née Rajecka (1762–1832),[2] portrayed Potocki as a patriot decorated with the star of the Order of the White Eagle, the Crown's highest honor (fig. 1). Like his brother Stanisław Kostka Potocki (1755–1821)—author of the first major art-historical text in the Polish language—he saw a direct relationship

FIG. 1   Anna Gault de Saint Germain, née Rajecka, *Portrait of Ignacy Potocki*,
1783–84. Pastel on paper, 61 × 50 cm. The Museum of King Jan III's Palace at
Wilanów, Warsaw.

between the survival of the Commonwealth and the cultivation of architecture and the arts, to which may be appended related rules governing taste. To read Ignacy Potocki's work is to consider the nature, variety, extensions, and limits of Western culture in an area geographically remote from the Italian lands that produced the buildings and architectural ideas the Potocki brothers most admired, but intellectually connected to its traditions. The *Remarks on Architecture* should be understood in the context of social and political reform at a moment when Stanisław Kostka Potocki's interests in aesthetics, art, and the relationship of the two to self- and national improvement appeared. Motivated by their commitment to education and together with other individuals in their circle, such as Grzegorz Piramowicz (1735–1801) and Hugo Kołłątaj (1750–1812), the Potocki brothers worked to reform the monarchy and citizenry through a variety of means.

While the text of the *Remarks* is chiefly a didactic treatise designed to educate a nobleman about best practices in architecture, the grammar of ornament, the origins of "true architecture," and standards and beauty, the ideas recorded within it allude to the need for cultural preservation during a protracted political crisis and period of national eradication, when the constitution was overturned shortly after its implementation and the Commonwealth was by 1795 partitioned in its entirety among Prussia, Russia, and Austria. In spite of their catastrophic political consequences, the partitions had a tangible and positive effect on independent cultural expression. Potocki's text presents the present-day reader with an opportunity to consider the extent to which Continental theoretical literature—the Vitruvian canon[3]— informed the attitudes toward architecture of like-minded members of the *szlachta* estate, who shared the author's interests in building a stronger republic through the mechanisms of reform. Architecture could signify and embody cultural values, bearing the traces of the ideals and principles of their practitioners and of the writers on architecture who formulated the relationship between form and content.

Potocki's treatise also stresses the role of architecture in the formation and critique of broader national traditions in a moment of intensive postmortem regarding the status of the *respublica*. Architecture was directly affected by problems of impermanence and instability and what some theorists criticized as the transient fashions born of mere taste; as tangible cultural property, it represented the outward expression of identity and allegiance to theoretical, practical, and aesthetic norms. Polish authors of art and architectural literature seeking solutions to impermanence and instability were cognizant of both the durability and liability of tradition.

The transcription of the treatise that follows its translation is based on a manuscript in the Archiwum Publiczne Potockich at the Archiwum Główne Akt Dawnych in Warsaw. While I believe it circulated in its day in manuscript form, to my knowledge it has never been printed in any language and has received only passing mention, by Polish scholars concerned with Potocki's activities as a politician and educator. There has been no art-historical analysis of the document.[4] The few Polish historians who have mentioned the *Remarks on Architecture* have limited their observations to Potocki's own modest description of his treatise as a "mosaic" comprising references to other sources and have stated that this dependence upon other sources demonstrates a lack of originality.[5] But a treatise of this kind, in which its author announces and sometimes credits his sources while establishing his own positions relative to the subject at hand, reveals the ways in which culture and ideas travel and how they are received. The value of Potocki's treatise lies also in what it reveals about the way a Pole, or someone living in and working from the eastern borderlands of Europe, would recognize, acknowledge, and assimilate foreign ideas and concepts, betraying a sense of affinity with a canon of ideas that shaped the classical tradition in other regions and embracing the pragmatic tone of its dicta. The text of the *Remarks on Architecture* embodies Potocki's comprehension of architecture's historical trajectory and the reasons for its rise and fall, intimating larger lessons for his compatriots and their legacy. Throughout, Potocki makes it plain that decline could be averted only through knowledge of the past combined with experience itself. This thinking echoed that of his colleague Stanisław Staszic (1755–1826), who in his *Warnings for Poland* (1790) made clear to his countrymen his positions about the dangers of their ignorance and fixed attitudes regarding tradition.[6] Correct architecture, Potocki held, provided evidence of cultural fortitude in the face of uncertainty. His work is guided by an autodidactic approach to the theoretical tradition of architectural writing and instruction to which he felt anyone interested in architecture would and must refer.

Knowledge of foreign languages, as well as the accessibility of ideas through the medium of engraving, enabled Commonwealth citizens interested in architecture to understand, assimilate, and transform ideas arriving from beyond the Polish-Lithuanian borders. The advances in architectural education made by the Piarist and Jesuit orders beginning in the 1730s in turn enhanced interest in architectural theoretical writings. Polish works did appear, such as those by the Jesuit professor Józef Rogaliński (1728–1802) and by students as well, who were exposed to French and German works by the likes of Delorme (1567), Blondel (1683), Perrault (1676), and Laugier (1753), among the French sources, and Penther (1745), Goldmann (1696), and Sturm (1717), among the German.[7] The appearance of these texts within Polish intellectual circles, where they were discussed or used and where the indigenous theoretical tradition was uneven, points toward Potocki's assimilation of that tradition and use of it for local but not exclusively Polish ends.

Educated at the Colegium Nazarenum in Rome from 1765 to 1768 and later at the Colegium Nobilium in Warsaw, Potocki was a product of the reformed Polish Piarist pedagogical tradition whose exponents promoted and wrote about the tenets of good citizenship as early as the 1740s and held assemblies in which students put forth their ideas on how to improve Polish customs— "how to make our fatherland a happier place."[8] Of central importance to the curriculum for the Colegium Nobilium was character building and love of the "fatherland," as well as instruction in Latin and other languages;[9] the curriculum also emphasized Polish history, geography, and rhetoric. As a man of letters, Ignacy managed the Załuski Library, Poland's first public and national library.[10] He was a close cohort of the statesman Adam Kazimierz Czartoryski (1734–1823) and the "Familia," who gathered frequently at Czartoryski's estate in Puławy (near Lublin), and was a central figure in politics during the reformist Four-Year Sejm (parliament) of 1788–92. His involvement in the reform of the Polish education system in the 1770s and 1780s reinforced his natural inclination to embrace the didactic potential of architecture to improve the citizenry. He had accomplished a great deal in the civic realm by the time he died, in 1809, at the age of fifty-nine. His pursuits, both recreational and professional, included politics, pedagogy, dramaturgy, poetry, and historiography; like his brother, he demonstrated a serious interest in architecture and maintained associations with the most important architects working in the Commonwealth, both before and after the partitions.

Celebrated as an author of the Commonwealth's 3 May 1791 Constitution, he was also famous as a member of one of the Commonwealth's most prominent families, whose art collections and libraries were among the nation's most extensive and esteemed, rivaling those of the king himself. Potocki's travels to Italy and France in the early 1770s and from Vienna to Italy in 1783 contributed to his familiarity with Continental writings about function, beauty, and proportion in architecture;[11] his collaborations and conversations with his brother further shaped his thinking about architecture's principles. In no

other Polish library of the time were there so many Italian architectural treatises as there were in his sibling Stanisław's library; the brothers shared ideas
on architecture, and each left behind many drawings, some of which survived
the bombardments of the Second World War.[12] While in Rome in 1769, Ignacy
began an album of his own architectural drawings, including a plan of Bor-
romini's church of Sant'Agnese (fig. 2) and a signed drawing of a plan for the
ground floor and *piano nobile* of a palace that in its disposition of rooms
echoes Palladio's recommendations regarding size, placement, and symmetry
(fig. 3). Drawings for a Greek-cross church display his engagement with Palladian approaches to sacred architecture (figs. 4 and 5) and also recall structures in Warsaw itself he would have known intimately, such as the Church of
the Holy Sacrament (1688–92), by the Dutch Palladian architect Tylman van
Gameren (b. Utrecht 1632, d. Warsaw 1706).[13]

His experiences abroad were fairly representative for most influential Polish *szlachta,* in spite of the Commonwealth's size and the difficulties of crossing it. Literature and travel facilitated the Potocki brothers' collecting activities;
the Potocki library also contained extensive eighteenth-century travel writings

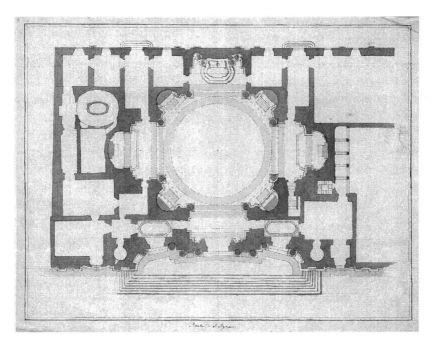

FIG. 2   Ignacy Potocki, plan of Sant'Agnese, Rome, ca. 1769. Pen, graphite, ink on
paper, 34.3 × 45.2 cm. Warsaw National Library.

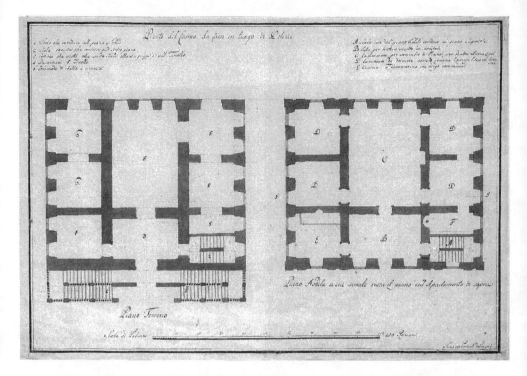

FIG. 3 Ignacy Potocki, plan for the ground floor and *piano nobile* of a palace. Signed "Ignazio Potocki disegno." Pen, graphite, ink on paper, 34.2 × 49.3 cm. Warsaw National Library.

that would inform Stanisław Kostka Potocki's *On the History of the Art of the Ancients, or the Polish Winckelmann (O sztuce u dawnych, czyli Winkelman polski,* 1815).[14] Several early modern editions of Vitruvius's *De architectura* appear in the library inventory;[15] the collection included *Vitruvius Britannicus* (London, 1701, and Campbell's 1725 edition), *Le Vitruve danois* (1740), and *M. Vitruvii Pollonis de architectura libri decem* (Rome, 1586; Amsterdam, 1649). Like most European writers on architecture before him, Ignacy Potocki would designate Vitruvius as the fundamental authority, though not without qualification. Also in the collection were a 1663 Venetian edition of Sebastiano Serlio's *Architettura,* the *Architettura di M. Vitruvio Pollione colla traduzione Italiana e comento del marchese Bernardo Galiani* (1758), *L'idea della architettura universale di Vicenzo Scamozzi* (1615), *Architettura di Palladio di Vicense a Venise* (1740), and *Architettura di Alberti di Cosimo Bartoli* (1726), to name but a few tomes.[16]

8

FIG. 4   Ignacy Potocki, *Project for a Central-Plan Church*, ca. 1772, plan. Pen, graphite, ink on paper, 34.0 × 23.6 cm. Gabinet Rycin, University of Warsaw Library.

FIG. 5   Ignacy Potocki, *Project for a Central-Plan Church*, ca. 1772, elevation with Tuscan pilasters, four attic statues, and cupola with lantern. Pen, graphite, ink on paper, 34.5 × 24.2 cm. Gabinet Rycin, University of Warsaw Library.

Architectural Theory in Early Modern Poland

In the fifteenth century, Vitruvius's *Ten Books on Architecture* had circulated in the humanist circles of Gregory of Sanok (1403–1477), archbishop of Lwów, as well as the Jagiellonian court in Cracow, where Copernicus studied Vitruvius's ideas on astronomical observatories.[17] Fra Giocondo's 1511 edition of Vitruvius and Daniele Barbaro's 1556 edition have been traced to Renaissance Polish collections; the works of Serlio and Alberti were also known within humanist circles. Just as Łukasz Górnicki adapted Castiglione's *Il cortegiano* to Polish customs and requirements in his work *The Polish Courtier* (*Dworzanin polski*), of 1566, sporadic writings on architecture also transposed inherited knowledge and advice to a Polish readership. This reveals the central role writers active in the Polish territories assigned to foreign authorities on matters of local significance. Practitioners' engagement with a foreign tradition in architectural thinking, including consideration of license, ornament, and the rules governing the architectonic orders, was a barometer of social thought in the same way as the "transposition"—to employ Peter Burke's term[18]—of a literary text into an interpretive community answered the cultural needs and perceptions of that group. The first "Vitruvian" Polish architectural treatise, the *Brief Study of the Construction of Manor Houses, Palaces, and Castles According to the Polish Sky [or Heavens] and Customs* (*Krótka nauka budownicza dworów, pałaców, zamków podług nieba i zwyczaju polskiego*), appeared in 1659; it is thought to have been written by the important statesman and writer Łukasz Opaliński, who also served as Court Marshal to the Crown. The work includes Scamozzi's early seventeenth-century designs for a *palazzo in fortezza* in the town of Zbaraż (Ukrainian: Zbarazh), about 150 kilometers east of Lwów (Ukrainian: L'viv), for the magnate Krzysztof Zbaraski (1579–1627).[19] Ignacy Potocki's eighteenth-century work is thematically linked to the *Brief Study* in the sense that both writers discuss elements of a specifically "Polish way" of building based on local custom and needs. These Polish authors may have gravitated toward Scamozzi's *L'idea della architettura universale* for its humanist undertones and its grounding of architecture in philosophy, and also because that architect's own travels north, to destinations including Paris, Prague, Budapest, and Colmar, "often led him to reflect upon matters of building and the connections between form and local materials."[20] Potocki's treatise demonstrates that the Polish reception of Vitruvius and other Italian sources was by no means uncritical, which in turn indicates that Polish writers and readers were active interpreters, rather than passive receivers, of the ideas therein. Interestingly, the Jesuit Bartłomiej Nataniel Wąsowski's *Callitectoni-corum seu de Pulchro Architecturae Sacrae et Civilis Compendio Collectorum* (Poznań, 1678), with drawings after Scamozzi's *L'idea,* rejected Vitruvius as its authority according to "what the custom of the Republic discards," starting its discussion instead with Scamozzi "for the ways in which he does a service to architecture."[21] Potocki too would echo the notion that the lessons espoused by Vitruvius were not foolproof and were at times in conflict with local needs.

Potocki's *Remarks on Architecture* thus appeared long after Polish writers and practitioners had already experimented with the Italian architectural theoretical tradition, and in part followed the trend in Piarist and Jesuit education, beginning in the second quarter of the eighteenth century, to introduce architecture and its elements to young noblemen, drawing upon not only Vitruvius but a wide range of Continental sources. Until the end of the eighteenth century, the Poles did not embark upon translations of foreign treatises, not even Vitruvius—in part because the *szlachta* were well versed in foreign languages, as letters and library inventories reflect. The first Polish translation of Scamozzi did not appear until 1791, and it was not a "faithful" translation, because the ideas of other theorists had been added. The author of the *Brief Study,* however, did publish Scamozzi's illustrations in his own text. Just as architectural drawings circulated elsewhere through the medium of printed treatise illustrations, in Poland too printed designs were fundamental to the reception of the Vitruvian canon. As Mario Carpo observes, "For some moderns, beginning in the sixteenth century (or rather as early as the mid-fifteenth century . . .), the mass production of identical architectural elements was considered to be neither a calamity, nor an abomination, nor a sacrilege."[22] Styles were transmitted to Poland via prints much as Palladio's *Four Books on Architecture* circulated widely in foreign lands, largely owing to the appeal and utility of its demonstrative illustrations. Polish scholarship has long recognized the early modern transmission of Palladian, Serlian, and Scamozzian ideas through prints. Architectural historian Jerzy Kowalczyk, for example, notes that although Vitruvius and Alberti were known in Poland before Serlio, Serlio's work was particularly important because it was more concise and was richly illustrated. He adds that the adaptation of Serlio meant a reduction of the elements, not an elaboration upon them; at times, Kowalczyk claims, substitutions were made according to the desires of patrons, although he does not substantiate this point. He deems Łukasz Opaliński and Bartłomiej Wąsowski the two main authors inspired by "Serlian" example.[23] In general, an assessment of the relative importance of architectural theory to Polish practitioners and writers cannot be based solely on the paucity in archival records of direct translations of foreign treatises into Polish. It was not until the third quarter of the eighteenth century that scholars, writers, and educators began to attend to the reform and purification of the Polish language in order to eliminate foreign elements and expressions from it. This "belated" consciousness of the inherent national importance of the native language constitutes further evidence that those who owned foreign texts had knowledge of other languages—particularly Latin and French. What the *Brief Study* and Ignacy Potocki's *Remarks on Architecture,* as well as Stanisław Kostka Potocki's *Polish Winckelmann,* share is their conscious assessment and transformation of the ideas contained in the source texts to suit Polish needs and situations.

Polish scholars have claimed that based on conservative inventories of sixteenth- and seventeenth-century libraries, Polish collections do not reveal excessive interest in the books that treat the theory of architecture, except in special circumstances.[24] In the second half of the seventeenth century the classic treatises in French, English, German, and especially Italian started to be used didactically, as manuals for the education of the young nobility. The religious orders, being the centers for education, used architectural treatises thus. Attempts such as Potocki's to assess the lessons of the Vitruvian canon as the universally authoritative source for architectural theory are, by extension, evidence of tradition formation and reflection upon it. Architecture could serve as a corrective to the ignorance of tradition remarked upon by foreigners, such as the French ex-Jesuit Hubert Vautrin.[25] At or around the time Potocki composed the *Remarks on Architecture,* the Polish nation was mired in political crisis, disdained by its neighbors, and pitied by its allies. In his memoirs one English traveler rendered a sketch of the Polish state of affairs in 1777:

> I contemplate this country as the most instructive and awful of political lessons: I even esteem myself fortunate in being able to survey it, before it sinks and is erased from the list of nations . . . an event which, according to every appearance, cannot be very distant. . . . What else could rationally be expected, as the natural death of a country, where the crown is at once elective, venal, and powerless; where the nobility are independent, uncontrollable, and tyrannical; while the people are sunk in slavery, ignorance, oppression, and poverty? . . . The great Nobility are depraved, corrupt, and destitute of enlightened patriotism: their education and habits extinguish every spark of public virtue.[26]

In the face of damning impressions such as this, the efforts of reformers like Potocki to return the country to a proper course through a program of enlightened education and the cultivation of individual responsibility may have seemed Herculean. Potocki and others of like mind would work to promote the reform process initiated earlier in the century. In large measure the reforms were aimed at members of the early modern *szlachta* estate who sought to protect their political and social privileges at all costs—most notably by taking advantage of an elected monarchy deliberately kept weak. Those who sought reform embraced the notion that it could be achieved only at some cost to themselves and to their historic freedoms, and they framed change within the by-then-familiar Continental rhetoric of the emancipation of the nation's population, both from foreign domination and from the yoke of serfdom.[27] A lack of consensus about these ideals in turn demonstrates that the Enlightenment in the ideological sense was not universally embraced by the entire estate; philosophical proclamations did not appeal to all. It did not help that the *philosophes* themselves took contradictory stances in their attitude toward Poland, depending on who was paying attention, and in some notable instances even found it deserving of dismemberment.[28]

A Climate of Reform

The circumstances of Potocki's life and the rhythm of his work suggest that the treatise could have been written between 1775 and 1785 or possibly later. Potocki's use of the present tense in referring to Emperor Joseph II of Austria in a closing remark about the Italian portrait painter Pompeo Batoni (1708–1787) suggests a date of composition before Joseph's death in 1790, although he may have used this grammar for emphasis: "Giving us a fresh example of this is the happily reigning German kaiser Josef II."[29] Irrespective of the precise date of Potocki's treatise, Potocki's activities undertaken under the aegis of the National Commission for Education (Komisja Edukacyjnej Narodowej)[30] indicate his didactic bent and his commitment to education reform for the betterment of the citizenry. Within the commission, Potocki also founded and led the Society for Elementary Textbooks (Towarzystwo Ksiąg Elementarnych). While Potocki's political allegiances are well documented, scholarship has been more reticent on the full extent of his architectural pursuits and their connection to his interests in education.

Our understanding of the precise context to which his treatise belonged and the circumstances that brought him to write it might be greater were it not for the destruction of significant portions of Warsaw drawings collections and archival holdings at various points in the nineteenth and twentieth centuries. The state of Polish archival collections is anything but uniform. For example, the Warsaw University Cabinet of Prints (Gabinet Rycin), the city's primary repository of early modern architectural drawings, comprising the collections of Stanisław August Poniatowski, Stanisław Kostka Potocki, and the Society of Friends of Learning (Towarzystwo Przyjaciół Nauk), suffered losses when Russia confiscated portions of the collection in 1831 and transferred them to St. Petersburg. The collection suffered extreme losses during the German occupation from 1939 to 1945. Among the many items destroyed was a volume of drawings by the Polish architect Stanisław Zawadzki (1743–1806), who had left designs for several Jesuit churches in Poland and had been hired to transform the Jesuit college in Warsaw into the buildings that would house the National Commission for Education. King Stanisław August Poniatowski had founded the National Commission for Education on 14 October 1773, in the wake of Pope Clement XIV's dissolution of the Jesuit order. The project for the commission and Zawadzki's association with the Polish Patriots (who staged the Kościuszko Insurrection in 1794), as well as his letters to Poniatowski in which he expressed his concerns about national reform, tie him to Potocki's social milieu. A letter from Zawadzki to Potocki dated 13 February 1782, commenting on the positive progress of the controversial faculty replacements of secular clergy at the Szkoła Wojewódzka in Lublin, recalls their association.[31] Zawadzki's architectural training at the Accademia di San Luca in Rome between 1769 and 1776[32] and his familiarity with Italian and French architectural theory informed his projects; Potocki in turn would have found a valuable resource in Zawadzki as he cultivated his own interests in architectural theory and practice as an amateur. The commission also took over the supervision of the Załuski Library, originally founded in 1747 by the brothers Józef Andrzej Załuski and Andrzej Stanisław Załuski, Roman Catholic bishops, in the seventeenth-century Daniłowicz Palace; a surviving drawing attributed to Piotr Aigner dating from 1788 depicts the general plan for the library, with reading rooms, offices, and a geometric-style garden.[33]

Enlightenment-era reform in Poland-Lithuania is traditionally associated with Jesuit and Piarist education, the latter under the leadership of the bishop and pedagogue Stanisław Konarski (1700–1773), as well as with the briefly reigning king Stanisław Leszczyński (r. 1704–10), presumed author of the tract *Głos wolny wolność ubezpieczający* (A free voice insuring freedom, 1749). Not long before the formation of the National Commission for Education, Jean-Jacques Rousseau had written his *Considérations sur le gouvernement de Pologne et sur la réformation projetée en avril 1772* (London, 1782), in which he recommended the overhaul and regeneration of Polish education.[34] The formation of the commission marked an important shift in the manner in which Polish education was organized, as it also entailed the absorption of Jesuit resources by the Crown and a redefinition (though, importantly, not a secularization) of the religious educational system under the auspices of the state.[35] In the commission's early days its leader, Bishop Ignacy Massalski, claimed that the poor state of education was the primary reason for the Commonwealth's political weakness; it was commonly held among commission participants that reform of the nation went hand in hand with reform of education. That message also informs Potocki's treatise as well as the works of Piarists who made the first proposals for a "civic education."[36] One of these figures, Adolf Kamieński, in his work *Edukacja obywatelska* (1774), advocated instruction of civil and military architecture, painting, wood carving, and other arts, in addition to philosophy, math, theology, and law, within academic curricula.[37] Many ex-Jesuits were eventually brought into the commission, including Grzegorz Piramowicz, who served as secretary to the Society for Elementary Textbooks and with whom Potocki led the society's work.[38] Potocki's treatise opens with a verse by Piramowicz. The treatise may have been composed while Potocki was the head of the society and working with Piramowicz closely. On the other hand, letters to his brother after Piramowicz's death reflect his preoccupation with the loss of his friend and with the writing of the commemorative lecture, which was delivered by Stanisław Kostka Potocki before the group known as the Society of Friends of Learning on 15 May 1802.[39]

Architectural writing provided Potocki with a platform for his reformist principles. A member of the *szlachta* estate possessing resources and education should take responsibility himself, Potocki held, to direct these intellectual and financial resources in ways his privileged position permitted:

> [W]hen it comes to our fatherland in particular, I agree with everyone who believes that we have to put more thought into public structures. Over time, the Commonwealth should establish official residences for state dignitaries, befitting the dignity of the office. . . . For even if individual citizens enjoy building, as is often the case, the opportunities for

fulfillment of their desires would be greater and more honorable if they expended the same sums to build churches, hospitals, schools, and public toilets, necessary for hygiene and rarely used here. . . . [I]f the rich learned more diligently the art of managing their money, I assure you that idleness, poverty, and vices everywhere would turn into industry, financial self-sufficiency, effort, and work.[40]

By extension, Potocki maintained that the knowledge of architecture could lead directly to the elimination of social problems; expenditure on architecture should not be a mere exercise in excess or indulgence for those with resources. In this sense he shared the goals of Stanisław Leszczyński (1677–1766), the enlightened former Polish king and Duke of Lorraine and Bar, whose plans for the renovation of public space in Nancy during his dukedom appear in the Potocki library.[41] Potocki had passed through Nancy while in France in 1771 and would have seen Place Stanislas, as well as the work of the architect Emmanuel Héré (1705–1763),[42] Leszczyński's court architect.

But while it is true that Potocki's motives included the broad Enlightenment concern with the improvement of his society, as a Commonwealth citizen and lawmaker he had little fondness for abstract proclamations concerning the forfeiture of freedoms and resources for the sake of the "general will." As fervently as he rejected relativist positions, Potocki made clear throughout his *Remarks on Architecture* that he had yet to be persuaded by the fashionable notion articulated by Rousseau that man was free but everywhere in chains; nor, in keeping with Joseph Rykwert's assessment of Laugier's positions, did Potocki "see any particular moral virtue in returning to a 'natural' condition." For Laugier, Rykwert notes, the primitive hut is "*notionally* primitive. . . . it never spills over into an advocacy of 'primitive life.'"[43] Potocki voices similar sentiments:

[P]lease let no sylvan philosopher get angry, warning everyone that cities are prisons, and fortresses veritable cages. It is easy only to mention to such a philosopher that in the absence of society and cities, one would be hard-pressed to find on earth either justice or friendship or love or any other primary virtues that keep the entire human nation together. . . . True, it is often easier for rulers, at least when it comes to speed and efficiency, to conquer people living in the comfort of cities and harder to quash the wild and those spread throughout forests. But it is also true that [the latter condition] would be a sad and false privilege of savagery and that not everybody is so hostile to freedom as always to want to lose it irretrievably. . . . However, choosing according to the precepts of common sense, of those arts which bring people the most benefit and the least harm, I believe that even the most exacting of philosophers would concede that architecture would be one of the first among them.[44]

The freedoms sanctified by Commonwealth law also informed the social and political context in which Potocki worked, the *szlachta* ethos. The *szlachta*'s "Golden Freedom," understood best as a set of privileges enjoyed and consecrated by the nobility, protected the estate from control by the monarchy. It has been said that these privileges rendered the country politically weak and provided the impetus for reformers such as Konarski to advocate their curtailment or elimination.[45] The most famous of these statutes and the principal target of reformist goals was the right of *Nihil novi* (from 1505), which dictated that the monarch could not enact any major legislation (literally, "nothing new") without the consent of the *sejm* (parliament). Among the most wealthy of the estate, revenues derived from the ownership and management of hereditary latifundia, lifelong leases of Crown lands (*królewszczyzny,* which constituted 30 percent of the Commonwealth's territory),[46] and commercial enterprises. A wealthier nobleman would also have a sizable palace, usually evocative of neo-Palladian, French, or English style. Cultural and ethnic diversity, a by-product of the 1569 Union of Lublin, meant that there was in effect no single language or religion outside the noble estate,[47] which by the mid-seventeenth century was predominantly Polish speaking and Catholic. Significantly, as the historian Janusz Tazbir points out,

> [in] no other country in Europe at that time did a set of privileges, forming a kind of legal and political institution, seem to exert such a strong influence on the shape of national consciousness among the ruling class as it did in Poland. . . . The share that [the nobility] had in this political community—a state having an enormous area, of which they felt themselves to be the owners—created a certain link among all noblemen throughout the country. That led, in turn, to their common commitment to defend the republic against external enemies as well as against internal opponents of their "golden liberty."[48]

This political and social context in turn informed Potocki's *Remarks on Architecture,* disclosing the nature and customs of Potocki's intended readership.

Potocki was orchestrating architectural knowledge for the purposes of correction: "[I]n particular, I dedicate this work to those of noble birth, driven by the conviction that to them the knowledge of architecture in the country where it has not yet blossomed completely is not only useful but necessary."[49] This is significant because it positions Potocki in an informative, didactic role vis-à-vis his own countrymen and reveals an awareness of the need to clarify not only matters of architectural know-how but also architecture's origins; it also demonstrates that currents traveled more slowly into this area of the Continent, in keeping with the relatively late appearance of the Renaissance architectural vocabulary to the Commonwealth in the early sixteenth century.

With the advent of the Four-Year Sejm, in 1788, Potocki's attention turned toward the more urgent matter of political reform and leadership within the Patriotic Party. In 1789 he authored the *Project to Reform the Government*[50] and around the same time gradually overcame his differences with Poniatowski, promoting an alliance (albeit temporary) with Prussia to guarantee the Commonwealth's protection from neighboring aggressors Russia and Austria while the Poles undertook this reform. This is also the period during which Potocki coauthored the Constitution of the Third of May.[51] Political turns, including the Kościuszko Insurrection against Russia's military response to the Patriots' ambitions (which resulted in the repeal of the 3 May Constitution), as well as two periods of arrest and imprisonment before his death, dilute the possibility that Potocki could have written the *Remarks on Architecture* after 1788.[52] On the other hand, from 1800 until his death, he was a member of the aforementioned Society of Friends of Learning, the first Polish society of its kind, which his brother cofounded in 1800. The society served as a public forum for the presentation and discussion of scholarship and politics. Five departments encouraged scholarship across the disciplines of philosophy, mathematics, physics, chemistry, medicine, natural history, economics, history, geography, poetry, and fine arts; cultivation of the Polish language and literature formed an important part of its "national" agenda during the era following the partitions, until the society's closure, in 1832. It is possible that Potocki had written and presented portions of the *Remarks on Architecture* to colleagues in the society or that the society's environment provided him with the incentive to write on his subject. The architect Chrystian Piotr Aigner (1756–1841) was also a member and had worked closely with Stanisław Kostka Potocki; Aigner also authored several architectural texts, including a dictionary of architectural terms (undated), with which Ignacy Potocki would have been familiar. Other architects in the ambit of the society produced similar texts.

The personal, social milieu of the Potocki brothers provides further context for understanding Ignacy Potocki's commitments to education and reform. About 125 kilometers southeast of Warsaw, just northwest of Lublin, site of the constitutional union between Poland and Lithuania in 1569, lay the estates of the Czartoryski family at Puławy and of the Potocki family in the towns of Kurów and Olesin.[53] Until the late eighteenth century Ignacy owned the town of Kurów and its outlying parts, along with the towns of Klementowice, Michów, and Świdry, all of which he had inherited from his parents. Stanisław Kostka Potocki took a liking to the marshy area of Malownicze, not far from the Kurów residence, where he established an English-style garden—one of Poland's earliest—and called it Olesin after his wife and son. The most serious work in Kurów began in 1782; the original garden design, however, does not survive *in situ*.

In his "Memoirs of My Times," the Polish poet Julian Niemcewicz described his association with these important hubs for Poland's intelligentsia: "We returned . . . to Puławy, where the prince [Adam Kazimierz Czartoryski] had already set up with his whole summer residence. . . . Like Puławy itself, the neighborhood was most pleasant. About two short miles away lived the marshall, [Ignacy] Potocki, in Kurow, *ad unguem factus homo,* and nearby at Olesin the Potockis [Stanisław Kostka Potocki and his family], who for a year honored me with their friendship."[54] This close-knit community set an agenda for the education of young citizens, most notably at the Puławy estate, where Prince Adam Czartoryski designed a curriculum to impart the lessons of Polish history to the young. After a scandal in 1785 involving a supposed plot by the king's chamberlain, Franciszek Ryx, to poison him,[55] Czartoryski abandoned the directorship of the Knight's School (Szkoła Rycerska), or Cadet Corps of His Royal Majesty and the Republic (Korpus Kadetów Jego Królewskiej Mości i Rzeczpospolitej), founded 1765, which offered military and civilian education over a seven-year curriculum that included drafting.[56] The family then cut its ties with the king and exiled itself from Warsaw to Puławy, whose classical Temple of the Sybil (fig. 6) and palace grounds (fig. 7) were designed by Chrystian Piotr Aigner and depicted by the painter and professor of perspective Zygmunt Vogel in his *Recueil des Vües de plus Célèbres Monumens Nationaux tels que: Ruines, Châteaux, Temples, Mausolées, Édifices antiques, et lieux memorables de la Pologne* (1806). The residence there would become the most

FIG. 6   Jan Zachariasz Frey (engraver) and Zygmunt Vogel
(draftsman), *View of the Temple of the Sybil at Puławy*, 1807.
Engraving, 36 × 24 cm. Warsaw National Museum.

important site of magnate cultural patronage and political activity, both anti-monarchical in tone and patriotic in its leanings.[57]

The matriarch of the estate, Izabela Czartoryska (née Fleming), cultivated a renowned botanical garden and assembled a collection of artifacts and images relevant to national history in the so-called Gothic House on the palace grounds;[58] this collection served as a quasi-public museum accessible to those within the family's social circle.[59] There was a pronounced moral component to the curatorial program of the collection; pupils were to learn lessons

FIG. 7   Jan Zachariasz Frey (engraver) and Zygmunt Vogel (draftsman), *View of Puławy*, 1806. Engraving, 24 × 36 cm. Warsaw National Museum.

of the Polish past—most important, the causes of the weakness of the Polish nation that led to the partitions, as well as how those maladies should be cured. Chronology per se was not an organizational imperative.[60] In noting that the objects contained in the Temple of the Sybil were assembled just after the partitions, Francis Haskell has described the collection as "more a giant reliquary than a museum. Its contents were varied in character, but all had one feature in common: they provided tangible proof that a great Polish Kingdom had once existed. The purpose of the Temple was to display a coherent view of history in visual form."[61]

Criticism leveled at Poniatowski for his exorbitant expenditures is captured in a related caricature of ca. 1784. The *Tableau alégorique de la Direction des Bâtiments de S. M. le Roi de P[oniatowski] . . . avec ce qui y est relatif* (fig. 8) serves as a counterpoint to the contemporary language of reform promoted officially by the monarchy and its adherents. The French artist Jean Pierre Norblin de la Gourdaine (1745–1830), active in Warsaw in the late eighteenth century, mocked the king's freewheeling spending and the seemingly haphaz-

Tableau alégorique de la Direction des Bâtiments de S. M. le Roi de P. ... avec ce qui y est relatif

FIG. 8   Jean Pierre Norblin de la Gourdaine, *Tableau alégorique de la Direction des Bâtiments de S. M. le Roi de P. . . . avec ce qui y est relatif,* late eighteenth century. Pen and ink on paper, 39.3 × 55.5 cm. Warsaw National Museum.

ard plans for sumptuous architecture intended to bolster the nation's public image. It is likely the king's court painter and superintendent of buildings Marcello Bacciarelli (1731–1818), with his palette, whom Norblin depicted with ass's ears, demonstrating and explicating an image that describes the major projects under way at the behest of Poniatowski. The sketch displayed on the easel within the drawing portrays a haphazard arrangement of these commissions, a commentary on Poniatowski's notoriously uncontrolled spending and the absence of concrete plans for their execution and construction. A figure underneath the giant easel, with his back toward the viewer—a Potocki? August Moszyński, the king's artistic agent?—cranes his neck upward to examine the image, an open book in hand (we might imagine a foreign text or treatise on architecture). In a sense, the caricature renders the process of artistic transmission—in the translation from print to plan—as determined, absorbing, and confused. A sagging carriage bearing a bloated king and transporting sacks of money arrives on the unpaved road and collides with the lecturer, its passenger receiving an impromptu lesson on the works in progress. Is this Izabela and Adam Czartoryski to the right of the carriage, turning to flee the scene in dismay? Groups of peasants in the foreground—kept in shadow, inhabiting the world of unmaintained dirt roads littered with magnate money—observe the scene before them. In the distance, two carts stuffed full of "projects for Łazienki" and "projects for Ujazdów" head south to their destinations.

Norblin disparaged those of Stanisław August's projects and priorities that distracted him from political matters, for which distraction he was also criticized publicly. In spite of his best intentions, the king was never able fully to realize his goals, dwelling at length on his aggrandizement of the city to the neglect of more pressing social and economic realities. Whatever the artist's original connotations, the critique of the king's fiscal policy is clear. And yet architecture under King Stanisław August Poniatowski and reform-minded *szlachta* flourished in Poland more than in any previous era. During the time of Warsaw's burgeoning, an array of foreign and native architects, artists, and craftsmen contributed to the formation of a capital that presented "all the refinement of Paris, the arts of Florence, and the splendor of Petersburg," as Nathaniel William Wraxall (1751–1831) wrote during his visit.[62] It is conceivable that in sponsoring architectural projects, Poniatowski was looking westward to Nancy in particular, to the enlightened agenda of Leszczyński. In the frontispiece to the account books for the French projects, Leszczyński was depicted on site, conversing with his architects and taking a central role as an initiator of political reform at the construction site of the Hôtel de Ville in Place Stanislas. One wonders whether Norblin adopted that image and the propaganda it espoused as a source for his ironic and scathing visual commentary on Poniatowski's lack of financial restraint. Ultimately, it is the weakness of the monarch he chose as the target of his artistic wit.

The imperative undertaken at Puławy by Czartoryski, Potocki, and their associates in the context of reform to study native history is essential to the understanding of Potocki's context, which above all else embraced the notion that an understanding of the past was essential to the durability of architecture and to society itself. The architects of reform held that students of all disciplines should receive material for reflection on the perceived reasons for political failure, with the goal to envision the possibility of a "repaired Republic" and, in the words of Adam Czartoryski, to find "a remedy to take away the present evil."[63] They found the intellectual bases for a curriculum in Polish historical writings by Marcin Kromer, the bishop Andrzej Załuski (whose library Potocki would direct), and others, supported by an independent analysis of consecutive tomes of the *Volumina Legum,* the Polish legal code and guarantor of estate freedoms.[64] Czartoryski's suggestions about the position the study of individual epochs in Polish history should occupy within the curriculum, as well as the role of general history, were nearly identical to those conceived by Franciszek Bieliński in 1775 for the National Commission for Education.[65] Czartoryski's aim had been to consider the root causes of the Crown's weakness, the flexibility of Polish law, the personalities of the rulers, and finally the causes of the Commonwealth's decline. History would serve civic education directly and would assist in the training of a future political elite. In the realm of home teaching, the curriculum emphasized the history of ancient Greece and Rome as well as earlier epochs in Polish history. These lessons took place in the form of conversations "without dates, without order, without progression."[66] The chronological presentation of history would be subordinate to the translation of historical lessons and caveats. The educational methods and aims pursued at Puławy, and the society in which Potocki participated there, help to explain other projects designed to use knowledge of history and national resources as means not only of civic improvement but of cultural defense against future incursion from without and errors from within.

Precedent and Adaptation

The significance of Potocki's manuscript resides in its use of architecture as both a yardstick and a point of reference for national culture. In his desire to preserve national culture in a period of great uncertainty, he promoted architecture as an effective bulwark against decline. Though the efforts of Potocki and his associates did not prevent political annihilation, they did highlight education as the means through which the dormant state could reconstruct and conserve itself in the wake of political disaster.

Although Potocki's treatise was not printed, the ideas it engendered were important to their moment. It is possible that the work circulated among Potocki's peers in the form of manuscript copies. The writing may be by a hand other than Potocki's, and the clarity as well as size of the text on each page suggests that it was intended to be copied, or had already been copied, for distribution. Manuscript culture had persisted into the eighteenth century in the Commonwealth, alongside print. It is also possible that the publication process had been interrupted by the urgent matter of the Four-Year Sejm and the events that followed. It is also not beyond the realm of possibility that copies in any form were destroyed in the conflagrations of the nineteenth or twentieth centuries. The diagrams to which Potocki refers in the text, for example, have been separated from the text and to date have not been located.

The writings and shared interests of Potocki's cohorts, as well as the significance of the National Commission for Education as an institutional patron under whose aegis reform efforts took shape and didactic texts appeared, illuminate the nature and context of the work. Potocki's text should not be seen as an anomalous or exceptional development in an architectural landscape otherwise untouched by writing of its kind; the scarcity of comparative studies of the Commonwealth's architectural and cultural history in relation to the broader currents of architectural theory and practice produces the false sense of a barren landscape. The ex-Jesuit and Cracow canon Sebastian Sierakowski (1743–1824) practiced and wrote about architecture extensively, finally publishing his significant work *Architecture, Including Every Type of Masonry and Building* (*Architektura obejmująca wszelki gatunek murowania i budowania*) in 1812. He had begun this text some ten years before its publication and practiced architecture throughout his entire adult life, beginning with restoration projects at the Wawel Cathedral in the 1770s. In the volume, Sierakowski establishes his architectural lineage by noting his close associations with the Potocki household, dating back to the days when he served as a member of the National Commission for Education. He notes the direct influence the Potocki brothers' ideas and unfinished works had on his own architectural thinking, and as a close adherent he continued their unfinished work. Sierakowski also received several assignments from the commission's Society for Elementary Textbooks during the period of his participation.

Other figures among Ignacy's cohorts, in addition to the aforementioned Stanisław Zawadzki and Chrystian Piotr Aigner, include Vincenzo Brenna (1747–1820) and Jan Ferdynand Nax (1736–1810). Brenna worked together with Stanisław Kostka Potocki on designs for the reconstruction of Pliny the Younger's Villa Laurentum, for which extensive drawings and a description survive.[67] Polish collections also contain plans, sections, and elevations for a fine-arts museum Stanisław Kostka Potocki wished to commission from Aigner, designed in a distinctly Palladian idiom (fig. 9). Ignacy Potocki also created plans and elevations for a porticoed villa "of a monumental and public character," with a central rotunda and cupola topped with an allegorical sculpture of Fame and faced with a clock on one side and the Pilawa coat of

FIG. 9   Stanisław Kostka Potocki, *Design of a Museum of Fine Arts*, section, late eighteenth century. Pen, ink, watercolor on paper, 58 × 92 cm. Warsaw National Library.

arms, which the Potocki family bore, on the other (fig. 10).[68] In the domain of architectural language Nax wrote a Polish-Latin-French-German glossary of architectural terms, to which Sierakowski and others would refer. Nax, a professional architect himself, also designed a national order that featured on its capital the white eagle of the Polish coat of arms (fig. 11).[69]

    In both visual and linguistic terms, these collective efforts undertaken by a group of close associates point toward their desire to define a national approach to architecture that had a distinctly public purpose and could be articulated in the Polish language. Before their pursuits were stymied by the politically desperate situation in which they found themselves, this group was well on a path to formulating clear principles for architecture that were steeped in their learned understanding of the tradition inherited from the Continent through the circulation of architectural treatises. What united these thinkers in the domains of arts and architecture and of politics alike was their goal to interpret, formulate, and disseminate their ideas to a Polish audience in need. For

FIG. 10   Ignacy Potocki, attr., *Design for a Palace with the Pilawa Arms,* ca. 1774. Pen, graphite, ink on paper, 33.6 × 49.8 cm. Warsaw National Library.

at the end of the eighteenth century these heirs to the defunct Commonwealth engaged in an intensive postmortem. Their reform efforts, which included the study of waning power and its ultimate loss and acknowledged a drastic shift from centrality to marginality on the European political stage, provided the opportunity deliberately to shape present and future conduct. Potocki's writing emerged within the context of the Commonwealth's decline and partition and the ensuing debate over that state's disappearance in the writings of the Commonwealth's thinkers ca. 1800–1815. Unable simply to accept the status quo, Potocki and others who participated in government seemed to embrace one of two positions: the nation could either cleave to a sense of its former political greatness or reexamine itself and reconstruct its cultural relevance and place within the wider Western context and European tradition. Importantly, they chose to perform this postmortem through arts and letters. In effect, the Commonwealth, absent statehood, would become a state of mind. Potocki and his circle shared an explicit desire to create national monuments

FIG. 11   Jan Ferdynand Nax, *Project for a National Architectural Order, Tab. 1, Fig. 1.*
Inscribed below frame: "Projet d'un Colonne de nouvel ordre par Nax." Second half
of the eighteenth century. Pen, graphite, ink, 41.1 × 50.6 cm. Gabinet Rycin,
University of Warsaw Library.

of their writings while announcing to the estates the universality of the ideas contained within them, connecting them to precedent, and generating new forms that embodied their patriotic goals.

Ultimately, observations on Polish art and architectural theory during the early modern period reveal how cultures that straddle or bridge very different, often opposing worlds fit into the modern Western conception of what ccnstitutes the history of European culture and artistic value. Poland, literally "between East and West," was in a position to explore, define, and evaluate both the extensions and limits of the classical inheritance. Throughout his text, Potocki asks that his reader consider observations on architectural theory in the Commonwealth "according to the Polish sky," or "heavens," and "customs"—a phrase borrowed for the present purposes from the aforementioned *Brief Study of the Construction of Manor Houses, Palaces, and Castles According to the Polish Sky and Customs* (*Krótka nauka budownicza dworów, pałaców, zamków podług nieba i zwyczaju polskiego*) of 1659,[70] which refers to both the Polish "way" of making culture and the local aspects of that process, including the sanction to do so by God. Potocki's treatise, among the variety of writings emerging during the era of reform and partition referenced here, shaped a dialogue about cultural centrality the Commonwealth's intellectuals frequently invoked. The extant works share a certain ambivalence about whether culture itself provided fortification against the loss of native traditions or was a permeable membrane enabling intellectual exchange across it, specifically permitting foreign "influence" to cross national cultural boundaries. The result is multivalent. What these thinkers stated was conceived "according to the Polish sky and customs" was sometimes particular to Polish culture and at other times in line with broader European traditions. Nor was this differentiation lost on outsiders; it resulted in a mixed perception of the nature of Polish culture by Europeans, and also by Poles themselves. The very durability of traditions—both received from without and generated from within—ultimately yielded the peculiarities of Polish culture, including its official Christian identity within a broader multicultural and multiconfessional population.

In light of the historical dimensions of the adaptation and circulation of architectural ideas within the *szlachta* estate, it is notable that the unknown architect-author of the *Brief Study* placed a premium on the value of personal experience and observation in domestic architectural construction. Individual need and choice, by extension, allowed for a departure from strict theoretical canons of proportion familiar through the writings of Vitruvius, Serlio, Scamozzi, Palladio, and Vignola. The *Brief Study* was the first Polish treatise to employ Vitruvius's precepts, referring to them as a form of practical advice with theoretical underpinnings.[71] Further, its author adapted Italian sources to conditions particular to the situation and customs practiced by the nobility at the time; Palladio, for example, served as the model for the resolution of most practical matters. The widespread custom of building manor houses of wood lent particular importance to the study of construction, materials, and durability—and consequently regional climate and place. It was composed during a time of extensive reconstruction after the Swedish wars (1655–60)[72] and was intended as a manual to assist the upper and educated nobility in becoming self-sufficient in the language of building. Roughly a hundred years later, Ignacy Potocki's manuscript reinvoked this practical genre of architectural writing, but more methodically and thoroughly.

Potocki's treatise addressed both the necessity and the difficulties of reconciling the Vitruvian tradition in architecture with the "Polish sky and customs." Taking his cue from Enlightenment authors such as Winckelmann and Montesquieu, who theorized about the relationship of climate to cultural needs, Potocki too regarded climatic conditions in his practical considerations of architecture: "Vitruvius, whom I quote often, particularly mentions those issues in his writing, urging that all buildings have sufficient light. Without air it is impossible to live; without light it is impossible to work."[73] To anyone acquainted with the harshness of the region's winters, Potocki's invocation of Vitruvius's point about the relationship of climate to building would have seemed only natural. Eighteenth-century travelers complained about the cold and the hindrance to movement and safety posed by the lack of light; newspapers reported on such topics as the number of lamps needed to illuminate public spectacles adequately; darkness facilitated the abduction of King Poniatowski in 1771, during the Barist assassination attempt.[74] Potocki hoped that architecture could play an important role in the rescue of his society from the metaphorical darkness into which it had been descending precipitously since the era of Saxon rule. The *Remarks on Architecture* announces repeatedly that architecture itself was immune neither to the disease of social decline (which could be corrected) nor to the inconveniences of physical location and political geography (with which one was obliged to contend). By writing the *Remarks on Architecture,* Potocki wished to put architecture back on its proper course.

The *Remarks:* Form and Content

In the first pages of the *Remarks on Architecture,* Potocki expresses his concern for and sympathy with his audience, addressing their apprehensions in the face of the daunting task of learning the architect's trade. Informed by his personal experience as an amateur, he admits that the work of his predecessors and other models of architectural writing are intimidating to unstudied minds. Potocki's central challenge resides in rendering accessible a body of knowledge he deems necessary to the improvement of his nation's landscape; he sets out to ensure that "every reader may easily understand what architecture is all about."[75] A reduction of architecture to essential principles and concrete rules follows. He includes a frank admission of his indebtedness to the architectural theoretical tradition that inspired his own effort, humbly denying himself any credit for the wisdom his work contains: "I am not claiming that the remarks contained herein are entirely my own. In fact, I readily confess that I took them from only the best writers, so much so that if this booklet, like a mosaic, can even boast of something, it is that it is out of many and various pieces artificially conjoined."[76] Potocki's most frequently cited and conspicuous theoretical sources are Vitruvius, Vignola, Palladio, Scamozzi, Milizia, and Laugier,[77] who inform the passages on the technical explanation of the orders, decorum in decoration, rules governing proportionality, and the overall relationship of parts to the whole.

Early modern Polish authors on art and architecture readily admit to borrowing from other European sources but do not strictly imitate them; absolute originality was not a priority for Ignacy Potocki or his brother, who intended to adapt and aggrandize inherited models, namely Winckelmann's *History of the Art of Antiquity,* in his own way. The authority of texts belonging to the Vitruvian architectural canon as communicators of that tradition is fairly general and rests upon the cumulative truths and observations across theoretical works that Polish authors cited, summarized, and in turn adapted to local circumstances—namely, the Polish environment and social customs. As such, for Potocki, the body of knowledge contained in the texts that formed the canon was universally applicable to a broader vision for culture yet was prescriptively porous and subject to interpretation so as to be adaptable to a specific environment or place. Two overarching processes took place in the absorption of or encounter with that tradition—that of differentiation, or recognition of separateness from it; and that of concord, or recognition of long-held common cultural vantage points. It is the conjunction of these that yielded the multivalence of early modern Polish culture.

The treatise itself is divided into a preface and six sections that discuss, in turn, typology, beauty, the benefit of the discipline of architecture, ornament, comfort, and the branches of knowledge necessary to the architect.[78] The first three sections are historical and broadly conceptual in content; sections four and five present technical information drawn directly from others, with adjustments based on Potocki's own practice; the sixth section offers a commentary on the skills and education necessary for a good architect. Potocki's closing statement makes clear that he deemed architecture a noble art, one that dignifies and elevates the status of cities and rulers alike:

> [I]f we want to equip our fatherland with architecture, let us not begrudge spending anything on those who bleed to work for it. Let us respect all those who apply themselves for it. Let us imitate Francis I and Charles V, who were so committed to learning that the first attended to his painter's deathbed and the other handed Titian his brush when it fell from above. Sometimes this esteem constitutes a reward more appreciated than money. Giving us a fresh example of this is the happily reigning German kaiser Josef II, who not only visited the good painter Batoni frequently while I was in Rome but later, after granting him many awards, made him a nobleman, apparently doubting whether this nobility decorates the painter or the monarch more.[79]

His closing remark on the nobility of architecture resonates with the treatise's opening. A verse written by the Jesuit pedagogue and poet Grzegorz Piramowicz, Potocki's librarian and friend, announces the chief problem, in Potocki's eyes, befalling architecture at the time, namely, the corruption of form resulting from excess and indulgence:

> To Architecture.
> Mother Need brought you to this world;
> Her first attempts were huts alone.
> Through excess into such perfection you grew
> That palaces you erect out of their inhabitants' loss,
> Palaces in shapes magnificent and wondrous,
> Like gargoyles, a travesty of true need.[80]

The verse is a seven-line sketch of the trajectory of architecture, from its dawn in the Vitruvian primitive hut to its lamentable decadent phase in the present day: the production of forms entirely divorced from necessity, contorted expressions not found in nature. Interestingly, the same poem appears at the beginning of Chrystian Piotr Aigner's treatise on rural architecture, *Country Building from Sun-Baked Bricks, with Methods for Making Permanent Rural Cabins, as Applied to National Properties* (*Budownictwo wieyskie z cegły glinosuszoney z plantami chałup wieyskich, stosownie do gospodarstwa Narodowego*). The paragraph that follows the poem duplicates almost word for word a passage that appears in Ignacy Potocki's text. Unless Aigner and Potocki collaborated directly on the *Remarks on Architecture,* or unless Potocki had seen Aigner's text in manuscript before its printing in 1791, Aigner likely used Potocki's text in shaping his own. During the time Aigner wrote his pamphlet, he had been collaborating closely with Stanisław Kostka Potocki. If Emperor Joseph II was indeed still living when Ignacy Potocki made reference to him, the treatise could not have been written after 1790.

Piramowicz's poem stands as a prelude to a topic important to theoreticians of architecture at the time, that is, architecture's origins and their relationship to contemporary practice. Potocki claimed,

> In the end, we can easily find natural architecture that, although already masked or hidden, can nevertheless be discerned in the greatest homes and even in royal structures. In Roman palaces the architect-philosopher will first find beggars' huts; he will find logs incorporated in columns and other ornaments. And if he will not find them, then that fact rightly will allow him to make a judgment about this style of building. For even if those buildings are to be hidden or covered, their architecture should always seem natural. Let us remind ourselves of the beginnings of architecture as mentioned; let us analyze civil architecture, and we will certainly find that our discipline also has its own grammar all the more dignified in its simplicity.[81]

Laugier, from whose work Potocki borrowed extensively, had also discussed architecture's origins. And Laugier's ideas were in turn strongly influenced by those of Etienne Bonnot de Condillac (1715–1780). Both Jean-Jacques Rousseau and Condillac advocated a return of "all subjects to their 'natural' and therefore 'principled' origins," Condillac with regard to language and Rousseau to society; Laugier's ideas were especially influenced by Condillac's thinking.[82]

As Joseph Rykwert has noted, Laugier situated the origins of architecture within the realm of necessity and reason, which provided "a guarantee against outworn, capricious custom as well as the vagaries of individual taste. . . . It was a theory of architecture out of Newton (and Locke) by Condillac."[83] As it turns out, the affinity between Condillac and Potocki was also close.

Condillac himself was asked to compose a text on logic for the Society for Elementary Textbooks, and Potocki translated a portion of this text. Letters Condillac wrote to Potocki express his great interest in seeing the Polish education project succeed.[84] The imprint of Laugier's and by extension Condillac's influence on Potocki's text aligns the project with the turn among eighteenth-century French writers toward "primitive functionalism," whereby "the organization of the plan, the division of built space, was isolated as a tool of social control and reform, while the characteristics of the legible façade were identified in order to make of the building a school of sensations and morals." Laugier's "reduction of architecture to a 'single principle'" led him to assign to the Vitruvian primitive hut "a paradigmatic status for all architecture."[85]

As James McQuillan has noted, the Vitruvian treatise underwent important reevaluation in the late seventeenth and eighteenth centuries, in part because the rules governing the orders came to be seen as no longer fixed and writers had begun to discard the notion that beauty was absolute.[86] The former adherence to Vitruvius began to transform into something more amenable to the needs of eighteenth-century audiences, whose interest in architecture's roots was "animated by frustration at the riot of conflicting contemporary opinion as to proportion and ornament in architecture."[87] This frustration is clearly echoed in Potocki's text, but he nonetheless remained committed to the notion of absolute beauty.

The problem of architecture's origins as connected to Vitruvius's primitive hut also captured the imagination of Freemasons, whose institutional interests in the origins of happiness found natural connections with the search for "primitive purity" in architecture, which Vitruvius's primitive hut—expounded through Laugier—had offered. Freemasonry, it has been noted, "exploited architectural imagery and language far beyond the antique properties of the Vitruvian treatise."[88] Potocki, like many members of the *szlachta* estate, had been a Freemason. Thus, though the attention he paid in the *Remarks on Architecture* to the question of architecture's origins may have arisen out of his attraction to the ideas in Laugier's treatise (it remains unclear whether Laugier himself had been a Freemason),[89] it may also have reflected the kinship his reformist agenda found with the metaphorical rhetoric of the lodges, which emphasized the relationship of architecture to the larger issue of the reconstruction of society. The connection between Freemasonry and architecture in the eighteenth century, however, has yet to be fully explored in the context of Polish architecture.[90] Nevertheless, it is not surprising that members of the education commission and textbook society were also members of Masonic lodges throughout the Commonwealth. Ignacy Potocki joined a lodge in 1779, becoming grand master of the lodge Catherine of the North Star in 1780;[91] Adam Czartoryski served as one of the deputies. Of twenty-four members of this lodge, thirteen were Poles. Freemasonry gained momentum in the Commonwealth during the early 1780s in particular, for the society of the lodges provided a moral model for the reform-minded, and private spaces for discussion following the trauma of the first partition.[92] Lodge members would gather to read scholarly lectures and patriotic speeches. For example, Potocki's associate, the Swedish mathematician Simon Antoine Jean L'Huillier (1750–1840), read his piece "On Electricity" at the lodge on 29 April 1782.[93] L'Huillier was also a member of the Society for Elementary Textbooks and in 1819 became a foreign correspondent for the Society of Friends of Learning. From 1777 to 1788 he was a tutor and librarian for the Czartoryski estate, and from 1777 to 1780 he wrote handbooks on geometry, arithmetic, and algebra.[94] His example was not unique, and it is conceivable that the *Remarks on Architecture* was written for presentation and dissemination within the context of lodge meetings.

Beauty, Judgment, and Progress

One of the most interesting features of the *Remarks on Architecture* is Potocki's treatment of the ideas of authority and tradition in architectural precepts and practice. His identification with his social group suggests itself as a compelling force behind his attitudes and disposition. After Potocki describes those for whom the booklet is intended, the subject resurfaces time and again as a source of irritation and reprimand, on the one hand, and inspiration and motivation, on the other. Assuming the mantle of educator, he ruminates on architecture's historical contours, the cyclical peaks and valleys of architecture's progress and decline. Echoing Winckelmann and hence his exchanges with his own brother, he draws upon the achievements of the Greeks and Romans, as well as the Egyptians, for purposes of comparison. The passages in which Potocki makes observations about the architecture of other cultures relative to architecture's overall progress or decline recall that historicist vein of writing which claimed "that every culture had a unique character of its own," a viewpoint founded in a kind of "thoroughgoing cultural relativism."[95] However, his protracted discussion on the nature of beauty and proportion makes clear that beauty itself was innately and universally intuitive, constant and divorced from more superficial and widely varied matters of taste or convenience.

Potocki devotes considerable space to his philosophical concern with beauty (ladność) in architecture, based on both inherent and externally assigned properties.[96] He states that unlimited architectural freedom leads to disorder, emphasizing in particular the Saracen and Moorish architecture of Spain, where "the whim of every architect became the rule for any given building," where "there were as many architectures as there were buildings."[97] But while taking this critical stance toward architecture not based explicitly on the Greco-Roman model (a position he maintains against Gothic architecture as well, contra Jean-François Félibien [1658–1733], who admired Gothic forms), he recognizes that form and function differ with both geography and historical moment: "For as the Egyptians marveled the human eye with size more than shape, so the Greeks on the contrary put all of their efforts into the smoothness of their designs, the beauty of their form, and exquisite perfection to impress the viewer. Taste thus described was already well established in Periclean times and blossomed uninterrupted under Alexander the Great, expanding ever more."[98] In this sense Potocki draws on Jacques-François Blondel, who also acknowledged that architectural style differed depending on national and cultural conditions.[99] Potocki explains that even the most beautiful of Greco-Roman buildings were not perfect, because they had not yet been subordinated to the rules of "reason and reflection";[100] this leads him to consider whether beauty is to be governed by taste, as is proportion, or by Nature, as are geometry and symmetry. Here he displays a familiarity with Claude Perrault's ideas concerning positive and arbitrary beauty.[101] While he challenges the idea that the rules of proportion are governed by Nature, as had Perrault and Scamozzi, Potocki declares that Nature does give us a sense for good proportion (thus echoing Blondel), but he qualifies this idea by saying that our ability to see beauty comes in part from custom and daily experience. His Polish terms *porządek, układ,* and *proporcya* correspond to Boffrand's *ordonnance, convenance,* and *proportion*—the elements of *bon goût*[102]—and also to Vitruvius's *firmitas, utilitas,* and *venustas.* Nature, Geometry, and Experience are to be the three sources for architectural rules, Potocki declares;

Nature and Geometry are exempt from *dowczyp,* or our invention and spirit, while Experience informs our taste.[103]

Potocki maintained that the abstract notion of beauty was constant and inherently understood by the senses. Paraphrasing Yves André's *Essai sur le Beau* (1741), he reflects on whether beauty is constant and unchangeable or is subject to the whims of fashion. Linking the discussion of beauty with a historical model of progress and decline, he appears deeply unsettled by the idea of an unstable beauty and muses on the future of contemporary architecture: "Who knows how much those who come after us will hold our architecture in contempt." He continues,

> We can see so far how the Muslims have contempt for Greek architecture in countries under their control. If therefore architecture depends on taste alone, then who is fit to judge? Who has better taste: a Greek, an Italian, or a Turk? Each loves his own structures, each considers his own manner better than those of others, one makes a wry face at the other. And what can we take from that? Only the fact that the beauty of our art does not depend on taste or any particular fashion. For it is different fashion and not architecture that would be considered beautiful.[104]

The theme of cultural specificity arises again in connection to taste. In a passage throughout which he complains about those who hold that beauty is neither universal nor fixed by rules, he rejects the notion that those peoples deemed to possess "miserable" architecture are content in doing so: "They claim that a Tatar is equally content with his miserable abode as a German, a Frenchman, or an Italian with a magnificent structure. And on this they base the belief that each should remain within his own borders and each should enjoy this architecture that blind luck bestowed on him."[105] He implies, in other words, that some people understand beauty and others disregard it or simply do not need or care about it, and his points of reference are his neighbors—the Europeans to the west and the Tatars and Ottomans to the southeast. While critical of the implication that types should not mix, he acknowledges a kind of natural segregation of styles based on locale, people, and culture. Pointing out that the Pyrrhonists believe that "each should remain within his own borders and each should enjoy this architecture that blind luck bestowed on him," he suggests that, instead, men should base their taste on reason, and presumably on selection. The Pyrrhonist view works for those who believe in fate. On the contrary, he writes, "a prudent man should restrain his taste with reason."[106] Where there was reasoned imitation of nature, beauty would be constant. In this sense he adheres to the reductive rationalism of Laugier.

Turning from the theme of beauty, Potocki then contemplates the authority of Vitruvius to discover why it was that architecture had fallen into decline. Custom interferes with "correct works" due to uncritical adherence to ancestral authority; because of this, architecture had become "contaminated" (*splamiona*) and the need had arisen to "purify" (*oczyścić*) it.[107] In keeping with Laugier, he takes a critical stance toward the slavish followers of Vitruvius, linking the historical process of the decline of architecture with the blind following and copying of the master. He makes specific reference to the situation within Poland, inviting practitioners to follow not just the ancestors but also the desire for personal glory that would in turn elevate the state of architecture in the land:

> [I]n seeking all things for the benefit of my fatherland, I briefly remark on how architecture can spread among us. Indeed, the love of fame and emulation among the scholars may have a significant effect here. For it is not enough to examine old structures and to follow in the footsteps of our own ancestors; we should endeavor to exceed even them. Neither Raphael nor Buonarroti would ever have reached the perfection that they did if they had followed any other route. Not imitation alone, but virtue and the love of glory are what raise and disseminate all learning. Therefore, when here the educated will endeavor to challenge fame with their name, at that time they will blossom with general benefit for all.[108]

Perhaps making reference to Laugier, he notes that Vitruvius, "however great a man he proved to be, was also susceptible to error,"[109] and that Scamozzi suggests Vitruvius is not to be totally trusted, insofar as the proportions he gives for columns are "false and far removed from beauty proper." He continues, "As a matter of fact, to tell you the truth, sometimes Vitruvius contradicts himself. Sometimes what he first criticizes he then praises."[110] His dilemma does not stop there:

> [I]f one has to be careful with Vitruvius, what does one say about others, respectable, in truth, but inferior to him as architects? Alberti, Serlio, Palladio, Scamozzi, Vignola, Philibert de l'Orme—all have merit, but they disagree with one another, each makes mistakes, and none is faithfully and absolutely followed by his imitators. This reasoning perfectly

demonstrates that a weaker architect would be unlikely to attain proper beauty. The image of ancient buildings, though somewhat helpful to architecture, nevertheless cannot become its first principle.[111]

For Potocki the very nature of architectural practice itself, if not grounded in first principles, endangered theoretical clarity and was by definition flawed. Insisting on a departure from ancient example as well as from matters of taste, he proscribes looking for answers in philosophy, defined by its constants; order and proportion, he claims, can be recognized and admired by everyone. There is, in a sense, a recourse to instinct governed by physiology, which he explains with reference to optics and perception.

Pertinent here is Laugier's statement that "the greatest men have sometimes gone astray—to take their example always as a rule is therefore not a safe way to avoid errors."[112] Emulation of the past clearly did not come without controversy. Potocki refers to the process of invention in ancient architecture, writing that it is always harder for the innovator to create the perfect model, because he is working out his problem for the first time: "Those who are the first to invent find it too difficult to avoid all mistakes in their undertaking, while those who only slavishly imitate others choose the good and bad elements equally and do not doubt that everything is already in the right proportions, that everything has been confirmed, that everything has been validated with the dignity and name of the ancestors and even the long-established and unbroken customs."[113] He continues, "There was thus a great and urgent need for remarks to clean contaminated architecture through the clear identification of the original errors, introducing harsh critique of old works, using words to prevent errors or mistakes from being validated by [both] the blind custom of their use and the credit and fame due the original inventors."[114] The result was an architecture, as seen in the period of Constantine, removed from progress and worsened rather than improved.[115] His criticism of others for imitating their predecessors too closely led him to the obvious conclusion that he who emulates uncritically adopts both the good and bad elements of his example, without improvement. His historical observations and remarks serve to amplify his strongest sentiments about the responsible use of authority, with the ultimate aim of halting further decline, much in the same vein as his opinions in the arena of political reform. His tone is not one of overwhelming optimism.

Potocki's invocations of the example set by Vitruvius continue where he asserts that it is individuals who should be held responsible for the demise within contemporary architecture. Outlining the achievements of the six-teenth-century Italian architects, he explains that the studies of Roman ruins along with the maintenance of old proportions helped to promote improve-ments in architecture, naming Bramante, Peruzzi, Sangallo, Michelangelo, and Vignola as exemplary practitioners. In this too he clearly borrows from Laugier, who, with reference to the sixteenth-century recovery of architecture, writes, "We have had our Bramantes, our Michelangelos, our Vignolas. The last century produced masterpieces in architecture worthy of the best ages because at that time nature almost spent itself by lavishing upon us a gift of talent. But at that very moment when we were approaching perfection, as if barbarism had not lost all its claim on us, we fall back into a low and faulty taste. Everything now seems to threaten us with a complete decadence."[116]

Importantly, Potocki observes that Italy, like Greece and Rome previously, created for "all of Europe" the new rules and values for architecture that everyone should follow. He acknowledges the primacy of Italy, whose influ-ence stretched to other countries: France, Spain, and "even" to St. Petersburg, Sweden, Denmark, Poland—and England especially.[117] Here he speaks both as a Pole and as someone belonging to the Republic of Letters addressing the Vitruvian tradition—one of many places where elisions of the term "we" color the text. Citing the authoritative theoretical works and the ideas of his own countrymen, sometimes without differentiation, and bringing the broad brushstrokes of architectural history to bear on his prescriptions for the Pol-ish nobility's own architecture, he infuses the text with these two stances and renders his disposition clear.

A discussion about the effects of climate and location on architecture natu-rally leads Potocki toward contemplation of site specificity, echoing Palladio's instructions in *The Four Books*. One challenge was the need for reconciliation of the idea of universal beauty with site and inhabitants. Indeed, the Potocki brothers shared with Johann Gottfried von Herder an interest in the differ-ences between peoples and places and in the cultural, geographical, and lin-guistic explanations for those differences.[118] Stanisław Kostka Potocki met both Herder and Goethe in Vienna in 1785, as he reported to his wife in a letter written in July of that year.[119] Gottfried Ernest Groddeck (1762–1825), the stu-dent of the philologist Christian Gottleib Heyne (1729–1812),[120] served as pro-fessor at the University of Vilnius (Wilno) from 1807 to 1825 and is credited with introducing the discipline of classical philology into Poland, basing his ideas on those of Winckelmann, Herder, and Lessing. Herder had recom-mended Groddeck to Adam Czartoryski as a tutor in Greek and Latin for his sons.[121] The extent to which Herder's ideas may have influenced the Potocki milieu is a subject for further development, but it is not unreasonable to propose that as the Polish writers explored the connections between climate and custom, his ideas likely resonated with their theories regarding the nature of culture.

Like Winckelmann, Ignacy Potocki notes that "under the mild Greek sky, the Greeks could keep the pediment at a mild angle, which in Italy grew slightly greater, combining beauty with need in that country." The Egyptians, "who on the contrary rarely experience rain, make use of homes without roofs and buildings without pediments. And is this not an obvious example of a tight relationship between nature and architectural ornaments?"[122] Simply put, and evocative of Montesquieu and others, climate determines necessity;[123] Potocki argues, therefore, that the relation between architecture and nature is obvious. What we do not realize, he concludes, is that we merely ape our ancestors, not necessarily to our benefit, and fail to take local needs into consideration, forgetting or disregarding the specific reasons for doing something that might have arisen from the dictates of a specific climate and resources.

A point of comparison is instructive. Whereas Ignacy Potocki in his *Remarks on Architecture* would explicitly question the dangers of conforming to certain traditions steadfastly adhered to by the nobility, Chrystian Piotr Aigner also approached architecture in a practical fashion, according to the Polish situation, and in the mode of Palladio. Aigner wrote as a theoretician, cultural commentator, and builder, with pragmatic solutions to the problem of impermanence in mind. Like Ignacy, Aigner too was motivated in part by Poland's problematic image abroad and use of counterintuitive practices such as the long-standing custom of building in wood. He stated the "well-known fact" that his country suffered "from continuous fires, which burn towns and villages, a result of a common but inappropriate way of building houses. This causes damage to both the owners and the country."[124] In his treatise on brick building, he writes that "truly only Poland, according to an author on building, is a miraculous phoenix that rises again and again from the ashes to continuously rebuild itself, in order to be more widely burned down."[125]

In his text *Project for Ordering Construction Policies That Would Establish and Enforce Rules Including Ways of Preventing the Decay of Cities and Simultaneously Ensuring Their Enlargement,* Aigner casts doubt on the prevailing idea that the practice of building in wood persisted solely on account of the ease of construction and the availability of materials:

I have mentioned in general how careful with the available building materials each builder visiting his province should be. In speaking about cities, this should be considered even more carefully. As in countries abroad, so it is a respectable custom here as well, that the attention of the government should be on enforcing the habit of planning stone towns throughout the entire country and getting rid of wooden ones. This is what the builder should keep in mind to facilitate achievement of the goal: all of his designs should promote this easy way of building cities in brick . . . , sparing the forests, which should be easy [to do] in our country due to the large amount of stones and other materials that are perfect [for building] in masonry.[126]

Aigner suggests that the practice of building in wood could be phased out, at least in the cities, because other, more durable materials were in fact readily available. For what other reason than tradition and expedience did the Poles continue to turn to wood as the preferred material for construction? Aigner states that tradition could in fact be a liability and that by extension education and technology would provide the solutions enabling the Polish built environment to be raised from its so-called primitive or regressive state. The troubling state of building in the towns and cities, he notes, was obvious to Poles and foreigners alike.

This is a critical point for determining whether wooden architecture was maintained more as a matter of custom than because wider theoretical principles, that is, the Vitruvian precepts of building, were adapted to local needs, dependent on place. In this way, the problem of tradition returns to the fore. Did Poles habitually build in wood simply because they lacked the architectural technology and skills to adapt their practices to stone and brick construction in the architecture of towns and the countryside (as opposed to that of the royal court, where it was commonly practiced), or because they preferred long-standing customs, or both? In "Early Modern Ideas About Artistic Geography Related to the Baltic Region," Thomas DaCosta Kaufmann asks in a related vein, "[C]an we infer that general geographical conditions, including such factors as local circumstances, climate, and materials, as they relate to particular locations, that [the writers of architectural treatises in the Baltic region] discuss are the major determinants of the characteristics of the art or architecture of the Baltic?"[127] Perhaps to some extent. But how these local physical characteristics compare in significance to social customs and traditions, as well as the extent to which social customs and traditions were shaped by them, is more difficult to determine. This issue lies at the core of what ultimately constitutes a particular local approach to architectural thinking and practice and therefore the histories of architectural undertakings.

In remaining critical of blind adaptation, Potocki held that such practice merely led to architecture divorced from necessity, with no connection to local circumstances. In his *Remarks* he grapples with the problem of tradition and how to use it; mistakes arising from ignorance and uncritical approaches to building ultimately yield architecture that is totally inappropriate to the demands of location and circumstance. Paying homage to his predecessors ("our ancestors"), he to some extent acknowledges the universal validity and truth in what they did, but simultaneously argues that the factor of place separates his contemporaries from these ancestral authorities. Necessity, in other words, is born of that geography. As an example, he invokes the use of arches in connection with roof construction and protection from the elements. He refers to a drawing he has produced, unfortunately lost, to illustrate the point directly: "In that olden time of those first inhabitants, joining two trees at an angle with an architrave at the top relieved significant weight. We veritably ape our ancestors, whether the need exists or not; it is from that that we use arches between columns, gladly and sometimes in vain doing what the ancients did with drudgery of labor and not without reason (Fig. IX), but probably out of necessity to free themselves of rain, bad air, and harmful winds."[128] Pedestals, he writes, were employed to raise a building off of swampy ground or else to correct the view for the spectator.[129] The conjoining of necessity and specific conditions with the abstract qualities or requirements of architectural beauty appears again and again throughout the *Remarks*. In this too he finds mentors in Palladio (most conspicuously) and Laugier. Taking the subject further, to the issue of site and town planning, he notes that if one wishes to reside in a city, he "should choose fertile land or at least a place close to a river to assure ease in importing food."[130] Echoing Vitruvius, he reminds the reader that "everybody agrees that good air, which is the first requirement of good health, should not be the last thing for a builder to consider; and its quality depends on all cities' local ground or soil, on exhausts and fumes, and also on winds, which can blow with them bad and septic atmosphere from other places."[131] The geological factors that make settlement feasible and comfortable appear in the discussion, but the problems posed in Poland by humidity and dampness had a particular resonance that one could not dismiss, as seen in the grounds of the royal Łazienki Park. These designs, proposed by the superintendent of buildings to the Crown, August Moszyński (1731–1786), in imitation of Thomas

Whateley's ideas for English landscape gardens, included canals and complicated hydraulics systems.[132] The *Remarks on Architecture* also contains Vitruvian- and Palladian-style instructions on how to tell good soil from bad, differentiating between the kind of soil that contains only a small amount of moisture and that more fertile soil which contains a large amount of mineral elements:

> [T]o recognize a good or harmful air, we have tools both certain and reliable. Chemical experiments make it possible to measure salt particles in dew mixed in with the air, because thick mineral vapors alter the proper colors of metal and silk, causing rust. Therefore, wherever those changes can be observed, the air should be considered suspect. . . . The diligent and wise architect will want to learn about the health of earlier inhabitants, or at least of those who live nearby, and also about the diseases found among the livestock. The ancients were particularly attentive to that when erecting their cities, carefully examining the entrails of sacrificed animals, considering their colors and possible spoilage, not without reason, as indicative of the fitness of the air for human settlement.[133]

Like Vitruvius, Potocki notes that unhealthy winds should be avoided when planning streets. Referring to Palladio, he explains that in warm countries houses should be high and streets narrow in order to avoid the summer heat. Palladio "confirms this opinion of his using the words of Tacitus, who avers that in Nero's Rome the air became far more harmful when that Caesar, for the sake of the city's shape, broadened the heretofore narrow streets."[134] Referring to private houses, he admits not only that wider streets are conducive to better air circulation but also that the view of private houses in every town is more beautiful, the more space there is to let in light and to observe the distance between the buildings.[135] Describing the layout of buildings and the choice of location for individual structures and rooms, he stipulates that "the view of private homes in every city is all the more elegant, the more exposed to air and light each proper part of the home is, according to its use. Storage spaces, granaries, and all other places that serve to store perishable goods should be facing north. Libraries and study rooms should be facing east, both to catch the earliest possible light and to ensure the long-lasting and good conservation of the volumes." Similarly, rooms should be open on the south during winter and on the north during summer.[136] By comparison, Laugier had written that once the site has been chosen, the position of the building remains to be decided and this means finding the best protection against too much cold and too much heat. Generally speaking, east and west are two uncomfortable positions; in summer people are scorched by the sun which shines almost half the day. North is too cold and always a little humid. South seems to be the best position. In winter the sun shines and reduces the cold, in summer it skims the walls and does not give too much heat. However, in every country there is usually one part of the horizon from which strong winds and constant rains come; if one wants to be comfortably housed, good care must be taken not to turn the house towards such a troublesome part of the sky. . . . The convenience of the position depends on many other circumstances relating to the climate, none of which an architect ought to ignore.[137]

Laugier clearly recognized the influence of climate on architecture and acknowledged that building choices would be directly affected by the specific climate of the surrounding country. He did not, however, associate the progress or decline in the art with this factor. In Potocki's text a discussion about the placement and number of windows in a house follows an acknowledgment that it is easier to design a building when there are no other structures around it to take into account. The author also recognizes that the conditions of place and the solutions it demands may trump a general rule. After explaining the ideal proportions of windows, Potocki notes that "these are the first rules that have to be considered very diligently in the context of each country's nature. For what I put forth here is only general, and it is to them that the particulars should be applied."[138] Thus the conditions of physical location (e.g., climate, topography) and the requirements generated by them drove decision making in building—in any place at any given time. What differentiated cultures and histories of architecture were not only these physical variables but the kinds of solutions applied in order to create appropriate buildings. This level of awareness speaks of a way of conceiving history across both place and time, in a trajectory of development and decline.

In the closing section of the treatise, Potocki couples Vitruvian ideas about what qualities make for a good architect with those about what kind of education the architect needs to have, explicated in section III of the *Remarks*. In "Remark on the Benefits Coming from the Discipline of Architecture" Potocki proclaims architecture a part of philosophy. It follows that architecture "should be judged not only by architects themselves but also by others."[139]

Promoting the active involvement of the property owner and the amateur, he notes that "kings who first erected cities without seeking strangers to establish their walls determined all things on their own." Claiming art as a "king's game," he refers to "one of the German princes"—most likely his contemporary, Frederick II of Prussia—who "decorates his cities with structures imitating pictures of Venice, Rome, and Vicenza."[140] Noting specifically the new funerary chapel at the Charlottenburg Palace and a "magnificent ballroom," which were the German monarch's inventions, he asks by what means such monarchs were able to conjoin the powers of Mars and Apollo—the warlike and the artful—in order to use "a pen and a weapon, a compass and a ruler," equally well.[141] Frederick II had hired his favorite architect, Georg Wenzeslaus von Knobelsdorff, to renovate his residence at the Schloss Rheinsberg and later the Schloss Charlottenburg (1740–ca. 1746), which included the Golden Gallery, or Banquet Hall (completed 1746), possibly the "magnificent ballroom" to which Potocki refers. If Potocki was referring to Frederick II (Frederick the Great) of Prussia (r. 1740–86), the treatise would have been written before 1786, lending support to the idea that he may have composed it for the compatriots of his lodge and/or within the milieu of the Society for Elementary Textbooks, discussed earlier.

After mentioning that many noblemen in Italy practiced architecture, further to demonstrate his point about the universality of the amateur's active hand in architectural practice, he invokes Sweden: "In Sweden, I gather, Count Tessin, following in the footsteps of his father, erected a structure the like of which would be hard to find in northern countries."[142] He undoubtedly refers to Count Nicodemus Tessin the Younger (1654–1728), who had trained in Rome in the circle of Bernini and was responsible for the design of the Stockholm Royal Palace (1696–1753).[143] A reference to a place that, like Poland, was far from Italy but to which Italian and French tenets had spread would have made for a fitting analogy and demonstrates the reach of Potocki's knowledge of architecture elsewhere; Saxon, Swedish, and Prussian neighbors exercised their own architectural idiom within the Latinate tradition. In referring to architectural practice through example, cultural affinities for Potocki were, then, more local, whereas his theoretical inclinations were more "universal."

Potocki also cites English patrons, including Lord Pembroke and Lord Burlington, as noteworthy examples of amateurs who took architecture seriously and into their own hands.[144] Referring to Poland itself, he notes that "we can even find our own examples in this matter, for some of our own also imitate this now-common but noble custom, seeking to improve architecture more and more."[145] It is generally useful for kings, noblemen, wealthy people, and also clergy to know the rules of architecture, so that one might at least be able to choose a good architect for one's commissions, "for how can one not at all conversant in architecture choose a good architect or a good design?"[146] For Potocki, architecture was a matter of public good and civic responsibility; in the text, he promotes the view that architecture is to be undertaken and supported by the government of nobles:

> And because we know well from experience that the shape of structures preserved, not only whole but also in parts, brings fame to each individual citizen and to the entire country, part of the orderly organization of a city would be to place architecture under public management. For it is one thing to say, "A nice city," and another to say, "Nice architecture." If so, through the establishment of a ruling standard for the façades of palaces by a group of architects designated for the purpose, each city would certainly contain fewer unshapely structures.[147]

He expresses interest in the idea that a ruler should commission one or two architects at most to plan the façades of palaces along the streets, citing the example of Turin, one of the most beautiful and orderly of cities. In contrast, he does not hesitate to make known his frustration with Poland for thus far being unable to learn from Turin's example.[148] He notes that even in Cicero's time private buildings and buildings of magnificence brought dishonor to the city: "I am aware that this great rhetorician does not count private buildings among needs, that he criticizes churches, even magnificent ones, that he claims that buildings such as these bring infamy instead of glory to cities. I believe that these severe civic thoughts occurred to Cicero only when he saw freedom and liberty in his fatherland collapse from excess."[149]

Both Ignacy and Stanisław Kostka Potocki were convinced that architecture could serve a people without a state and could hold within it the potential for national rebirth. Stanisław's ideas on the role of architectural education in the inculcation of the values of citizenship in the young concerned architecture not only within the broad categories of art-history writing and linguistic reform but also in the relationship of these fields to the cultivation of the true Polish citizen. Conversely, his national political stance also informed his art-historical and architectural writing. His attempt—like his brother Ignacy's—to demystify the architectural process and transform it into something each nobleman could and should use to construct the world around him reflected his aim, outlined in *On the History of the Art of the Ancients, or the Polish Winckelmann,* to endow the noble citizen with the skills necessary to his station in life, or, put another way, the skills necessary to elevate himself, regardless of his net worth, to a state befitting his title. Knowledge of architecture, like knowledge of the arts and the history of cultures, brought with it a certain dignity and self-sufficiency. In an atmosphere of political instability in which the property a nobleman owned could by 1795 not even be said to occupy the ground of a Polish state, the firmer the noble's grasp on these skills of self-definition, the greater his strength to resist the erosion of native, local culture in his daily life, however illusory the notion of political autonomy may have been.

Like Ignacy, Stanisław had arrived at certain convictions about the education of young people in Poland. Extant architectural drawings made by his young son Aleksander (to whom Ignacy, who died without an heir, bequeathed his estate) suggest that Stanisław had dreams and plans for his offspring; his manuscripts reveal his general opinion on the value of architectural learning to children:

> Most of the time, we are trying to bring up children properly and bring to fruition future talents that will not cause much pleasure and might not be useful at all. Parents feel obliged to add to a child's education certain things like music and drawing, and children do not usually want to do these things, and do not yet have the talents to pursue them. In doing that, we are overlooking architecture. Architecture is, among all of the liberal arts, the most fun and also the most useful for the children of citizens.[150]

Stanisław's agenda for the nation's young was both straightforward and pragmatic: learn about architecture, not only because it is fun to do so, but because it is one's duty as a citizen. As with knowledge of the arts, the strength of architectural understanding and practice in turn would serve as a testament to the strength of the citizenry and of the nation. Architecture, then, was an authority capable of articulating the desires of the estates and was representative of their accomplishments, intellect, goals, and progress. It had a distinctly public face but had to be cultivated within the private domain of every good nobleman's domicile.

Within the theory and practice of architecture, traditions could be explored, maintained, and revisited so as to yield ideas about what constituted

Polish architecture and distinguished it from that of other nations, places, and peoples. The study of the history of architecture and art, in turn, was born in part of utilitarian needs and interests and had very pragmatic ends.

It would seem that in spite of political tumult and a bloodless revolution in the social order, little had changed in architectural thinking since the conception of the *Krótka nauka budownicza* in 1659. At the same time, as the Potocki brothers cast their glance over the history and theory of architecture, they asserted that now there could be no excuse for ignorance. For the amateur builders among the nobility, a national architecture in the late eighteenth century still meant a domestic architecture, a country house that was durable and comfortable. No special talents were necessary for citizens to renovate and shape a decrepit country house, decorate it with their possessions, and organize it so that it was comfortable and could be protected and given permanence. And so Stanisław Kostka Potocki stated, "You do not need to be a Vitruvius or a Palladio, and the ability to fix things is easy to acquire. You need basic geometry, which is the basis for architecture—which I call rural architecture."[151]

For the brothers, common sense reigned among the most important principles for the practice of architecture, for a commonsensical knowledge of architecture's precepts was not only useful on its own, it also satisfied the needs in a person's life. Without much effort, basic knowledge could lead to higher knowledge of architecture based on proportions and dimensions that, they added, were already well-known, if not perceived naturally. The amateur builder only had to understand what other architects had already done. Given the knowledge that was readily available, any architect who willingly ignored it committed a grave sin. Should the rules of proportion and construction be neglected or altered, architecture was bound to be incorrect and its difficulties never overcome. According to Stanisław, architecture, unlike painting, was a well-defined practice; success would follow observance of its rules.[152] Understanding the rules and rejecting an "anything goes" attitude were essential.

With regard to the mechanics of learning about architecture, Stanisław's writings informally outline the basic necessities. Following statements on the importance of learning architecture's fundamental principles of construction and proportion, he writes, "I am going to mention one more remark about architecture that might at first glance seem fairly surprising, but the fact that it might surprise people does not make it any less true. Architecture requires drawing to such a small extent that you can be a great architect without really knowing how to draw."[153] Ignacy seems to agree: "To all [required skills] needs to be added the ability to draw a person. This final art is by some so essential that they understand that it is impossible to be a good architect without being a competent painter. I completely disagree with this opinion. I know that the rules for drawing and architecture differ, and although they mutually support each other, they are in many ways opposite to each other."[154] Stanisław then describes how he understands architects' work: "Mostly . . . they carefully think about the appearance—outside and inside—of the structure that they are planning to draw; they cast on paper the outline of this first thought, and accordingly they adjust the measurements that they usually mark only by numbers to signify the different sizes of parts. They are not adding more work for themselves by drawing clear lines, shading parts, and adding notations for decorations; they are suggesting the mechanical structure."[155]

A longer study would be needed to discuss Stanisław's architectural practice together with his extensive art-historical writings.[156] Neither brother would have considered theory disconnected from practice, and in fact both argued that their ideas about aesthetics and history, as well as the utility of practice for the improvement of the citizenry, would bring mutual benefit to the noble estate and, it was hoped, the state alike. Stanisław's architectural undertakings may be taken as a case in point. Both independently from Aigner and in collaboration with him, Potocki demonstrated his interest in public buildings and villas; the façade of the Church of St. Anne in Warsaw was a collaborative effort designed in a style evocative of Palladio's Il Redentore.[157] With Vincenzo Brenna he produced the designs for the reconstruction of Pliny the Younger's Villa Laurentum and for the renovation of the interior of the Palace of the Republic (Pałac Rzeczpospolitej), formerly the Krasiński Palace, in central Warsaw.[158] His proposals for the Temple of Divine Providence (Świątyna Opatrzności), meant to commemorate the 3 May 1791 Constitution, merit a separate study.[159] The Villa Laurentum project in particular sheds light on his antiquarian and archaeological interests. Also extant are designs for a public library, a museum, a theater, a villa for Izabela Lubomirska, and sketches of Italian architecture. He also wrote another tract, *Rural Architecture (Architekturze wiejskie)*.[160] The range of projects in which he was involved reveals Stanisław's many interests, his facility with the language of architecture, and the harmoniousness of his ideas with those of his brother. Together, their impact upon eighteenth-century Polish arts and culture cannot be overemphasized, nor can they be separated.

Conclusion

By the seventeenth and eighteenth centuries, Polish writers on architecture had proclaimed their allegiance to a canon of architectural theory and practice informed by Vitruvius and his followers; Ignacy Potocki questioned the unequivocal authority of Vitruvian ideas and in that sense expressed affinities with French theoretical literature that had begun to do the same beginning in the late seventeenth century. In practical manuals addressing local needs and directly influenced by fundamental works, these professional and amateur architect-authors instructed the nobility residing in the Polish-Lithuanian Commonwealth on architecture's principal precepts: only on firm foundations could the discipline of architecture flourish; readers ought to embrace the Latin tradition of architecture without imitating it slavishly, while simultaneously rejecting relativist approaches to architecture's conception, beauty, or value. For the most part, the standards and rules informing arts and architecture were, in their essence, unchanging and permanent; patrons needed to be informed of those standards, and practitioners should heed the lessons of the past. Only then could architecture in the Commonwealth improve.

Another lesson imparted to contemporary readers by the *Remarks on Architecture* is that it does not suffice to generalize that an architectural tendency or form is simply "northern" or "southern" European in timbre and custom, especially as regards places that annex elements from multiple regions concomitantly onto their own local practices. The idea of a "center" in relation to European borderlands like Poland is therefore difficult to embrace. In effect, Potocki addressed human needs and the conditions of natural environment— a topic he returned to again and again—together with the way that natural environment imposes itself upon us. On one hand, he wished to tame it, to make it a more livable place; and on the other, he sought both to shape and to express customs through a response to natural limitations and through innovation. For Potocki himself, blind adherence to traditions had detrimental effects on the environment, the durability of towns, and the stability of the social and political autonomy of the state.

In an important way, this introduction has been concerned with the problem of perception—namely, what others think of things and peoples they can only understand approximately, through reading and through putting inherited practices to work. The problem emerges from the sense of unease evident in the sources produced by encounters with things familiar and unfamiliar— indeed, travelers to Poland were perplexed by the fact that much of the architecture they did see was somehow familiar and up to Continental standards yet was simultaneously very foreign. Polish writers on art, architecture, and culture revealed themselves to be as aware of the role foreign perception played in the Polish standing on the European cultural stage as they were of their own urban deficiencies. Views about the role and position of foreign traditions in the ever-changing Polish cultural landscape represent different ideas about how to rejuvenate patriotic ambitions and respect for the *ojczyzna* (fatherland) within the realm. The anxiety of writers such as Stanisław Staszic about the prevalence of foreign ideas in Polish culture was quite pronounced; Stanisław Kostka Potocki, on the other hand, embraced what could be learned from foreign example and applied that knowledge to his vision of reform, imparting an understanding of the tenets governing beauty and good taste in the arts and emphasizing the necessity for basic knowledge of art and building. Borrowed traditions exerted their own imperatives upon the formation of aesthetic taste and architectural knowledge; the Potocki brothers were determined to put scholarship in the service of a culture that would find itself without a state.

The *Remarks on Architecture* yields the distinct impression that among Polish Enlightenment-era intellectuals Potocki was motivated to create a program of reform and restoration against the backdrop of national annihilation. He believed firmly that architecture could play a fundamental role in that program. Since the mid-seventeenth century, repeated foreign invasions of the Polish-Lithuanian Commonwealth had challenged both the permanence of the territory itself and the architecture within it. Geographical vulnerability stunted the growth of the discipline's theoretical framework and enabled foreigners to lay waste to the built environment with every incursion. The custom of building in wood rendered the towns and cities vulnerable to easy destruction, while the fortress towns in the south, such as Zamość, Kamieniec Podolski, and Chocim, had been strong enough to withstand incursions from Ottomans, Cossacks, and Tatars. Potocki's awareness of the state's vulnerability partly informed his general motivation, as well as his lifelong devotion to improving the Commonwealth through social and political means. Drawing attention specifically to the deficiencies in architecture that resulted from a lack of knowledge and a blind adherence to ancestral authority, Potocki revealed a concern central to all writing on the arts in Poland at this time: namely, the place of native authority and received authority within the Polish artistic, architectural, and intellectual spheres and, by extension, their role in the articulation of cultural identity and choice of affinities that accounted for the multifaceted nature of visual expression throughout the realm.

It is clear that the two brothers also believed love of the homeland, as an inspiration for the arts and architecture, could lead directly to the improvement of cities. Stanisław writes, in a tone familiar from the *Remarks on Architecture:* "All the miseries that befell Greece contributed to establishing its greatness. The Persian invasion and demolition of Athens demonstrated that after great victories people focused on decorating the country anew. Love for the fatherland caused competition in rebuilding and in making cities even more beautiful. Many monuments were raised in memory of the victories."[161] Given their inclinations, it is easy to imagine why the brothers held up ancient Athens as an example for Poland to follow. As representatives of a social estate whose political values shared Continental ideas concerning natural law and the importance of education to social progress and political strength, the work of both Ignacy and Stanisław represents an important contribution to Polish Enlightenment architectural histories and elevates the place of such histories within the broader framework of European Enlightenment studies. The long-neglected artistic and architectural projects of Polish intellectuals should be seen, at least in part, in light of the political instability through which they lived and against which they worked, during a period that had positive and lasting implications for literary and artistic culture. To these efforts Aigner contributed his practical ideas for the establishment of construction policies in the cities. Each province, he suggested, should have its own general builder; each county should have its own conductor to assign the best builders to the task of improving the towns. Skilled architects, in their designs for public projects and monuments, would aim for perfection, durability, comfort, beauty, and economy. Among these architects, one would compete for the position of builder of the republic. The profits and benefits that would come from this competition, he stated, were so obvious that they need not even be stated.[162] Potocki's ideas, stated in his third chapter, "Remark on the Benefits Coming from the Discipline of Architecture," are virtually identical.[163]

Aigner shared with the Potocki brothers the conviction that the cultivation and dissemination of the fine arts improved the nation and enhanced its citizens' happiness; the fine arts also represented the legacy of their royal patron, brought fame to those who created them, and served as the standard by which future generations would judge the past. Acknowledging that other countries were ahead of where he felt Poland should be, he recommended that promotion of the arts be accelerated, so that they might flourish, and that artists and

54

architects be given stipends for the study of foreign models abroad. The National Commission for Education, he said, should sponsor these journeys, and a national academy of fine arts should be established in the capital, Warsaw. He spoke his mind, he said, out of a "great desire" to be useful to his country, hoping that "those to whom the people of the nation gave some sort of power" would, "for the love of their country," find his ideas desirable and useful.[164] Ignacy Potocki's text should also be understood as belonging to this realm of thinking, for it demonstrates how a Polish noble and reform-minded intellectual with architectural inclinations considered the authority of received tradition relative to building methods appropriate to Polish circumstances—whether cultural (Polish traditions and customs), geographical (the situation of the nation by itself and in relation to others), political, or physical. This kind of negotiation and stocktaking was not a specifically "Polish" phenomenon broadly speaking. Other architectural writers in the northern, Baltic region also inflected the Vitruvian canon of architectural theory according to local circumstances, as seen, for example, in the works of Vredeman de Vries and Salomon De Bray.[165] But precisely what *was* "Polish" was the set of concerns—historical, political, social, topographical—that, when taken together, shaped human thought and action in a way particular to Potocki's political and cultural context; they encouraged or reinforced sensibilities, habits, or customs that, when taken together, formed an architectural culture specific to its place and time. It is not surprising that authors such as Ignacy Potocki would take note of where their own ideas accorded with or diverged from those of their historical sources and contemporaries. Notably, the circumstances in which Poland's writers were working—in the political sphere as well the cultural, taking an active role in shaping and critiquing the Commonwealth's laws, codes, and traditions—must have heightened their sensitivity to considerations of durability and safety, historical cycles of rise and decline. As his letters and writings show, these things were central in Potocki's political and social consciousness, and how one settled, cultivated, and protected land was inextricably implicated in daily life. It was the authority of Vitruvius, however distilled or transformed, that would enable Potocki to gauge the history of architecture and its patterns of development or decline, to locate his own philosophical stance vis-à-vis those who followed Vitruvius, and to make contact with the building public in the *szlachta* estate in the hope that a high standard of architecture could be achieved and maintained. What is clear is that he reflected on the formal fundamentals of architecture and aspects of its history always with a mind toward improving the state of building at home. One does not look to raise a Polish Vitruvius from the ashes of a lost early modern past. Rather, resident in the *Remarks on Architecture* are traces of the impulse and determination to preserve and strengthen a culture that was being usurped from without. Caveats loomed large.

Eighteenth-century Polish reformers articulated their perceptions of the reasons for political weaknesses in a period when Poland was characterized by European observers as "regressive" or "conservative" in mentality and culture. Observations on its architecture were cast in similar terms. Polish historians have theorized that internal problems in effect paralyzed the nation's political and social structures, leaving the nation vulnerable to attack and encroachment by absolutist regimes.[166] Architecture provided a forum in which writing and design could be mobilized to solve problems related to permanence and stability through the examination and reform of traditions. The formal language Polish writers used both to describe Polish conditions and to prescribe solutions to cultural problems borrowed from other international sources and also exhibited a Polish inflection. As a political activist and publicist, Ignacy Potocki strongly believed in the social power of political writing and used it to shape public attitudes. While he and other publicists borrowed freely from other political writers, they always adapted those writings to their own context.[167] By extension, the brothers Potocki and their collaborators held that art and architectural theory could be used both to understand and to form culture. To see the circulation and transmission of ideas and forms according to the intersection of circumstances of time and place is to begin to understand received traditions and theories in a comparative fashion. The comparatist approaches to architecture, art, and aesthetics espoused not only in Ignacy Potocki's treatise but also in the letters, publications, designs, and informal observations of those within his circle served personal and patriotic ends. Importantly, they demonstrated an overt awareness of and interaction with the wider world around them.

REMARKS ON ARCHITECTURE

IGNACY POTOCKI

———◆▸✖◂◆———

(2)[1]
To Architecture.
Mother Need brought you to this world;
Her first attempts were huts alone.
Through excess into such perfection you grew
That palaces you erect out of their inhabitants' loss,
Palaces in shapes magnificent and wondrous,
Like gargoyles, a travesty of true need.
—Piramowicz[2]

(3) Beware.
The same fate to which other fields are subject befalls architecture. All the tomes written in this manner serve the master more than the student. And that is why those who without a mentor who wish to have any knowledge (4) of architecture whatsoever are at first intimidated merely by looking at the great tomes. And, so to speak, they lose desire to read them before they even begin to understand the subject.

That is what prompted me to collect some remarks on architecture which (5) every reader may easily understand what architecture is all about. For I have endeavored to the best of my ability to describe everything clearly and precisely, without indulging in verbosity, which introduces more confusion than improvement.

To improve the remarks, I have often embellished them with various historical and interesting facts, which will, combined with some qualifying remarks,
like a game, somewhat entertain (6) the mind of the reader.

I am not claiming that the remarks contained herein are entirely my own.
In fact, I readily confess that I took them from only the best writers, so much
so that if this booklet, like a mosaic, can even boast of something, it is that it
is out of many and various pieces artificially conjoined.

(7) Whoever will scrutinize this booklet, let him not forget the ends to
which the focus of all of my efforts was directed. Let him remember that this
collection will only serve those who desire to know the first and universal rule
of our discipline. Everything here is infused with first, elementary principles;
everywhere simplicity and ease shine through. But in particular, I dedicate
this work to those of noble birth, driven by the conviction that to them the
knowledge of architecture in the (8) country where it has not yet blossomed
completely is not only useful but necessary.

And finally, knowing from experience that this little booklet will fall into
the hands of varied and various people, I ask of those wise and prudent to
overcompensate with their kindness for the errors or omissions that everywhere inadvertently may have found their way in. But the timid and less
learned I humbly beseech to forgo the reading of this little work altogether.
This small effort, this little tome, (9) does not give them a significant opportunity to express their malicious critique. I assure you that such reactions to my
work from both types of readers will serve me as the most generous reward for
my efforts and will effectively encourage me to undertake more ambitious
works more suited to my advancing age.

(10) [blank]

(11) I. Remark on the Types of Architecture[3]

The first citizens of this world threw themselves into agriculture seeking freedom from hunger, and into architecture seeking shelter from rain and heat.
Both of those arts have their origins in need, their growth in the demands of
comfort, and their improvement in the excess of means and innovation. As
long as people were content living under trees, (12) in dens, and in caves, they
did not seek greater comfort and were perfectly capable of doing without
architecture. But as the population grew over time and small communities

developed, [so too grew] a need for more decent and more spacious home-steads. Hence architecture. But what kind? Sheds, huts built of simple logs and covered with straw or weeds, are the images of the newly begotten art. For a long time even in Athens, the Areopagus, instead of a magnificent roof, had a simple covering of straw even though Athens (13) could already call itself the custodian of all disciplines. In Rome, among the magnificent buildings of the Capitoline Hill, the first palace of Romulus had its place, made of simple wood resembling in design a shepherds' shed. Hence the beginnings of our disci-pline are not magnificent by any measure, but they are nevertheless very much deserving of our memory, so that architecture itself would not have to be reminded of them in the manner of the nobility, who, forgetful of who their ancestors used to be, no longer remember who they themselves are.

That learning (14) and liberal arts took their first beginnings from Egypt is nearly universally understood. Is it as though the Asiatics[4] or the Chaldeans or the Chinese were not equal to the Egyptians? In my opinion, if Egypt had Memphis, Thebes, labyrinths, pyramids; Asia had Enoch, Babylon, Nineveh.

It is difficult to prove who was first. And since, to spare time, uncertain things are better briefly mentioned than lengthily elaborated, I believe that to whatever nation those peoples belonged who first threw themselves into archi-tecture, (15) what is certain is that they expended a significant amount of time in making their minds—the innovators of new things combining need with beauty—traverse so great a distance as that found between a shed and a palace built to Corinthian proportions. For indeed others put in no less, if not more, effort when they tried to clean up our discipline and free it from the disorder into which it was beginning to fall through the unlimited freedom of archi-tects. I have to praise the Greeks in part here. For as the Egyptians (16) marveled the human eye with size more than shape, so the Greeks on the contrary put all of their efforts into the smoothness of their designs, the beauty of their form, and exquisite perfection to impress the viewer. Taste thus described was already well established in Periclean times and blossomed uninterrupted under Alex-ander the Great, expanding ever more. When the Romans, even toward the end of the Greek Republic's independent rule, got hold of architecture, they demon-strated that the student, by combining what he found with the greatness (17) characteristic of Augustan times, became equal to the master.

However, up to that point architecture had not entirely been subject to the rules of reason and reflection. The greatest challenge to this truth could be found by anyone in the most beautiful buildings of that time. And no wonder. Those who are the first to invent find it too difficult to avoid all mistakes in their undertaking, while those who only slavishly imitate others choose the good and bad elements equally and do not doubt that everything is already in the right (18) proportions, that everything has been confirmed, that everything has been validated with the dignity and name of the ancestors and even the long-established and unbroken customs. There was thus a great and urgent need for remarks to clean contaminated architecture through the clear identification of the original errors, introducing harsh critique of old works, using words to prevent errors or mistakes from being validated by [both] the blind custom of their use and the credit and fame due the original inventors. But everything happened in the opposite way; everything turned upside down.

(19) The successors of the famed architect Vitruvius imitated one another one after the other, each far removed from any progress or improvement, regressing instead. And as usually happens, the decline came more rapidly in every way than the original creation. Architecture was already outright bad under Emperor Constantine, worse under Justinian, worse yet and even more bizarre when the Barbarians embarked on the process of destroying Roman might.

What changed over that time? After Greco-Roman architecture, (20) another succeeded, heavy, devoid of any natural shape and proportion, and, for reasons I do not understand, referred to as the Gothic. For according to those more competent in the matter, the Goths knew neither bad nor good architecture; they had neither the time nor the proclivity for it. It is true that the Italian king Theodoric of the Goths ordered construction in Ravenna, Pavia, and Verona of amphitheaters, baths, and aqueducts, but in a style that had already been introduced and commonly used due to love of novelty. (21) For where and when in their own countries would the brave, bellicose Barbarians have built structures for play and romance? The Italians are all too generous in distributing and ascribing their own mistakes to others. Anything they consider unattractive they immediately attribute to the Goths, conveniently allowing themselves to point out, not their own errors, but ostensibly those of others. We see the opposite, that is, that the Goths adopted the taste they found, and directed their structures following the country's ancient customs, (22) shapelessly, for the manner of tasteful ornament had already been lost [by the Italians].[5] The problem had grown even worse under the Lombards, the Franks, and the Germans, when even the general sense of proportion was abandoned, so great was the prevailing blindness.

Some threw themselves into the task of changing the above-mentioned architecture of the tenth and eleventh centuries, but in vain. Each of them moved from one extreme to the other, and beauty that depends on proportion and decorum (23) could not emerge. While up to that point heavy and enormous structures were being erected, their builders embarked on the opposite—buildings light, airy, perforated with holes, playful, decorated with filigree, and [having] small roofs. They seemed to be constructing pyramids with heavy joints, while the structures themselves seemed delicate enough to be toppled by the lightest breath of wind. But even that was not enough. The unrestrained greed for embellishments spread further. To this new Gothic architecture were added still other, even sillier Barbarian decorative incongruities, (24) which delight the layman as much as they horrify the learned. One can see examples of them in some of the palaces in Spain erected by the Saracens and the Moors, where the proportion and measure would more appropriately be called a disproportion and lack of measure. For at that time the whim of every architect became the rule for any given building; there were as many architectures as there were buildings. For him who wanted only to surpass others in his art, to reach beyond, it was enough that (25) his building or his church simply surpass the structures of the others in height. For it was on this that the shape and beauty were based, but even that did not last. Finally, the architects found themselves in a very uncomfortable position. To the extent possible, they started to return to the old sense of proportions, imposed some limits on themselves, and drew up certain rules whose observance improved our discipline somewhat. The church of San Marco in Venice is a good example built according to the new Greek (26) architectural style. For that is the name that was given to the style at the time.

And although, with such a change afoot, it would seem that the time had come for the human mind to emerge from the deep lethargy in which it seemed to have been drowning, nevertheless, up until the sixteenth century, only small steps were made in that direction. It was only with the unexpected, surprising, and rapid renaissance of learning in Italy that architecture, among other things, improved. From then on, the Roman ruins were carefully regarded, and the measures and proportions of old were kept together, which, along with their successful demonstration in (27) the St. Peter's church project, contributed not insignificantly to the change. Bramante, Peruzzi, Sangallo, Michelangelo, and Vignola made the utmost efforts to imitate the beauty and magnificence of ancient architecture while distancing themselves from the new. The example of great men happily followed: the age of the Medici Leo X was soon to equal the centuries of Alexander and Augustus. Like Greece and ancient Rome before it, Italy issued statutes for the branches of learning for all of Europe, to which all needed to subject themselves. (28) The power of beauty over our mind is not insignificant, and therefore significant improvements were soon visible everywhere. Good architecture came under the roofs of France and added much ornament to the era of Louis XIV. It was not neglected in Spain; it spread all the way to Petersburg. It beautified Sweden, Denmark, Poland, and, even more, England. In a word, it flowed like a great river, which, though at one point it runs as a narrow brook, at another, gaining in strength, makes for itself a (29) wider bed. But as much as the discipline of architecture gained in the northern countries, it lost in Asia, Egypt, and Greece, where for ages now it could not be reborn. But such are the travels of itinerant learning.

Having considered that, allow me to say that we should be careful, in a way the successors of Vitruvius were not. Our architecture is now shapely, but to make sure that it does not exceed its measure, effort and (30) watchfulness are needed. The time is right. This era calls itself the philosophical one, and if it errs in any way, it is that everyone philosophizes about everything. However, architecture merits analysis and attention. Do not Frézier, Algarotti, Laugier, and others demonstrate what philosophy can do for this art? And who knows whether [philosophy] could not do more, if others following in their footsteps considered more harshly the effort of (31) the architects, let no error go unnoticed, and sought first causes in all things—in other words, if they were to combine theory with practice more and to pay more attention to experience. I realize that at the present time a great number of active architects must necessarily include many poor ones. But that is not why I am judging so suspiciously that our discipline is already in decline. For Vitruvius also complained about his contemporaries (32) and their number,[6] and he did so with greater regret and with deeper fear than ours for the fate of architecture. Even the enlightened age of Augustus promised a reversal in the future. Similarly, even Greece heard the lamentations of Plato. But where, and in what nation, has everyone taken responsibility for his duty? Always and everywhere the number of experts is few. (33) They are easier to find where many pursue a given discipline. It is true that we do not now count among ourselves the likes of Michelangelo, Bernini, and many others. But what can we deduce from that? Nothing except that some periods in history give birth to great men, but possibly under such circumstances in their field, in which they can show their innovation and their talent is neither free nor spacious. Indeed, it is also possible that anonymity through silence (34) or lack of knowledge about an exceptional person comes from the fact that there are no differences between architects as a result of the equal distribution of knowledge and talent across the field.

Though it is hard to contradict that as night follows day, so often a dark age follows an age of light, it is (35) easy enough to ensure that we find ourselves at the dawn of that bright day but also that that day cannot be fixed with any mathematical calculation. The golden age of architecture lasted for almost six centuries in Greece; the opposite has been with us for more than 1,300 years. And who knows when it will end. Everything is reversing itself now in Europe. For three centuries now this liberated art, along with other (36) disciplines, has experienced renewal, gaining in importance and clarity. And indeed it is to be expected that if the press, the academies, and even more the philosophical mind do not lead architecture to the anticipated improvement, they will at least very effectively delay its decline and fall.

(37) II. Remark on What Should Constitute Beauty in Architecture

It is an unmistakable fact that the things in nature people most frequently discuss they understand the least. Among thousands of those things, this is the case with beauty. Almost everybody talks about beauty; everyone everywhere has an opinion about it. But as a matter of fact, (38) if we cannot recognize beauty, then the blame is at least partially with our blindness and with us.

However, to enter the labyrinth of metaphysical meditation, which is commonly considered, is not only dangerous but altogether unfitting in our remark. A reader curious about this matter has the books of Plato, some remarks by Saint Augustine, or the conversations of recent times past published in French, the *Essai sur le Beau par P. André*.

Hence in this remark I want (39) to discuss beauty only as it pertains to architecture, remarking first on what does not determine beauty and then on what should constitute it. For whoever wishes to, let him ask architects themselves: What is beauty in their art? What is its basis? What is its nature? Is beauty in architecture constant and unchanging? Is there beauty that should appeal to all nations alike? May an image be found that would allow us to come close to the most natural beauty and give us a prescription for it? Whoever wishes to, let him ask (40) the architects themselves about all of it; and let him see that their understanding of the matter, when expressed, will confuse them. For the less they think about what they already perfectly know, the clearer it is. And that is why the greater number of them—if, at the moment when they are being asked, a certain je ne sais quoi with which they usually defend themselves will not come to their rescue—will demonstrate a shocking ignorance of beauty. For everybody knows that it is nature that imbued us with the affinity for (41) objects of proportion. But allow me briefly and clearly to explain what causes that affinity.

First of all, as one can surmise from everyday experience, considering something beautiful or ugly is often a consequence of custom. It is also from this experience that we can easily claim that beauty in architecture should not depend on taste introduced through custom, (42) for Greco-Roman architecture, respected for a long time, lost its property of beauty in the eyes of Gothic architects. In Italy, in Rome itself, it was the Gothic style of architecture that was considered beautiful, as if to offend ancient beauty. We of this age can hardly look at Gothic architecture once so favored. Who knows how much those who come after us will hold our architecture in contempt. We can see so far how the Muslims have contempt for Greek architecture in countries under their control. If therefore architecture (43) depends on taste alone, then who is fit to judge? Who has better taste: a Greek, an Italian, or a Turk? Each loves his own structures, each considers his own manner better than those of others, one makes a wry face at the other. And what can we take from that? Only the fact that the beauty of our art does not depend on taste or any particular fashion. For it is different fashion and not architecture that would be considered beautiful.

I am also far removed from those who seek the shape of architecture in its taste and use as determined by architects themselves. For (44) more often than not, the beginning of use is such that one respects everything that comes from one's teachers, believing in their knowledge and often lacking the courage or opportunity to discern the bad from the good. The architects themselves are susceptible to those who command them to build; either because of their intellectual limitations or their need to flatter, they have to place the most wondrous idiosyncrasies in the structures that they erect. And even without that, whom can we imitate with certainty and without the possibility of error. (45) Perhaps Vitruvius, the lawgiver of the Latin architects? Even Vitruvius, however great a man he proved to be, was also susceptible to error. Scamozzi warns against trusting Vitruvius completely and indeed assures us that his measurements of columns are false and far removed from beauty proper. As a matter of fact, to tell you the truth, sometimes Vitruvius contradicts himself. Sometimes what he first criticizes he then praises. So if one has to be careful with Vitruvius, (46) what does one say about others, respectable, in truth, but inferior to him as architects? Alberti, Serlio, Palladio, Scamozzi, Vignola, Philibert de l'Orme—all have merit, but they disagree with one another, each makes mistakes, and none is faithfully and absolutely followed by his imitators. This reasoning perfectly demonstrates that a weaker architect would be unlikely to attain proper beauty. The image of ancient buildings, (47) though somewhat helpful to architecture, nevertheless cannot become its first principle. This truth could easily be recognized by anyone who would remember that it is architects who erect those structures and therefore can have no more importance than they and possibly less, for practice effectively always lessens the purity of theory. And it is rare that we would find those structures without a flaw, often in fact with great errors. The Roman arches, the Baths of Diocletian, the Theater of (48) Marcellus did not perfectly follow the rules of architecture. In my opinion, if all the [ancient] buildings were to serve us as examples of beauty proper, each and even the most egregious error would have its defender in an ancient example.

And therefore, because neither in human tastes nor in architectural use, not even in the buildings of the ancients, can we find the image of beauty proper, let us abandon these frequently alluring paths (49) and seek the image of beauty; only there will we know to find it without an error. One should not doubt that it can be found where pure, unprejudiced, and indeed natural philosophy reveals it.

Even the weakest and most elementary remark should demonstrate to anyone that order, arrangement, and proportion are everywhere more pleasing than disorder, confusion, and lack of proportion. Why, even natural (50) geometry explains that a figure is more shapely, the more smoothly its lines interact; that when any drawing consists of many parts, all should be arranged to avoid any confusion, placing the single ones in the middle, the double ones on the sides; placing equal parts in equal numbers insofar as possible, equally removed from the center, the unequal parts on both sides in a way that allows them to correspond with one another. In other words, (51) to connect all those parts in a manner that creates unity without accentuating any striking difference. Taking from experience, it is enough to look at two homes, one regular and one irregular, to remind oneself not only of beauty but also of the prescription for it hidden within.

Above all, there are three sources for the rules of architecture: nature, geometry, and human experience of certain proportions not contrary to (52) the organization of a human being. Outside of nature and geometry, rules are not dependent on our varied cleverness. However, prescriptions collected from experience may appeal within certain limits to our taste, but they should be applied in a manner consistent with the laws of geometry and nature, whose combination should provide a tempering influence according to what decorum dictates. *Hic murus aheneus esto.*[7]

Take, for example, the simple line of a column, (53) the choice of figures more convenient, more even, and you see that first and fundamental rules in our art come from geometry. Nature teaches us about the organization of fitting ornaments, of columns slender on the top and heavier on the bottom, of the use and height of frontons, and of their incline, and a thousand other similar elements. The choice of the arches, windows, and columns according to the Doric, Ionic, or Corinthian order, the relationship between the height and width—in a word, all ornaments and their measures (54) consistent in their proportions and organization come from experience.

And although thanks to the use of figures in our art anyone can understand the tight connection between geometry and architecture, it is less obvious what those proportions consistent with the human organization of the human body are, what the rules for imitating them are, and what images in nature help us to grasp them. To begin with, I believe that proportions that agree with the enjoyment of our senses (55) depend on harmonious relations, the same harmonies on which music draws in a performance. Another remark will explain the art of harmoniously dividing a line.

For now, I want to mention that the resulting proportions are not only in agreement with the comfort and reliable construction of erected structures, but they are also—indeed they must be—pleasing to the eye. If it is considered a certainty in anatomy that veins conveying the sense of hearing lead to our soul, not (56) only are they of the same measure as the veins of the human eyes (or other objects moved in the opposite direction), but also each vein in its vibrating movement is responsible for equal sensation. However, a small deviation in their movement does not cause any error. Combining optics and perspective with need and circumstances allows a clever architect, artificially and sometimes necessarily, to draw on geometric and arithmetic proportions. (57) And this is what I meant when I said, "pleasing to the eye."

Second, there is another thing many cannot understand: in what sense do I derive the laws of architecture from nature? How can nature possibly be the image of this art, when Mother Nature, present in all the world's things, has never produced anything resembling architecture? I confess that this is but illusory criticism, and not so (58) strong as immediately to abolish our argument. There are three ways to imitate nature: by imitating nature itself, by imitating the manner in which nature runs its course, and finally by imitating natural architecture. I will explain this more clearly.

First of all, nature presents us with visible images; we are able to imitate nature in and of itself not only in water arts, but in the arrangement of our gardens, in the arrangement of rocks and terrible grottos that, frequently employed in Italy, (59) produce the most pleasing of sights. In Rome the Trevi Fountain used to be much more pleasing to the eye when its water followed the traces of nature, neither easily nor evenly, but instead in spurts, struggling as if running in grooves off to the side with a rushing sound toward a steep fall in a natural manner, as if pushed off of a cliff. Even now, it is a pleasure to look at the Navona Fountain, so called from the (60) square on which it is founded in Rome, and the pleasure is all the greater that the rock anchoring a large obelisk is not carved with a human hand, but together with the obelisk it was broken from Egyptian rocks and brought as if seemingly on purpose. With all of this [. . .] I can't understand [. . .] that not a single example has nature given to architecture.[8]

Let us take note that of the same nature whose (61) own course we imitate, we may just as well imitate the manner in which it progresses. If for better effect[9] one took two disciplines not only remote from each other but in fact opposites of each other and took one to be the model for the other, this strange decision would seem insufficiently thought through, but possibly might serve as a form of preparation or of seeking the beginnings of architecture. The philosophers apply such thinking to law. Nowadays law and geometry are taught together even though they seem remote, and indeed the (62) origins of geometry and law are indeed opposite. In this way, although most certainly we are not likely to find herbs or leaves expressing arches or columns, we do have, and consider certain, the actions and works of nature, which we should usefully imitate, all the more so that they are derived from the Highest for the decent arrangement of the world. That is what imitation is, that is what derivation is, to be able to use what one sees. All of these various colors in the sky, (63) connected in this unity, can they not teach us that in buildings there should be various elements of which the entire structure consists, with different elements introduced and interwoven only gradually and step-by-step, showing the variety?

In the end, we can easily find natural architecture that, although already masked or hidden, can nevertheless be discerned in the greatest homes and even in royal structures. In Roman palaces the architect-philosopher will first find beggars' huts; he will find (64) logs incorporated in columns and other ornaments. And if he will not find them, then that fact rightly will allow him to make a judgment about this style of building. For even if those buildings are to be hidden or covered, their architecture should always seem natural.

Let us remind ourselves of the beginnings of architecture as mentioned; let us analyze civil architecture, and we will certainly find that our discipline also has its own grammar all the more (65) dignified in its simplicity.

Columns are derived from the shafts used in those arts which in the beginning of time used to support roofs and other coverings. And because in the beginning those shafts used to be dug directly into the ground, we also have an example of Doric columns without any base in the Theater of Marcellus (see Fig. i). When, however, their weight and moisture caused the said shafts to sink deeper than necessary, it marked the introduction of the base and support; hence in columns (66) bases are introduced (Fig. ii).

And the heads, or the capitals, only slightly express parts of the architrave so situated on the upper part of the column as to make it easier for the epistyle to be supported (Fig. iii). The architrave itself, now referred to by the architects as the epistyle, supports beams placed at right angles to one another, forming a crisscross pattern on the inside, which, covered with smaller planks, serve as a ceiling (Fig. iv).

Over time, the part of the entablature commonly known as the *frigium,* or (67) frieze, became the most ornamental among the ancients. The space in Figure iv marked with the letter x between the two beams, or the metope, which we could call *bałczyca* according to its own meaning [something substantial], differed in width from the beams (r) themselves and the triglyphs (m), which were shaped with channels or vugs as if carved by the water dripping off the roof. In this way, the human mind thought of a decorative use even for erosion or natural damage.

Also, the end of the cornice, known in Latin as the *cornix,* expresses (68) nothing beyond the natural slant of the roof, that is, the incline of the roof artistically covering the distance just beyond the wall, so that the rain falling off the roof is removed as much as possible from the wall (Fig. v). Dentils (d) used under that section of the cornice represent patches (s.s.) that keep the roof tiles in place. But the other pieces, known variously as the *mensulae,* modillions, or mutules (Fig. vi), serve as nothing but supports (m, m) between the end of the roof and the wall, strengthening the slanted roof. (69) If in the entablatures the *mensulae,* triglyphs, and spaces between, the metopes, are often not visible, it is only because in those early times, as now in the wooden buildings, the entire entablature used to be covered with smooth sheets.

Going further, one can discern that this incline of the roof, which on the façades of churches is decorated by the pediment known as the frontispiece (Fig. vii), is derived from the roof's natural slant. Under the mild Greek sky,

(70) the Greeks could keep the pediment at a mild angle, which in Italy grew slightly greater, combining beauty with need in that country. In the northern countries, even in ours, we make the roofs steeper still than in Italy. The Egyptians, who on the contrary rarely experience rain, make use of homes without roofs and buildings without pediments. And is this not an obvious example of a tight relationship between nature and architectural ornaments?

But that is not all. In the early beginnings of our art, (71) the shafts now known by their more glorified name of columns, used to be dug into the ground not far apart from one another in order to make it easier to support the higher beams to cover a home or structure, as I described earlier (Fig. VIII). Over time, however, as new needs arose, when the human mind sought new comforts, that distance [between columns] in the design of houses also increased, so much that it became almost impossible for the shafts to support broad beams. In that olden time of those first (72) inhabitants, joining two trees at an angle with an architrave at the top relieved significant weight. We veritably ape our ancestors, whether the need exists or not; it is from that that we use arches between columns, gladly and sometimes in vain doing what the ancients did with drudgery of labor and not without reason (Fig. IX), but probably out of necessity to free themselves of rain, bad air, and harmful winds. The entire distance covered by the shafts (73) surrounding the whole house was covered with sheets in such a manner that if the shafts were unfinished they would seem round, and if finished they would seem four-sided between those sheets. And is that not the obvious source of pilasters or engaged columns so often used? (Fig. x) But when it comes to stylobates, commonly called pedestals, they were used for no other reason but either to raise the structure and improve the view of those looking up from below or, when dealing with a swampy ground, to (74) free the structure from the harmful effects of moisture.

This is what I call natural architecture, which should take utility not only as its rule but as a measure for those who criticize it. From that on which I have been expanding so far, however, the purpose of my remark is easily disclosed here.

For indeed, I see two types of beauty in architecture: one not at all subject to our varied ingenuity, the other subject to it but limited (75) by its relationship to the first. I assume the first type of beauty to reside in its imitation of nature—that is, either in imitating nature itself or the manner in which it runs its course or natural architecture. The second type of beauty I take to be in the choice of proportions, whether harmonious or otherwise, but always in concordance with nature. Therefore, where those two types of beauties are found, architecture will be beautiful as well. For let anyone say (76) whatever one pleases, there is nothing more pleasant to the human eye than the sight of nature to which we are immediately accustomed from childhood and which exists not for anyone else but for us. Even the unthinking beasts have eyes; they have organs much like our own; their veins, just like ours, are moved by external objects. What then will the difference be between human and animal perception if we banish natural taste from the rules of proportions? What is our superiority over beasts (77) if we exclude the certain and unchanging origin of our taste? In my opinion, even if such exclusion were the case, we should be ashamed of our horrible humiliation, hiding it rather than announcing it to the world. And what now, when of course we can see that beauty rests in something else and does not depend on our taste? For even what we call a proportion cannot be a proportion if it is not (78) a natural thing, and we cannot find a natural thing that would lack proportion. For what is a proportion if not an easy confirming of external things with the organs of the person perceiving them? And can we doubt that the Creator of all things surrounded us with objects contrary to our senses, that He created things for us discordant to us; would it not be coarse blindness and hubris to accuse this world's first (79) Architect of such an error, which would offend even the lowest of architects? I would be eager to discover why some find it necessary to rebuke our noble art for something for which others are responsible. Why go against one's own reason? Why is it that those who think that way call nature the mother, caretaker, master, and image of all things? It is not even my opinion, but that of Cicero, that such enemies of nature imitate those legendary (80) and brave giants who rebel against their own gods and attack them with their gifts.

As it is every human being's duty to remember the proper origin of beauty, so too is it the architect's to reconcile that beauty of nature with need, comfort, and ingenuity. It will certainly come to them more easily when they follow these three rules.

First of all, architects should not distance themselves from nature, (81) but they should also not exaggerate in their imitation, maintaining proper restraint. For it is just as objectionable to have a column so twisted as to be unnatural as to have one that is not twisted but carved out of an uneven shaft and therefore all too natural. Lack of care can be noble, but it has to be as the ancient rhetorician proscribes: *Negligentia quaedam diligens.*[10] For if there is a happy middle (82) in beauty, what the Latins called the *modum,* the one who crosses that desired middle sins as much as the one who falls short of it. A building without any ornaments may not be pleasing to the eye. But is the Gothic eye human that would tolerate such decorative excess used in palaces and churches of old? I am not saying that there is insufficient artistry in the collections of small figures; indeed I propose that there is all too much of it, and it is because of that overabundance that (83) I criticize Gothic architecture.

Second of all, architects should maintain this famous rule, which merits to be carved out in bold letters in every academy: *An architect should not do anything,* Vitruvius says, *for which he cannot give a good reason.* Such an obvious and clear law does not require a long explication.

And finally, it is up to the architect to render the structure handsome. It is on this part that (84) Laugier, surprisingly well, expounds in his booklet, showing that nothing is more just than for there to be a relationship between the builder and the building—that is, between the home and the master. What often happens to those looking at the private palaces of great lords is what happened to an ancient Roman in Egypt: when looking at the external façade of a church, he understood that it must be devoted to a great deity, and entering with that assumption in mind, he found to his surprise a funny monkey (85) playing inside. If a mistake similar to this does not trespass against the essence of beauty, at least it is not consistent with its intelligent bestowal.

Let the Pyrrhonist philosophers desist in saying that beauty is only a matter of taste and that this taste is not and may not be subject to any rule. Let them stop announcing out loud what a good philosopher should be ashamed of, even if it were but a hidden thought. (86) Truly such enemies of architecture are not terrible, but they are bold and arrive in great numbers. Their entire doubt comes from the fact that they see in architecture, in all its diversity, great instability and variety. But they forget that if ever there were such instability, it was for no other reason than that some have opinions similar to theirs and claim that everything is subject to the variety of ideas. The authors of those opinions themselves turn out to be guilty of the very trespass of which they accuse (87) innocent architecture. They add that although architecture is needed, its beauty is entirely unnecessary. They claim that a Tatar is equally content with his miserable abode as a German, a Frenchman, or an Italian with a magnificent structure. And on this they base the belief that each should remain within his own borders and each should enjoy this architecture that blind luck bestowed on him. It is true that those who are governed by luck must (88) like such a thought; true that those who gamble with life should enjoy such architecture. But it is also certain that common sense should not stop at that, and that a prudent man should restrain his taste with reason.

Let us therefore conclude, along with all philosophers of architecture, that architecture is not entirely subject to our unrestrained will; that nature is its (89) image;[11] that beauty will be constant or unchanging where taste is tempered by the reasoned imitation of nature; and that our art will use all the help that it can use, not only from geometry but also from all much needed philosophy.`

(90) III. Remark on the Benefits Coming from the Discipline of Architecture

Architecture, being a part of philosophy, should be judged not only by architects themselves but also by others. According to some, (91) those kings who first erected cities without seeking strangers to establish their walls determined all things on their own. This art used to be a royal game, although even now one of the German princes so decorates his cities with structures imitating pictures of Venice, Rome, and Vicenza that his capital can already be called not only the school of Mars but of Apollo as well.[12] But can the hand of that great monarch [not] use equally a pen and a weapon, a compass and a ruler? (92) For are not the new funeral chapel, the completion of the Charlottenburg Palace, including the magnificent ballroom, his own ideas? It is no wonder, then, that following those examples, it is the noble ones who are entertained with the noble art. Many nobles born in Italy always used to have training in architecture. In Sweden, I gather, Count Tessin, following in the footsteps of his father, erected a structure the like of which would be hard to find in northern countries. And the English lords, (93) among whom we count Pembroke, the Earl of Northumberland, and Burlington, show perfectly that this liberated art is much respected in their country. And we can even find our own examples in this matter, for some of our own also imitate this now-common but noble custom, seeking to improve architecture more and more. As a matter of fact, it would perhaps be beneficial for those who are able to build (kings, nobility, the affluent, even the clergy), not necessarily to (94) get to know this discipline thoroughly, but to become acquainted with it. For how can one not at all conversant in architecture choose a good architect or a good design? Who can explain certain rules to an architect, certain comforts, without having any idea about the discipline's beginnings and its governing rules?

And at the same time, with any understanding of it all, not only building but also other arts with design (95) would improve. For paying no heed to others, the woodcarvers, according to their own will, now do with us as they please, in furniture, in wood paneling, creating silly ornaments, all the worse for being expensive, without the least attention paid to the naturalness of the effect. They charge us steep prices for their mistakes, often gilded as if out of spite.[13]

But the consequences of the misunderstanding of architecture go further still. Let us look not at the builder or the decorator (96) of a home, but at the one who, for his own convenience, seeks new forms in tables, cabinets, and bureaus. Our everyday experience immediately shows us that one gripped by such a fearful forgetfulness, weak of thought, rushes to the craftsman as quickly as possible, half dead from unstable ideas changed and renewed every step of the way; [he] finally arrives at the spot marked where our comedy only just begins. For the new caller starts a conversation (97) with the worker, yet one does not comprehend the other. Each spins someone else's thought upon his own, the conveniences of others applying to his own opinion. Hence the Babylonian confusion. And so several idle hours are spent in vain. The craftsman takes more time to talk than to do the work; it takes more time to understand each other than to perform the task at hand. Therefore, not wanting to suffer any longer in vain, and maybe even ready to forgo the profit, he already starts to assure [the client] that everything was perfectly (98) understood and that he will do the work as directed, specifying on top of this the day and the hour if not the minute of completion. At such time my caller is beginning to leave, muttering ceaselessly under his breath, in the doorway, on the stairs, and if necessary even on the street. But with all that, the craftsman still does not know what it is that he is supposed to undertake; he puts together parts of earlier directions and sees in them only contradiction and assumptions that cannot possibly lead to the desired effect. He therefore becomes impatient. (99) Without much thought he undertakes the work, putting all his effort into completing the effort within the promised time. Meanwhile the unpleasant caller again suddenly barges into the craftsman's shop, snatching up work that is possibly not yet finished. He looks at it, but even he himself is not sure if it is the thing he once desired. Slightly embarrassed, he does not dare say anything. From this he always reaps shame and silence as the craftsman praises (100) the nobleman's taste (about which he never thought) and his attentiveness in the blind imitation of the thought of another (which he never experienced); in a word, he is bamboozled and muddled still more: the craftsman would not get away with it if the nobleman had any knowledge of design drawing, more trust in his own ideas.

But that is not all there is. We visit foreign lands, traveling from one country to another, from one city to another. (101) The very first things that strike us are the buildings. Therefore we have to visit those, as long as we do not do it superficially. Otherwise, instead of clarity, we will walk away confused and with a false understanding of the thing growing in our minds. That often leads, as they often say, to *quid pro quo*. Taking one thing for another, one could be found with his own ugliness in tow; having returned to the fatherland, he would confuse a column with a pilaster, a dome with a tower, the portico of a church with the (102) church itself. I ask, what is the benefit of such sightseeing?

However, let it be a given that a noble citizen does not leave his home country, that for him the world does not exist beyond the walls of his own city. In short, let us turn all of our remarks to one such nobleman, looking at him as one who does not know such architecture. And from him probably, apart from the unpleasantness in praise, screaming both unbearable and incessant, one should also (103) expect wonderment.[14] For a person remaining in such a relationship to knowledge, even the smallest thing would seem magnificent, indeed most wonderful; another would seem base or worthy of all his attention for the simple reason that it is to him unfamiliar. For a person who understands architecture, the conversation would be completely the opposite: it would be intelligent, and the conversation would make apparent knowledge worthy of respect. As for unpleasant wonderment, that often comes from the lack of understanding in a mind (104) clogged with unrestrained love of one's own things and sometimes of things foreign.

And because we know well from experience that the shape of structures preserved, not only whole but also in parts, brings fame to each individual citizen and to the entire country, part of the orderly organization of a city would be to place architecture under public management. For it is one thing to say, "A nice city," and another to say, "Nice architecture." (105) If so, through the establishment of a ruling standard for the façades of palaces by a group of architects designated for the purpose, each city would certainly contain fewer unshapely structures. We know that Turin, in Italy, was built according to this useful manner, and it is considered one of the most beautiful [cities], a city more orderly than others, yet we do not seem to be able to use that knowledge.

But here, I fear, a student of (106) Tullius, armed with his master's book, would not fail to bring up opinions somewhat contrary to my Ciceronian interpretations. Even without that, I am aware that this great rhetorician does not count private buildings among needs, that he criticizes churches, even

74

magnificent ones, that he claims that buildings such as these bring infamy instead of glory to cities. I believe that these severe civic thoughts occurred to Cicero only when (107) he saw freedom and liberty in his fatherland collapse from excess. Overcome with regret and passion, Cicero complained about every manifestation, whether commenting on instances of something outright harmful or on something serving as a poor example. Therefore, while maintaining the deepest respect for him, I do not believe there is anything wrong, once a country has all the structures it needs, for it to have other buildings for greatness, enjoyment, and entertainment. However, when it comes to our (108) fatherland in particular, I agree with everyone who believes that we have to put more thought into public structures. Over time, the Commonwealth should establish official residences for state dignitaries, befitting the dignity of the office and tied to that office [rather than its officeholder]. For in this way, those private residences would almost strengthen into royal palaces, castles, and other similar structures by being passed on to the successors of the office, instead of (109) to successors by bloodline, for whom the inheritance often becomes more of a burden than a benefit. For even if individual citizens enjoy building, as is often the case, the opportunities for fulfillment of their desires would be greater and more honorable if they expended the same sums to build churches, hospitals, schools, and public toilets, necessary for hygiene and rarely used here. The mayor of Amsterdam, one (110) [Johan Witte], has few imitators; his entire income was spent on public building needs. With all this, if the rich learned more diligently the art of managing their money, I assure you that idleness, poverty, and vices everywhere would turn into industry, financial self-sufficiency, effort, and work.

These are the true benefits flowing from the understanding of architecture. But please let no (111) sylvan philosopher get angry, warning everyone that cities are prisons, and fortresses veritable cages. It is easy only to mention to such a philosopher that in the absence of society and cities, one would be hard-pressed to find on earth either justice or friendship or love or any other primary virtues that keep the entire human nation together. Philosophy would not be known either, nor other as-yet-unknown liberal arts. Our affinity for learning and forming communities would be abandoned and buried (112) in its entirety. True, it is often easier for rulers, at least when it comes to speed and efficiency, to conquer people living in the comfort of cities and harder to quash the wild and those spread throughout forests. But it is also true that this would be a sad and false privilege of savagery and that not everybody is so hostile to freedom as always to want to lose it irretrievably. Besides, there is to be found in this world not a single (113) thing that brings nothing but good. Everything has some small inconvenience about it, or at least creates an opening for possible consequences. However, choosing according to the precepts of common sense, of those arts which bring people the most benefit and the least harm, I believe that even the most exacting of philosophers would concede that architecture would be one of the first among them.

(114) IV. Remark on Ornaments in Building

All natural things, not only those we comprehend in our mind but also those we perceive with our senses, are subject to philosophical understanding. Therefore, philosophy of beauty proper cannot contradict good taste, discovering true origins in all things, (115) without confusing one thing for the other, but instead describing everything according to the heart of the matter. In fact, this first and common ability may offer significant help for good taste. It should therefore also be easy for me (having in another remark already explicated the proper aspects of beauty) to discover in ornaments of architecture much-needed cautionary remarks, unpleasant only in that they will often controvert the established custom and possibly thus-formed (116) example.

The ornaments of architecture belong to that aspect of beauty I associated with human taste as long as it is not contrary to nature. Among other architectural ornaments, the most important ones are the orders according to which various columns are carved, with their various manifestations. We can count five orders in architecture, although only three orders exist: (117) Doric, Ionic, and Corinthian. The quality of basic beauty lies in the Doric, of delicate beauty in the Corinthian, and of medium beauty in the Ionic. Whatever crosses the order in one way or the other will not have pleasing proportions. For example, the Tuscan order would seem to a good architect too simple; the Roman, or Composite, too delicate.

Each order comprises greater (118) parts, which in turn comprise lesser elements. The greater parts, starting on the top, are the cornice, the frieze, the architrave; then proceeding lower, the shaft of the column itself and its base. The stylobates, that is, the pedestals, do not constitute an essential configuration of all orders.

For brevity, the smaller parts, as they constitute the greater elements, are shown in Table I. I copied and marked each with its name. It will be easier looking at the attached figure (119) to understand and remember those parts from which almost all ornamentation in our architecture derives.

The ratio of the thickness of the column to its height, as well as to the height of the entablature, is not established so rigidly as to make it impossible for us to leave it aside for now. The configuration of the columns itself brings about significant variations in those ratios. And with all due respect to some honorable and known masters, I (120) deviate from them only in that I consistently designate the entablature as the column's fourth part, so that both in the Doric and Ionic orders, as I define them, my column will be only four times taller than the entablature. For to tell the truth, when the Doric and Ionic columns are of the same height, I do not see and I do not understand why the Ionic entablature is to be smaller and the Doric larger? (121) For the entablature, by its nature, should start at the line of the roof. And simply because a structure is to be built, for example, according to the Doric order, should the roof be raised without any other reason? If so, will somebody claim that in that way the Corinthian order would lose its delicacy compared to others? But nothing can be further from the truth, for the proper delicacy of columns depends on the ratio of thickness to height, which, following common custom, (122) I determine to be the following: in the Doric order, 1:8; in the Ionic, 1:9; in the Corinthian, 1:10. Though we will examine the proper proportions of each order in greater depth. Being the first, the Doric order is designated for buildings that even at first glance convey strength and simplicity. Hence it is obvious that a multitude of thin elements would not (123) agree with it. A big man, big members; a big tree, big branches bestowed to it by nature. The whole of Greek architecture was not divided into tiny pieces.

So too the Doric base, which is commonly in use, would be far more shapely if a small membrane,[15] marked in Figure I with the letter X, would not follow the larger and convex one, (124) as in Figure II, where after that part, called the torus, a simple listel follows. There is nothing to criticize in the capital of the Doric column. All proportions are decent, pleasant, and natural.

The ratio of the column's diameter to its height underwent much change among the ancients. The Greeks hardly ever raised their Doric columns (125) higher than five times the measure of the diameter; the Romans [raised them] a bit more. The column in the Theater of Marcellus was seven times [the measure of the diameter]; in the Diocletian Baths, it exceeds eight times [the diameter]. This last proportion is what I follow.

The Doric architrave should only be separated from the *frigium* (frieze) with one fillet, as shown in Figure II, where I have deliberately shown a column with some errors on one side and [a column] with those errors (126) cleaned up on the other. I have done so in the hope of making it easier to separate right from wrong.

So the Doric frieze has triglyphs, the spaces between which are decorated with metopes. Many unnecessarily leave out the metope in Doric columnia-tion, only because they do not work out correctly in a square figure. (127) I freely admit that if excessively elongated, they would not be very shapely. But such is the law as is the beginning, so that I do not see the reason why they necessarily have to be four-sided. I am, following the example of Vignola, much more critical of the dentil molding in the final part of the frieze, insofar as those tiny parts are too delicate for the whole.

In Figure II, therefore, among others, I have eliminated the dentil molding from the Doric frieze.

(128) I find far fewer mistakes in the Ionic order. The Ionic capital the ancient Romans used is not at all shapely. Ours and that of the ancient Greeks, whom, for reasons I do not understand, the Romans chose not to imitate, is far better. Two thin fillets slightly removed from the rolled part [the volutes] of the capital are a more pleasing sight than if they are placed immediately under it.

(129) Some divide the Ionian architrave into three parts, but such divisions are better left to the Corinthian order, for in [the Ionian] two will suffice (see Figure IV). The Ionian pedestal does not agree with the rule of architecture that says always to put thin on thick, and not thick atop thin supports. Far better therefore is the pedestal in Figure IV.

(130) The best model of the Corinthian order can be found in the ruins of Rome on the old Roman Forum behind the Capitoline. The column shown in Figure VI is taken from there. From it, anybody can infer the difference between its capital and pedestal and those used in contemporary times. But after such a long debate on the measures of those styles, is it not beside the point to figure out if it is fitting to compile one order out of many? (131) For example, could one give a column an Ionian capital, a Corinthian pedestal, and a Doric frieze? My answer to this question is only that each order, having its own proper character, is a useful order whenever it is derived from its properties. It is my opinion that such a compilation of disparate pieces is not only not useful, unnecessary, but also unnatural and ridiculous. (132) Would it not be ridicu-lous to see a statue of Hercules with a leg of Venus, or a happy Cupid with a

face of lame Vulcan? It is not without reason that the principal architect, Vitruvius, had contempt for mixing one order with another. Doing so is most often and most easily started out of a love of novelty and a lack of skills and intelligence (133) [required] to find something different. For why, with such a sense of affinity for the new, are we not looking for some new and heretofore unknown order? Why do we feel unable to do it, placing Greek invention above our own? We have two ways to come up with our own order, and we consider which one is the safer of the two.

Those two ways would be either to combine (134) different smaller aspects of an order or to invent an entirely new one. The first way is the one that the Romans undertook with great decisiveness when, taking the upper part of the Ionic capital, they combined it with the Corinthian. The French tried something similar during the time of Louis XIV. Both understood that to reach the desired effect, it was enough to change the capital. And none of these architects forgot about the Corinthian (135) capital. Instead of olive leaves, ostrich feathers mixed with decorations were added to the column in such a manner as to make this otherwise-known order pass for an entirely new order around the world, even though the change that was made was so small. Fruitful thinking! If this were all there was to the novelty, if a change in the capital were to be enough to make the order pass henceforth for a new one, then we would be begging the architects (136) not to try to come up with any new orders.

Which is why it is far better to approach this issue the other way—that is, to invent entirely new constituent parts. For however much we rearrange and move the old parts around, one thing is certain: there will always be similarity, and almost no difference will be apparent. The shape and figure of new parts can be excavated from the image of nature. Indeed, different forms and thousands (137) of varieties of leaves would greatly ease the necessary effort. Whoever does not believe it and considers me and the advice I give suspect will be more inclined to look at me with a kinder eye after reading what the famous Mr. Laugier, whom I have often praised, has to say about architecture. Because a careful reading of [Laugier's] book, together with the will and desire to [do hard] work, could go far in expunging from the heads of many people the false opinion that it is practically impossible to invent a new order in (138) architecture.

In construction, all the twisted and crooked columns should be moved as far apart as possible. The first model of crooked columns I found in a book by the famous Pozzo,[16] who was a better painter than he was an architect. First, the author himself confesses that columns like those are excessive.[17] But he endorses them with a reason that is contrary to him (139) and his opinion. He says that even the ancients quite often used human figures (in architecture called caryatids) in a seated position, which is, according to him, slanted and crooked. This is completely as though the example of the ancients had the privilege of approving errors and unnaturalness; as though it were a natural thing to present a person of strength and power in a seated position; and finally as though it were decent to present columns that have no similarity with (140) people whatsoever, twisted in a way you would never twist the human figure. Those sorts of columns are too unnatural, too unshapely to fit in—maybe I am not saying into *fabriques,* but not in those works in which an architect is allowed some more freedom. Here and there we can use twisted columns. They seem pleasing enough in the confessional St. Peter's, where they support the fabulous (141) baldachin. But I doubt very much that to support even a baldachin, crooked columns could have been used. (See Figs. VII and VIII, in which I have deliberately placed a crooked column.)

Any column of any order has a base, [. . .] and the uppermost part of the capital is four-sided, so it cannot fit where the angle is not square or is too skinny or too broad. (142) An angle would either have to be made smaller or larger so that the column could merge with the space, and great care has to be taken to choose [geometric] figures and to use anything but four-sided ones only in situations where the spot so dictates. When we are faced with this circumstance, then we need to rely on all the solutions that deep knowledge of (143) art reveals to us.

For we do have an easy way to avoid unshapeliness. When the angle of a figure is too narrow, like corners *xx* in Figure IX, then in the corner one builds up the wall until the edges of two columns put together form a straight figure.[18] Otherwise, the corners of a four-sided base not only protrude from the proper spot in which they should be contained, but they also do not (144) connect in a shapely manner with the other nearby columns. In Figure X the four-sided base "A" has its sides in a nonrectangular corner; they would not align evenly with the sides of nearby column [bases]. And whenever there is an obtuse corner, then you would similarly connect the columns in the shape of corners *dd* in Figure IX. So that these much-needed things (145) can be understood easily by a curious reader, I have reproduced other smaller and bigger corners, and in looking at them carefully, the reader will understand everything quickly. That is why I have added at the end a four-sided figure in which connecting two columns together is not necessary, as one can see just by looking at it (see Fig. XI).

It happens that architects themselves arrange columns in a round figure, and to make things worse, they line them up in several rows, as (146) you can see in Figure XII. Whoever looks at the base of a column will not see any mistake in this arrangement, despite the truth of it. For raising those columns off the base causes the first row to be disproportionately small (see Fig. XIII), and the last one at this height will be as wide as Figure XIV shows. What can an architect do in this situation? He should avoid the completely round and use instead roundish (147) figures; otherwise the last row will always be too wide.

Hence, whenever columns are arranged in one row in a round figure, the columns should be used without arches. An example of columns with arches is in Figure XV; without arches, in Figure XVI. The reason for this prescription is clear. For where the arches have their proper places, arch *bb,* is marked in Figure XVII with dots, (148) and it proceeds from line *dd,* that is, from the corners of the columns, on which the arch itself should be supported. This mistake is contrary to thoroughness, if not propriety, [and is] at least visually apparent. The moldings that we use in columns are not only for the decoration of the columns, but they also, in the upper part of windows and doors, interact with the figures with which they deliberately connect, easily bestowing proper proportions (149) on each.

In architecture, we have in the end other decorations that take their shape and pleasing aspect from drawing more than from anything else. In this respect, the ancient Greeks and Romans were superior to everybody else. Even in their moldings, ceilings, floors, their art is extremely pleasing to the eye. The Italians imitate the Greeks and Romans. It is my belief that nothing would be more useful for our art than a collection (150) of those decorations that were contained in Greek and Roman architecture. It is with great pleasure that I heard that one person in Rome is putting the greatest effort into assembling similar decorations. If this work goes forth into the world, it will be useful, interesting, and much needed. So far I have not found any author writing about it at length. Everyone who writes anything about architecture only touches [on this] superficially and does not explicate (151) this very much needed matter. In such a short piece, I could not discuss those things in great detail, and in particular I cannot discuss the thing that should be more greatly considered in figures. It is from experience, from good taste, and from the frequent observation of ancient structures, as well as from certain rules, more than from remarks or lengthy elaborations, that one understands it in general.

(152) V. Remark on Comfort in Buildings

In the remarks I have written so far, I have focused on architecture more in and of itself than as something applied to building. Organization now dictates discovery of the practical rules governing our art. In every building, it is necessary to observe comfort, solidity, and beauty. (153) So I will start with comfort and turn to solidity and beauty in further remarks. What I refer to as comfort depends on the good distribution of parts and their fitting placement. Many take it less dogmatically than I do, and indeed they understand the two to be completely synonymous. However, the distribution of parts means nothing more, really, than their quantity; that is: the appropriate size of pieces, which, whether separately or collectively, remain consistent with the workings of the whole and with (154) the outfitting of the building for its intended use. The placement, on the other hand, is nothing other than the quality, which is the decent choice in situating the parts in agreement with the final end the building will serve. In that way, comfort differs from utility in architecture in that comfort takes the drudgery out of the performance of the duties that should be carried out within, while utility atones for the use (155) that the builder assumed for the structure. A building may therefore be both useful and uncomfortable, and the opposite—comfortable but not in accordance with the will and the purpose of the builder. An architect should be able to reconcile the two.

In accordance with comfort so defined, I am going to attempt to explain the more helpful rules and (156) shall touch upon others to the extent that brevity demands. First of all, I believe that in deciding to establish a city, one should choose fertile land or at least a place close to a river to assure ease in importing food. Everybody agrees that good air, which is the first requirement of good health, should not be the last thing for a builder to consider; and its quality depends on (157) all cities' local ground or soil, on exhausts and fumes, and also on winds, which can blow with them bad and septic atmosphere from other places. Ordinarily, sandy soil emits few vapors, while fertile and oily soil produces thick mineral particles.

That first quality is desirable, while that second is harmful. (158) However, to recognize a good or harmful air, we have tools both certain and reliable. Chemical experiments make it possible to measure salt particles in dew mixed in with the air, because thick mineral vapors alter the proper colors of metal and silk, causing rust. Therefore, wherever those changes can be observed, the air should be considered suspect. In general, wherever water is good, the air is not bad either. But one should not stop there. The diligent and wise architect (159) will want to learn about the health of earlier inhabitants, or at least of those who live nearby, and also about the diseases found among the livestock. The ancients were particularly attentive to that when erecting their cities, carefully examining the entrails of sacrificed animals, considering their colors and possible spoilage, not without reason, as indicative of the fitness of the air for human settlement.

It is only after devoting such care to the choice of the air that in the building of cities we can start (160) thinking about the streets. When it comes to the streets, one must beware of unhealthy and contrary winds. He who is most often susceptible to the effects of winds will most easily get to know his own country through his ability to tell which wind is most harmful. The famed Palladio, while talking about streets, mentions that in hot countries buildings should be high and streets narrow, believing that such a design would limit the effects of heat. Indeed, he confirms this opinion of his (161) using the words of Tacitus, who avers that in Nero's Rome the air became far more harmful when that Caesar, for the sake of the city's shape, broadened the heretofore narrow streets. Despite all of that, it is always better to give the streets ample space,[19] for the gentle breezes will compensate for the discomfort of the heat.

The view of private homes in every city is all the more elegant, the more exposed (162) to air and light each proper part of the home is, according to its use. Storage spaces, granaries, and all other places that serve to store perishable goods should be facing north. Libraries and study rooms should be facing east, both to catch the earliest possible light and to ensure the long-lasting and good conservation of the volumes. Similarly, winter quarters (163) should be facing south, and the summer rooms should be oriented to the north.

Vitruvius, whom I quote often, particularly mentions those issues in his writing, urging that all buildings have sufficient light. Without air it is impossible to live; without light it is impossible to work. When the building is not surrounded by other structures, even a novice architect can handle the task without much effort, but it is different when he builds in the neighborhood of other nearby buildings. (164) First, to avoid all trouble that may come from such circumstances, one needs to strive to put only as many windows in a building as needed, because each opening weakens the structure. Second, make sure that the windows are neither too close nor too far from one another.[20] Third, make sure that the windows are equidistant from one another and, in a home that is multistoried, that the windows are vertically aligned with one another. Such distribution of windows (165) is not only pleasing to the eye but also consistent with the stability of the home.

The form windows take may vary. Wherever needed, round windows may be used, often oblong, or in the upper parts arched; but most commonly they will be rectangular, and in its essence this figure is most comfortable and ornamental. To facilitate the distribution of light throughout the rooms, it is not without merit to make the inner part of the window (166) broader than the outer one, as one can see in Figure I, where the opening *a,b* is wider than that of *c,d*.

To the extent possible, an effort has to be made to make the windows in a building neither broader than one-fourth the side of a regularly shaped room nor narrower than one-fifth. The width and the height of the window are mutually dependent, as marked in 12 or 13, and if a building consists of many stories, the higher we go, the shallower the windows should appear. Palladio has a particular (167) opinion on it, and he recommends that the second-floor window be one-sixth smaller than the first, and all others should be lined up according to the same proportion.[21]

And finally, one more thing needs to be observed when it comes to windows, and that is to make sure that the part called the *Lorica* is not lower or higher than needed for the comfort of one looking through, hence no more than three Roman feet up (Fig. XI). It is for the same reason that this *Lorica* is always made thinner than the wall. In Figure B, the *Lorica* is far (168) narrower than the wall of the house, marked with the letter *x*. But these are the first rules that have to be considered very diligently in the context of each country's nature.[22] For what I put forth here is only general, and it is to them that the particulars should be applied.

In construction the choice of figures more fitting to accommodate the end purpose of the building is of no small importance. And although of all geometric figures in geometry, that is, those delineated with a continuous line, (169) the most accommodating to a person is the circle, this should not be the rule in what we are now discussing, for a circle is entirely opposite in shape to that of good rooms. In a circular plan, one would have to suffer either many irregular rooms or walls all too often unnecessarily thick. It follows that the more a figure approaches a circle, the further it should be kept from any buildings (170) meant for habitation. I am referring to polygonal figures whose use is criticized by the first masters of our discipline. The famous pentagonal palace in Caprarola is respected not for its comfort but for its peculiarity. And there Vignola, who provided the design and a description thereof, as if as a warning for everyone, indicated deliberately in one inscription that it consumed much of his time not only to avoid (171) halls and voids but also to work out the distribution of the windows.

A rectangular figure is therefore more suitable than any other. Rhombuses or trapezoids may be used only when the circumstances do not allow anything more convenient. It is even possible to accommodate a round figure in a building as long as those spaces are used not for living quarters but for gatherings of people instead, as it is with almost all (172) public buildings.

It is difficult, indeed impossible, to issue particular rules for every individual building as circumstances demand, although it is certain that the distribution and placement of buildings can come in thousands of variations. In general, an effort should be made to accommodate smaller spaces to the needs of the bigger rooms, to make sure that galleries have rooms nearby. The reach [or stretch] of the building should measure the length of the (173) rooms. A small palace should have small living quarters; the large ones should not have meager ones. For who does not see that there is nothing less comfortable than to have a magnificent structure with tiny rooms, and small palaces with four rooms taking up the entire space? However, there needs to be an agreement between a fitting arrangement of rooms and the will and comfort of the builder, as long as it does not violate beauty. To tell you the truth, Italians live (174) magnificently but uncomfortably. Apartments are arranged in a long and straight succession of rooms.[23] [Witton][24] rightly rebukes Italian architects for this manner of configuring rooms. All foreigners criticize this custom as well. Even the Italians themselves bemoan it, but none of this will change the custom introduced and established with long use.

(175) There are also places in every building that attract others nearby, not only for comfort but also for need. The dining room, the kitchen, the pantry, etc.—these the architect should cluster together. Other parts must also be placed so that they can be used with comfort. I am referring here to doors, stairs, fireplaces, so very much needed in buildings. When it comes to doors, (176) the architect should use them sparingly rather than generously, moving them away from the corners of homes as much as possible, applying to them with ease and intelligence all that I have put forth about windows, with one caveat. The doors in private buildings should be not higher and not lower than six Roman feet. In public buildings, particularly in gates of cities, they should be not less than ten feet. As for prescribing the width of the gates of great palaces, there is no (177) rule. There, the size has to be consistent with the scale of the building and the purpose it serves.

Anyone can understand the need for comfort in the use of stairs and the limit they impose on the height of houses. It is not as easy to understand what care, diligence, and attention need to be paid to their arrangement. For whoever will consider that stairs first of all have to be lit decently and freely accessible, (178) that the steps themselves for easy passage should be wide and not steep, will comprehend the full challenge involved in the proper choice of stairs for a building. Only experience opens the way to meet that challenge. That is where even competent architects err most frequently.

The Vatican in Rome stood for a long time without stairs worthy of so great a palace. A pretty building (179) known as the *Capo di Monte* in Naples has been abandoned, among other reasons because of the unsuitability of the stairs.

The measure for steps is marked in such a way that almost everywhere a step should be seven inches tall and at least fifteen or sixteen in width. Ancient Romans, as Vitruvius testifies, made an effort to place an odd number of steps in stairs. For whoever stepped onto the stairs of a church with his right foot (180) could finish the climb with the same, which was considered auspicious not without reason.

The differing arrangement of stairs causes them to be called by different names. They are called straight when they go straight; they are spiral if the staircase is circular. If the conception of the stairs marked with x in Figure III is a quadrangle, the stairs are quadrangular. If the conception of the stairs is three-sided, the stairs will accordingly be triangular (see Figs. IV and V).

If the conception around which the stairs run (181) is entirely circular, so are the stairs. If it is oblong, the stairs would be called elliptical. In other words, even if one part is curved, the stairs are often called straight because of the many other figures of which they are composed and of which they form a part. This type of staircase is seen, for example, in Figure VI, but those should be used only when absolutely necessary and when the situation does not allow for the use of any others.

It is generally known that ancients (182) did not know about vented fireplaces for heating and that those are the brainchild of later architects. Although I do not deny that the ancients had various ways of heating their homes, I nevertheless consider it a certainty that they used something similar to our fireplaces and chimneys. For I have no doubt that it is to them that Virgil applies his saying, "Et iam summa procul villar [*sic*—villarum] culmina fuma[nt]."[25] For after all, even Appian (183) calls chimneys *fumaria sub tecto posita* in one of his treaties; even Aristophanes, in one of his comedies, introduces the old Polycleon, who, stronger in his legs than in his shoulders, thinks of escaping a chamber through the chimney.[26] Unless I am mistaken, this is an obvious confirmation that this errant though commonly claimed opinion [regarding the ancients' unfamiliarity with fireplaces] is mistaken.

Hearths should be sized to their rooms, and the proportion of the width of the hearth to its height should be 3:2. (184) Other rules concerning fireplaces and chimneys that determine the vents directing the smoke upward are far more difficult. The interested reader desirous of perfecting his knowledge of that should refer to *La mechanique du feu* by Mr. Gauger. After reading this book, his curiosity will be satisfied.

I merely want to advise you here that all of these rules that serve the various channels leading through the chimney may be applied to furnaces commonly used by us here. Palladio teaches us (185) that in olden times, instead of furnaces, they built vents in the inner walls in such a manner that they all led to a common station below, where a fire would be burning. I doubt if this economical way of using fire would be sufficient to protect from cold in the northern countries.

But if not for the demands of brevity and the purpose of these remarks, toward which I constantly turn and therefore remark only on the more necessary and most primary (186) rules of architecture, there would still be much left for me to write about—courtyards, wells, and gardens. But those subjects are too long, and I would not be able to explicate them all to perfection. And even if I were able to do it without too much drudgery, who knows if many readers would not become bored or at least confused by it. Most likely, it is better to combine brevity with (187) usefulness, and what is worth knowing and useful, as I understand it, I have sufficiently expressed. Other, deeper aspects of our discipline books will disclose. And for those who only want to have an idea about architecture for entertainment or out of honorable curiosity, it will be enough to read and remember all of these cautionary remarks.

(188) VI. Remark on Those Disciplines Which Are Needed for the Architect

There can be no better place than at the end of this little booklet for me briefly to describe the undertakings involved in all of architecture. From my clear explication of these many things it will be easy to understand what difficulties lie in our art, how great (189) a diligence it requires, and how noble it is. But not stopping there, I will also remark on some of the disciplines needed to achieve competence in architecture.

Right in the beginning, I see that for architects, among others, it is very useful to know those arts that deal with shape and pleasing appearance. Plutarch says that when two architects stood before the workers of Athens (190) to supervise the construction of a building, one of them so motivated the people with such speech that while they listened to him, they [became] contrarian toward the other. Although in our times we do not need our architects to be quite so skilled at speech, it would be good if contemporaries at least had a clear and easy style of explaining the things they are either doing or are about to do based on prearranged plans. (191) It often happens in Italy in particular that the judges arbitrating in cases dealing with the construction of buildings consciously draw on the arguments of architects. Therefore, if an architect cannot make his case with excellence and defeat [the arguments] of his opponent, he betrays both his duty and his patron.

But far more important for every architect than the skill of speech is the knowledge of history from which he takes not only (192) the understanding of the beginning and the middle, the rise and reasons for the fall, of his art, but also knowledge of ancient, magnificent, and expensive buildings, about the manner of their construction—in a word, about the architects themselves whom he should imitate in good things. The exacting Vitruvius demands a bit more; he wants an architect to know even the law, particularly that dealing with plumbing, windows, and other similar (193) things. Indeed, if our architects did not neglect this discipline, thereby avoiding all mistakes before the start of construction, the number of court cases coming from them would significantly diminish.

It is a particular issue, however, whether the architect needs arithmetic for drawing or construction. It is not enough to know the first four operations in math. (194) One has to attempt a deep understanding of this art if one does not want to make mathematical mistakes, which are sometimes also the source of six- or sevenfold cost increases over the given word. There was once a smart Ephesian law, concerning public buildings, that placed the architect under obligation to notify the magistrate about the cost and all expenses that could possibly be incurred. Once the construction was finished, (195) if the cost did not exceed the designated amount, the architect received his reward. But if the cost exceeded expectations, even by one-fourth, the expense was his own.

Geometry significantly serves the architect for the easy expression of the figures, drawing them to scale either smaller or bigger, magnifying or reducing them, for understanding various aspects of curves in arches and ceilings, and (196) finally for understanding the rules of proportion, on which all of architecture depends.

Mechanics also teaches the architect how to balance various opposite forces in the process of building, how to measure the thickness of the walls on which rest arches and vaulted ceilings. In a word, it is the art of ensuring that the structure has both superficial and essential (197) solidity.

After mechanics follows the science of water, that is, hydraulics; it serves for the construction of bridges, ports, aqueducts, mills; it serves for the excavation of canals, for facilitating trade, and for other needs difficult indeed but worthy of attention.

For the best placement of buildings, the architect very much needs optics and perspective; if (198) the famous Bernini did not know them, the stairs in the Vatican would never have had their perceivable shape. Optics, which belongs to the field of vision, has a significant relationship to architecture. It is odd, however, that after Newton and so many others nobody has yet applied practical optics to architecture.

For buildings, ancient Romans paid diligent attention to the ground and the site. (199) We are not as diligent about that and easily settle on the most convenient site in a place. Architects should manage and exercise judgment, using experimental physics especially in these times when this science is becoming commonly and widely known.

To all this needs to be added the ability to draw a person. This final art is by some so (200) essential that they understand that it is impossible to be a good architect without being a competent painter. I completely disagree with this opinion. I know that the rules for drawing and architecture differ, and although they mutually support each other, they are in many ways opposite to each other. But I am also not surprised that great painters were good architects, for they, having the need for this art[27] in their painting, necessarily made (201) some progress.

Even with all of this, an architect will never be good if he is short on genius, which is magnificent and great wit. For in any art, nature and reason give us certain prescriptions that our wit applies, as circumstances dictate, and spreads. Blind imitation is very much removed from wit so understood, and has only that result that the discipline, instead of progressing, (202) always remains in one place. Among other reasons the liberal arts, for a long time now, have not been dominant in China is the unreasonable, slavish respect among the Chinese for everything that they take from their ancestors.

But this and other things that are necessary for an architect may also well serve noble persons who have an affinity for this art, all the more if they are taught in schools, (203) even as part of philosophy. For even an architect is not under an obligation to have a deep knowledge of all things I mention. I do not require him to be a proficient physicist, a generally well-informed historian, a first-class mathematician, but I want him to have solid beginnings in all of those so that, in need, what is useful for him he can easily (204) draw upon and understand.

We should certainly not stop here, for in seeking all things for the benefit of my fatherland, I briefly remark on how architecture can spread among us. Indeed, the love of fame and emulation among the scholars may have a significant effect here. For it is not enough to examine old structures and to follow in the footsteps of our own ancestors; (205) we should endeavor to exceed even them. Neither Raphael nor Buonarroti would ever have reached the perfection that they did if they had followed any other route. Not imitation alone, but virtue and the love of glory are what raise and disseminate all learning. Therefore, when here the educated will endeavor to challenge fame with their name, (206) at that time they will blossom with general benefit for all.

But what can that emulation be among the learned, what prompting without incentives of rewards, which should be announced by the monarchs, the magistrates, the lords? For to express the truth more clearly, what else, if not this glorious generosity, awakens all people to observe their own duty? (207) This reward turns bad people into good, good people into better still. Let us only have a look at Greece, so rich in rewards, and we will immediately see [Stezikrates?], Praxiteles, Apelles. Therefore, if we want to equip our fatherland with architecture, let us not begrudge spending anything on those who bleed to work for it. Let us respect all those who apply themselves for it. Let us imitate Francis I and Charles (208) V, who were so committed to learning that the first attended to his painter's deathbed and the other handed Titian his brush when it fell from above. Sometimes this esteem constitutes a reward more appreciated than money. Giving us a fresh example of this is the happily reigning German kaiser Josef II, who not only visited the good painter (209) Batoni frequently while I was in Rome but later, after granting him many awards, made him a nobleman, apparently doubting whether this nobility decorates the painter or the monarch more.

TRANSCRIPTION OF THE MANUSCRIPT
"Uwagi o Architekturze Przez Ignacego Potockiego"

———◆►◆◄◆———

(2)

Do Architektury.
Potrzeba matka na ten świat cię wniosli
Pierwszą zabawą sameć były chaty.
Przez zbytek w takaź doskonałość wzrosli
Pałace stawiasz z ich mieszkańców straty
Pałace w kształtach wspaniałe i cudne.
Istney potrzeby maszkarki obłudne.
—Piramowicz,

(3) Przestroga.
Ten sam los któremu podlegają inne nauki, spadai na Architekturę. Wszystkie
księgi, którekolwiek w tym rodzaiu są pisane, mistrzowi bardziey, niż uczącym
się służą. Skąd i to pochodzi, że ci, którzy bez wodza życzą mieć iakakolwiek
architektury wiadomość, (4) na same tylko spoyrzawszy wielkie księgi, zaleki-
waią się pierwey (że tak rzekę) tracąc do nich ochotę, nim ią gruntownie mieć
poczeli. Wiem zaiste, że łatwo i w tey sztuce znaleść można małe Traktaty, ale te
nie które tylko w szczególności rzeczy, rzadko całą iaśnie wykładają architekturę.

    To mnie naybardziey pobudziło do zbioru pewnych Architektury uwag, z
których co o na iest łatwo każdy zrozumieć (5) może czytelnik. Starałem się
bowiem bydz według możności iasnym opisuiąc wszystko dokładnie, bez roz-
szerzania się, bardziey zamieszanie, niz upodobanie sprawuiącego.

Takie dla upodobania tegoż ozdobiłem często te moje uwagi rożnemi historycznemi i ciekawemi wiadomościami, które przeplatane potrzebnemi przestrogami, bardziey iak zabawnemi, rozerwą (6) nieco czytaiącego umysł.

Nieogłaszam się ani tymszczycę się, by te uwagi wcale moje własne były; chętnie owszem i dobrowolnie wyznaię, iż ie z dobrych tylko zebrałem Pisarzów. Tak dalece, że i ta książeczka, nakształt Mozaiki, ieżeli z czego będzie szacowna, to tylko, iż iest z różnych i rozmaitych kawałków sztucznie spoiona.

(7) Ktokolwiek iednak surowo będzie tę książeczkę roztrząsał, niech nie zapomina proszę o końcu na który zapatruiąc się całe moie łożyłem staranie, niech pamięta, iż ten zbior tym tylko służy, którzy pierwsze i powszechne nauki naszey chcą wiedzieć przepisy. Wszystko tu tchnie pierwiastkami, wszędzie się tu prostota i łacność przebiia. Osobliwie zaś szlachetnie urodzonym tę poświęcam dzieło; w tym mniemaniu, iż im znajomość Architektury w (8) kraiu, gdzie ieszcze dobrze nie rozkwitła, nietylko iest pożyteczna, ale i potrzebna.

Na koniec wiedząc i to z doświadczenia, że ta mała książeczka wpadnie w ręce rożnych i rozmaitych osób; mądrych i rostropnych proszę, aby nadgradzali dobrocią swoią omyłki które wszędzie niechcący nawet wśliznąć się mogą. Płochych zaś i mniey uczonych pokornie błagam, by wcale tego małego nieczytali dzieła. Mała robota, małe pismo nie (9) wielkie im pole daie do rozszerzenia się z uszczypliwemi zarzutami. Upewniam iz taki a nie inny obydwóch stron poztępek, będzie mi służył za sowitą prac moich nagrodę i do większych, a co raz bardziey wzmagaiące mu się wiekowi przyzwoitych dzieł, zapewnie wzbudzi, i skutecznie zagrzeie.

(10) [blank]

(11) I. Uwaga o Odmianach Architektury.

Pierwsi Świata obywatele do agrykultury na uwolnienie się od głodu, do architektury na schronienie się od deszczu, i gorąca rzucili się. Obydwóch Sztuk potrzeba początkiem, rozkrzewieniem wygoda była, udoskonaleniem zaś, zbytek i wmysły. Poki Ludzie Kontenci z pomieszkania pod drzewami (12) w iamach, i iaskinach wygodnieyszego nie szukali, wyśmienicie mogli się bez Architektury obeyść, ale gdy coraz więcey z czasem przebywaiąc Osób, wzrastały małe Społeczeństwa, dopiero potrzebowano porządnieyszych i obszernieyszych domóstw. Skąd architektura. Ale iaka? Szopy, Chałupy z pniaków prostych złożone, przykryte słomą, chwastem, wizerunkami są nowo zaczętey Sztuki. Długo w samych Atenach Areopag zamiast wspaniałego dachu, proste z Słomy miał przykrycie. Chociaż iuż Ateny w ten czas Opiekunką wszystkich (13) nauk nazywać się mogły. I w Rzymie między wspaniałemi na Kapitolu gmachami mieysce także swoie miał pierwszy Romulusa pałac z drzewa prostego, nakształt pastuchów szopek zrobiony. Nie są więc wspaniałe naszey nauki początki, lubo wszelkiey pamięci godne, by sama Architektura nie wpadała w słuszne napomnienie któremu podegli są Szlachetni Ludzie, kiedy niepamiętawszy, czym byli niegdyś ich Przodkowie, czym sami są zapomniaią.

Że pierwsze początki, umieiętności (14) i wyzwolone sztuki, z Egiptu wzieły, niemal wszyscy rozumieią. Wcale iak by iey Azyatycy, Chaldeyczykowie, Chińczykowie nie byli równi? Moim zdaniem, ieżeli Egypt miał Menfi, Teby, Labirynty, Piramidy; miała Azya Enoch, Babilonią, Niniwę. Ciężko ukazać kto od kogo pierwszy.

A ponieważ dla ochronienia czasu, niepewne rzeczy bezpieczniey krótko niż długo namienić, to tylko uważam, że któregozkolwiek Narodu byli owi pierwsi Ludzie, co do Architektury (15) rzucilisię, niemało nałożyli czasu, by ich umysł nowych rzeczy wynalazca, łącząc z potrzebą ładność, przez tak wielką przebiegł odległość która każden znaydzie między Szopą a pałacem na Koryncką budowanym miarę. Lubo zaiste inni, niemniey, a ieżeli niewięcey zażyli pracy, kiedy starali się oczyścić, i uswobodzić naszą naukę z tego nieporządku, w którem wpadać zaczynała przez nieograniczoną Architektów wolność, z czego po części Greków chwalić muszę. Jako bowiem Egipcyanie w tym (16) czalibyli aby przez wielkość bardziey, niż kształt oko ludzkie dziwili, tak Grecy przeciwnie wszystkie siły łożyli, by w ich rysunkach gładkość forma ładna i wyborna doskonałość patrzących bawiła. Tak opisany gust iuż był dobrze za czasów Periklesa ustawiony, kwitnął nieprzerwanie za Alexandra Wielkiego coraz bardziey rozszerzaiąc się, gdy Rzymianie nawet przy końcu wolnych rządów Rzeczy Pospolitej Greckiey, chwycilisię Architektury, i tyle dokazali, że łącząc do niey wspaniałość (17) właściwą za czasów Augusta, uczeń Mistrza wyrównał.

Niezupełnie iednak dotąd podlegała Architektura rządom rozumu i reflexii. Tey prawdy znaydzie każden, w nayładnieyszych owych czasów gmachach, naywiększe próby. I nie dziw. Ci co pierwsi wynayduią, nad to w zamierzonych rzechach znayduią ciężkosci do uniknienia wszelkich omyłek, ci zaś co tylko innych niewolnicze naśladuią, równie wybieraią złe i dobre rzeczy, nie wątpią, że wszystko iuż iest w powinney (18) mierze, wszystko potwierdzone i ugruntowane powagą, imieniem Przodków zastarzałym nawet i niezłamanym zwyczaiem. Wielka więc i nagła była potrzeba aby splamioną Architekturę uwagi oczyszczały odkrywaiąc iasnie pierwsze omylki, wprowadzaiąc krytykę surową na dawne roboty, słowem przeszkadzaiąc, by kredyt, i sława błędom mieysca nie dawala, lub ślepym używaniem [złego?] niepotwierdzała. Ale coż wszystko przeciwnie stało się, wszystko na wywrót.

(19) Witruwiusza sławnego Architekta sukcessorowie, ieden drugiego koleyno naśladował daleki każden od postępku, coraz na zad cofał się i iak bywa, że upadek prędszy we wszystkim nad powstanie wkrótce do tego przyszło, iż iuż za Konstantyna Cesarza zła była Architektura gorsza za Justiniana, i co raz bardziey osobliwa, gdy Barbarzyncy Rzymską ruinowali potęgę.

W ten czas co za odmiana? Po Grecko Rzymskiey Architekturze (20) następuie inna ocięzała, bez naturalnego kształtu, bez proporcii, niewiem czemu Gocka nazwana. Bo zdaniem biegleyszych ludzi, Goci ni złey, ni dobrey nieznali Architektury, niemieli nigdy czasu do niey, ani upodobania. Prawda ze tegoż Narodu Włoski król Teoderyk w Rawennie, w Pawi, w Weronie, Amfiteatra, Laznie, Akwedukty, budować kazał, ale w tym rodzaiu, który iuz był wprowadzony, i uzywany powszechnie przez miłość nowości. (21) Bo gdzie kiedy w swoim kraiu bitni, mężni Barbarzyńcy, do zabawy tylko i pieszczot budowali gmachy? Nadto są szczodrobliwe Włochy wrozdawniu i przypisywaniu innym własnych omyłek. Co tylko brzydkiego widzą, Gockie zaraz nazywaią, tym sposobem na cudze, nie na swoie krzywiąc się omyłki. My przeciwnie iasnie i oczywiście widzimy, że Goci kraiowy, iaki był przeieli gust, gruntownie budowali bo w tym Starodawny trwał (22) zwyczay, niekształtnie, bo iuz w ten czas zgubiono sposob zdobienia. A bardziey daleko za Lombardów, Franków i Niemcow, kiedy generalne nawet zarzucono proporcye. Taka iuz panowała ślepota.

Do odmiany wzmienioney architektury X i XI wieku nie którzy rzucili się, ale nadaremno. Każden z iednego końca do drugiego przechodził. Ładność, która między innemi w mierze i pomiarkowaniu zawisła, powstać (23) nie mogła. Budowano dotąd gmachy ciężkie i ogromne, zaczęto przeciwnie letkie budować wszystkie fabryki przebite, pełne dziur figlarnych, ozdobione śmiesznemi koronkami, daszkami, ciężkiemi wiezami Piramidami, zdawały się, że na naysłabszym wywrócą się wiatrem. Lecz i na tym niedosyć, daley niepomiarkowana zdobienia chciweść rozprzestrzeniała się. Dodano ieszcze do tey nowe Gockiey Architektury inne śmiesznieysze barbarzyńskie pstrocizny (24) które ile podziwienia nieumieiętnym sprawuią tyle nieupodobania znaiącym się. Widać to w niektórych w Hiszpanii pałacach za Saracenów, i Maurów budowanych, gdzie proporcyę, miarę, nieproporcią, niemiarą nazwać potrzeba. Wten czas bowiem humor każdego architekta prawidłem był na każdy z osobna budynek, ile budynków, tyle Architektur. Kto chciał celować innych w Sztuce swoiey, drugiego przewyzszyć, dość (25) było, by iego budynek, lub kościół, cudzy przechodził wysokością. Na tym bowiem cały kształt, cała zakładała się ładność, lube i to nie długo trwała. Postrzegli się na koniec sami Architektowie, że w złym bardzo znaydowali się stanie. Zaczeli do dawney, ile było mozna, powracać się proporcii, założyli sami sobie nie które granice, opisali pewne prawa, których zachowanie poprawiło nieco nasza naukę. Czego przykładem kościoł S. Marka w Wenecyi na nową Grecką (26) Architekturę budowany. Bo tak ią nazywać zaczęto.

A chociaż przy takiey odmianie zdawało się, że czas przyszedł by umysł ludzki z tak głębokiego, w którym zostawał zatopiony, wyszedł letargu, do XVI iednak niewielkie w tym uczyniono kroki. Dopiero nie oczekiwane, nie-spodziewane a raptowne w[e] Włoszech nauk odnowienie poprawiło także i Architekturę. Ruiny Rzymu od tąd pilnie uważane, proporcye i miary dawne zachowane, złączone z pomyślnym wystawienia (27) kościoła S. Piotra proiek-tem, niemało do tego dopomogły. Bramant, Peruzzi, Sangallo, Michelangelo, Vignola o to usilnie staralisię by od nowey oddalaiąc się Architektury, starożyt-ney ładność, wspaniałość, naśladowali. Przykład wielkich ludzi szczęśliwie wykonany (do emulacyi podaz) wiek Medyceuszów, Leona X, Alexandra i Augusta wieki wkrótce wyrównał. Włochy nakształt Grecyi i dawnego Rzymu, wydały w naukach statut praw całej Europie, któremu wszyscy poddać się muszą. (28) Niemałą ma moc ładność w umyśle naszym i przeto w krótkim czasie znaczne wszedzie poprawy widziano. Dobra Architektura wprowadziła się do Francji, dodała wiele ozdoby czasom Ludwika XIV, niebyła zaniedbana w Hiszpanii, rozszerzyła się aż do samego Petersburga. Ozdobiła Szwecya, Dania, Polskę, a bardziey Anglią. Słowem nakształt wielkiey rzeki płyneła, która ieźli w iednym mieyscu ścisłym idzie korytem na drugim większych sił nabieraiąc, obszernieysze sobie (29) ściele loze. Ile bowiem w Pułnocnych Kraiach nabyła, tyle w Azii i Egipcie, w Grecyi zgubiła nauka nasza, gdzie iuż od wielu wieków powstać nie może. Ale to są podróze przechodzących się Nauk.

To więc rozwazywszy iuż niech mi będzie wolno powiedzieć, że ostrozność mieć powinniśmy, którey nie wiem czemu niemieli Witruwiusza następcy. Kształtna iest teraz nasza Architektura, ale, by i w tym miarę nie przebrała, (30) potrzebuie starania iakiegoś i baczności. W dobrey do tego iesteśmy porze. Wiek ten Filozoficzny zowiesię, i ieżeli w czym błądzi, to tylko, że wszyscy, i o wszystkim filozofuią. Podpada iednak Architektura roztrząśnieniom, i ludz-kiey uwadze. Frezzier, L'Allgerotti, L'Augier, i inni rzeczą samą pokazuią, co może wtey sztuce Filozofia? A kto wie, czyby niewięcey mogła, gdyby i inni także w ich ślady idąc, surowie (31) Architektów rozważali roboty żadney nieprzepuszczali omyłki, w każdey rzeczy o przyczynę badali się, krótko mówiąc, bardziey praktykę z teoryką łączyli, więcey doświadczeniom uwag dodawali. Wiem ia że w teraznieyszych czasach, wielka Architektów liczba wielu złych zamykać musi, ale nie dla tego podeyrzliwie sądzę, by iuż miała upadać nauka nasza. Skarzyłsię także na Towarzyszów swoich (32) Witruwi-usz, na ich liczbę* i skarżył się z większym uzaleniem, z większą od nas o zgubę Architektury boiażnią, lubo Wek Augusta iasny wszystko przeciwnie obiecywał. Podobne i Grecya, Platona, słyszała Lamenty. A gdzie w którey Nacyi, każdy iako w tey swoiey pilnował powinności. Zawsze i wszędzie, nie wielka biegłych liczba bywa, (33) łatwieysza iednak tam gdzie więcey do tego Osob dąży. Prawda, że teraz nierachuiemy Michel-Angela, Berniniego, i tylu drugich. Ale coś z tego wnosić wolno? Nic innego, tylko, że choć niektóre czasy płodzą wielkich ludzi, w takich iednak przypaść to moze okolicznościach w których niewolne ani obszerne aż sami mają pole do okazywania dowcipu i przy-miotów swoich. Owszem bydz też może, ze pomilczenie, (34) nieznaiomość, ani osobliwa roznica iednego od drugich Architektów pochodzi z pospolitey powszechnie umieiętności. Jako trafia się w porządnym ogrodzie, gdzie niewidać wyższego[1] nad inne drzewa dlatego, iż wszystkie równie utrzymy-wane wporządku kwitną ładnie i okazale.

Chociaż zaś ciężko sprzeciwić się, że iak noc po dniu tak często wiek ciemności, następuie po wieku Swiatła, (35) łatwo iednak upewnić można, że my na poranku tego dnia pogodnego znayduiemy się, że dzień ten żadym Matematycznym rachunkiem nie może bydz ustawiony. Sześć prawie wieków trwał w Grecii złoty czas dla architektury, trwa iuż więcey iak 1300 lat przeci-wny. A to wie, kiedy ustatnie. Na opak wszystko teraz w Europie dziejesię. Od trzech wieków odowiła się z innemi (36) naukami i ta wyzwolona Sztuka, większą coraz bierze górę, większą iasność, I owszem spodziewać się trzeba, że Druk, Akademie, a bardziey umysł Filozoficzny, ieżeli nie do oczekiwanego udoskonalenia przyprowadzi Architekturę, to przynaymniey od zguby i updaku iak nayskuteczniey oddali.

*Rachowano za czasów Witruwiusza 700 Architektów.

(37) II. Uwaga w czym ładność Architektury zakładać się powinna.

Nieomylna rzecz iż ludziom przytrafia się, że tych rzeczy natury niewiedzą, o których nayczęściey rozmawiaią. Między tysiącznemi to się z ładnością dzieie. O ładności niemal wszyscy gadaią, ładność każden zawsze i wszędzie uważa. A w rzeczy samey (38) ieżeli gdzie ładności niewidziemy; to po części winie naszey i ślepocie przypisać należy.

Wchodzić iednak w labirynt medytacii Metafizycznych o ładności, w powszechności uważaney nie tylko iest rzecz niebespieczna, ale w tey tu uwadze wcale nieprzyzwoita. Ciekawy w tey mierze czytelnik ma ksiąszki Platona, uwagi niektóre Augustyna Stego. Rozmowy niedawnych czasów w Francuzkim ięzyku wydane, „Essai sur la beau par le P. André.”

Ja więc o ładności tylko Architektury tyczącey się krótko tu (39) rozmawiam, uważywszy naprzod na czym niezależy, potym w czym ta ładność zakładać się powinna. Niech się bowiem kto chce spyta samych Architektów, co to iest ładność w ich sztuce? Iaki iest iey grunt? Iaka natura? Czy iest w Architekturze ładność stała i nieodmienna? Ładność, która podobać się powinna wszystkim równie narodom? Czy znaleść można taki wizerunek, którenby nam pewne do zbliżenia się iak naybardziey naturalney ładności dawał przepisy? Niech się kto chce o (40) to wszystko samych Architektów spyta, a zobaczy że ta, którą maią w tych rzeczach wiadomość samych naypierewey plątać zacznie, i tym łatwiey, im mniey niegdyś myśleli o tym, co iuż doskonale wiedzieć, i iak naylepiey rozumieli. I z tąd też pochodzi, że ieżeli im w ten czas nieprzyidzie prędko na pomoc, pewne nie wiem coś którym nayczęściey bronią się naywiększa część grubą w sobie ładności niewiadomość pokaże. Wiedzą wszyscy że od natury mamy [własne?] upodobanie (41) w organizacyi naszey do rzeczy proporcyonalnych. Ale o tym co sprawuie te upodobanie, niech mi będzie wolno krótko iasnie wyłożyć.

Naprzód, iako z doświadczenia codziennego dorozumiewać się można, że poczytanie rzeczy za piękną lub brzydką skutkiem bywa zwyczaiu, tak też z tegoż doświadczenia i to twierdzieć nie ciężko, że ładność Architektury nie na tym upodobanie przez zwyczay wprowadzony, zakładać się powinna. Architektura (42) bowiem Grecko-Rzymska szacowana przez długi czas zgubiła ładność w oczach gockich Architektów. Gocka w ten czas ładną we Włoszech, w Rzymie samym, iak na obelgę dawney zdawała się. My teraznieyszego wieku na Gocką Architekturę iuż niegdyś ulubioną patrzyć niemożemy, kto wie iak naszą poźnieysi od nas gardzić będą? Gardzą widziemy dotąd,

Machometańczykowie Grecką w kraiach swoich Architekturą. leżeli przeto Architektura (43) w upodobaniu samym zawisła: ktoż nas osądzi? Ktoż iest lepszego gustu, Grek, Włoch, czy Turczyn? Każden swoie kocha budowanie, każden swoy sposob nad cudzy przekłada, ieden na drugiego krzywi się. Coż ztąd? To tylko, że nie w partykulaney modzie, ani upodobaniu zawisła ładność sztuki naszey. Moda bowiem odmienna, nie Architektura byłaby ładną.

Daleki także iestem od tych, którzy kształt Architektury w upodobaniu i uzywaniu samych Architektów zakładaią. A bowiem (44) nayczęściey są z młodości początki Nauczycielów swoich pewnie przez uprzedzenie o ich umieiętności, szanuią wszystko, cokolwiek od nich biorą niemając często śmiałości, a może sposobności złego od dobrego oddzielać. Sami do tego Archiektowie podlegaią tym, co każą budować, muszą albo przez słabość umysłu, albo przez podchlebstwo naywiększe budujących w fabrykach pomieścić dziwactwa. A choćby i tego niebyło, kogoż mamy naśladować pewnie i bez (45) omyłki? Witruwiusza prawodawcę łacińskich Architektów? Witruwiusz iednak wielki człowiek wielkim iak często bywa, podpada omyłkom. Nie każe mu zupełnie ufać <u>Scamozzi</u>, i owszem upewnia, że iego miary w kolumnach są fałszywe, dalekie bardzo od właściwej ładności. W rzeczy zaś samey prawdę mówiąc, czasem Witruwiusz sam sobie sprzeciwia się. Nie raz co pierwey gani, po tym skutkiem chwali. Jeżeli więc Witruwiuszem ostrożnie sobie często trzeba (46) obchodzić, coż dopiero powiem o innych, godnych prawda ale mnieyszych od niego Architektach? Szacowni są Alberti, Serliusz, Palladiusz, Scamozzi, Vignola, Bullan de l'Ormes, ale ieden z drugim niezgadza się, kazden ma swoje omyłki, swoich naśladówców, nikt nie iest powszechnie słuchany. To samo zaś doskonale pokazuie, że słabszy daleko byłby dla dostąpienia właściwey ładności, wizerunek dawnych Fabryk, któren chociasz (47) nieco pomocą Architekturze bywa, nie moze się iednak iey pierwszymi pewnym nazwać prawidłem. Łatwo tę prawdę każden pozna, kto sobie przypomni, że od Architektów te Fabryki są wystawione, a żatym że nie więcey mogą mięć wagi od nich, i owszem mniey ile że Praktyka w skutku zmnieysza zawsze czystość Teoryki. Ale rzadko tez bez skazy często zaś z wielkiemi omyłkami znayduiemy te gmachy. Arki w Rzymie, Termy Diokleciana, (48) Teatrum Marcella, nie są zupełne według Architektury reguł. Moim zdaniem gdyby dawne gmachy przykład nam właściwey ładności dawały, każda i naygrubsza omyłka miałaby swoją z przykładu dawnego obronę.

Przeto ponieważ ani w upodobaniu ludzkim, ani w uzywaniu Architektów, ani nawet w fabrykach dawnych nieznayduiemy właściwego ładności wizerunku, opuścmy więc w tym te często ludzące drogi, tam (49) tylko wizerunku ładności szukaiąc, gdzie pewnie i bez omyłki znayduie się. Ani wątpić trzeba, że tam stałe pewnie, i bez omyłki znayduie się, gdzie go nam szczera nieuprzedzona, i owszem naturalna nawet odkrywa Filozofia.

Naysłabsza zaraz o pierwszych wiadomościach uwaga to by powinna każdemu ukazać, że porządek, układ, proporcya, wszędzie podobać się musi nad nieporządek zamieszanie, i nieproporcyą. Wszak iuż sama naturalna (50) Geometria o tam odkrywa, że figura tym iest kształtnieysza, im iey linie gładziey obchodzą się, że kiedy rysunek iaki z wielu części składa się, wszystkie tak powinny bydz uszykowane, by naymnieyszego niesprawowały zamieszania, by poiedyńcze w szrodku, podwóyne po bokach były rozłożone, by równe części ile możności w iedney liczbie, i równie od szródka odstawały, części nierówne z iedney i drugiey strony sobie odpowiadały, słowiemby (51) te wszystkie kawałki tak były złączone, aby w nich związana iedność, bez naymnieyszey w oko biiącey różnicy znaydowała się. Bo iuż do doświadczenia przychodząc, dość spoyrzeć na dwa domostwa nieregularne iedno, regularne drugie, na przypomnienie sobie nie tylko ładności, ale i skrytych oneyze przepisów.

Trzy są naprzód reguł architektury żródła: Natura, Geometria, i doświadczenie pewnych proporcii człowieka organizacyom (52) nieprzeciwnych. Wyięte z natury i Geometrii reguły niepodległe są odmiennemu naszemu dowcipowi. Zebrane zaś wzmienionego doświadczenia przepisy lubo podpadaią gustowi naszemu z ograniczeniem, iednak uzyte bydz powinny bez naymnieyszego uięcia Geometrii i naturze, których złączenie hamować powinno, cokolwiek z przyzwoitości wychodzi. Hic murus aheneus esto.

Kolumn naprzykład prosty (53) spadek, wybiór figur, wygodnieyszych, równieyszych, i pierwsze a fundamentalne w sztuce naszey prawa dodaie nam Geometrya. Rozporządzanie przyzwoitych ozdob, kolumn u góry wąszych u dołu szerszych, używanie, wysokość frontonów, ich spadek, i tysiąc innych podobnych rzeczy, uczy nas natura. Arków zaś, okien, kolumn, według Doryckiey, Iońskiey, lub Koryntskiey miary, wysokość do szerokich, słowem ozdoby wszystkie, ich miarę, doświadczenie ugruntowane (54) z uwag proporcii organizacii nieprzeciwney oczywiście nam ukazuie.

A lubo uważywszy figur w sztuce naszey używanie łatwo każden ściśle Geometryi z Architekturą złączenie zrozumieć może, nie tak iest iednak łatwo poiąć, iakie to są proporcye nieprzeciwne Ludzkiey organizacii, iakie przepisy do naśladowania, iakie wizerunki od natury nam w tym podane? Mniemam naprzod, że proporcya zgadzaiąc się z upodobaniem umysłów (55) naszych zawisły od harmonicznych relacii, od tych samych, których muzyka w koncertach swoich zażywa. Da się widzieć w inney uwadze, iaką sztuką linię harmonicznie podzielić można.

Teraz to namieniam, że takie proporcye prócz tego, że zgadzaią się z wygodą i gruntownością fabryk, powszechnie takze sprawuią upodobanie, i sprawować muszą. Jeżeli te w Anatomii pewna, że zyły sensacyą słuchu do duszy naszey wprowadzaiące nie tylko (56) iedney są miary z zyłami ludszkich oczów, ale tez (lubo od innych i przeciwnych sobie poruszone obiektów) równie trząsącym biegiem każda swoje sprawuie czucie. Mała iednak w tym odmiana żadney niesprawuie skazy. Łącząc optykę i perspektywę z potrzebą i okolicznościami, może rostropny Architekt, sztucznie a czasem ypotrzebnie, geometrycznych także i Arytmetycznych zazyć (57) proporcii. Tym to znaczeniem część tę upodobaniu ludzkiemu podlegaiącą, nazwałem.

Wielu powture dociec niemogą, iakim to znaczeniem naturę za iedne reguł Architektury zrzódło policzam? Jakim sposobem natura wizerunkiem może bydz w tey sztuce, kiedy nic nam podobnego Architekturze niewydała na świecie powszechna wszystkich rzeczy Matka natura? Pozorne przyznaię, są to zarzuty, ale nie tak (58) mocne by z gruntu naszą obalały opinią. Troiaki iest sposób naśladowania naturę, imituiąc samą naturę, imituiąc sposób którym sobie postępuie, imituiąc na koniec naturalną Architekturę. Jaśniey to wykładam.

Mamy naprzod od natury widoczne nam podane wizerunki, możemy naśladować samą naturę, nietylko w wodnych sztukach, ale i w układzie ogrodów, w ułożeniu skał i okropnych iaskiń, które często we Włoszech (59) uzywane naymilszy sprawuią widok. W Rzymie Fontana Trewi daleko niegdyś była ładnieyszą, kiedy woda wślady idąc natury, niełatwo ani równie, ale przerwanym i mocującym się, a po bokach rozdzielonym strumieniem w różne biegącym kręty, z szumem, przykrym spadkiem z wysokości zepchnięta, przyrodzonym spadała sposobem. Do tych czas nawet i na Nawoną fontannę tak (60) od placu w Rzymie nazwaną miło iest spoyrzeć, i tym miley, ze skała duży obelisk utrzymująca nie ręką ludzką wyryta, ale razem z obeliskiem z skał Egipskich oderwana, sprowadzona na umysł, wydaie się. Przy tym wszystkim zmiarkować niemogę iakim czołem z iaką śmiałością mówić wolno, że zadnego nam w Architekturze Natura nie dała przykładu?

Ale i to przed oczy weźmy że tę samą naturę, która z (61) własnych wywodów naśladuiemy, naśladować możemy, i z sposobu, którym sobie postępuie. Gdyby kto dla większego kształtu dwie nauki nie tylko od siebie dalekie, ale i sobie przeciwne, iednę na model drugiey traktował, taki postępek dziwny zdawałby się mało myślącym, ale podobnie Architekturę w tym szukuiącym. A z tym wszystkim ta druga już iest do prawa od Filozofów stosowana, i prawo teraz Geometrii wykłada się, lubo dalekie, i owszem (62) przeciwne są prawa i Geometryi początki. Tymże sposobem chociasz zapewne zioł ani listków nieznaydziemy arki lub kolumny, wyrazaiących, mamy iednak i uważamy pewne natury postępki i dzieła, które pożytecznie naśladować powinniśmy, a tym bardziey, iż te od Naywyższego do ułożenia porządnego świata są zażyte. To się zowie imitować, to umieć zazyć, umieć z widzenia korzystać. Tyle różnych, kolorów na Niebie z tą iednością (63) złączonych nie mogę z nam pokazać, że w gmachach nawet powinny bydz różne cząstki, całą, fabrykę składaiące, ale przeplataną różnicą i po stopniach odmiany ukazuiące?

Łatwo na koniec znaleść możemy naturalną Architekturę, która lubo juz iest umaszkowana, da się iednak poznać i w naywięszkych domach, i w Królewskich nawet gmachach. W Rzymszkich pałacach Filozof Architekt, znaydzie pierwsze nędznych Ludzi szopy, znaydzie (64) pniaki w kolumny, i inne ozdoby poprzemieniane. A ieżeli ich nieznaydzie, to tym samym o gatunku budowania sądzić będzie sprawiedliwie. Ale bowiem okryte są te fabryki, zawsze iednak powinna w nich wydawać się naturalna Architektura.

Przypomnieymy sobie wzmienione Architektury początki zrobmy Analizę cywilney Architektury, a znaydziemy pewnie, że i nasza Nauka ma swoią gramatykę, tym (65) szacownieyszą ze niewykwitną.

Z tych sztuk pniaków które w pierwszych czasach, utrzymywały dachy, i inne przykrycia, wprowadzone są kolumny. A ponieważ były na początku pniaki prosto w ziemię wbite mamy także przykład kolumn Doryckich bez zadnego bazamentu w Teatrum Marcella [Patrz Fig. I], gdy iednak i ciężarem i wilgocią więcey nad potrzebę w doł wchodziły wzmienione pniaki zaczym dopiero dna i podstaw, zkąd tez w kolumnach (66) wprowadzone są bazamenta. Fig. II.

I głowice, czyli kapitele nieco innego wyrażaią tylko kawałki deszczek tak położonych u wyszey pniaków części, by tym łatwiey bałka na nich utrzymywała się. Fig. III. Balka zaś sama, teraz Epistilium, to iest Architraw nazwana wspiera inne balki poprzecznie i w krzyż rozciągnione, we wnątrz na sufit deszczkami okryty służące. Fig. IV.

Z czasem ta sama gzymsu część zoferus powszechnie i Fregium (67) lub fryz nazwana, u dawnych naybardziey była zdobiona Odległość w Figurze IV litera (X) znaczona, między balką a balką, metopą a u nas, między balczycą według własnego znaczenia, różniła się grubość zaś samey balki (r) wyrazała tryglify (m) to iest kanały czyli szpary, zwody z dachu ciekącey wyryta. Tym sposobem umysł ludzki że szkody nawet ozdoby wynalazł.

Także ostatnia część gzymsu z łacińskiego cornix nazwana (68) nic innego nie wyraza tylko spadek dachu, czyli spadku tegoz od muru odległość sztucznie przykrytą, by deszcz z dachu spływaiący, iak można był od muru oddalony (Fig. V). Ząbki (d) pod tą gzymsu częścią używane reprezentuią łaty (s.s.) na utrzymywanie dachuwek. Inne zaś kawałki według odmienney formy mensuły, modiliony, mutuły nazwane (Fig. VI) nic innego nie są tylko podpory (m.m) od końca dachu o mur podparte, by tym łatwiey nachylony utrzymywał się dach. A (69) ieżeli często nie widać w gzymsach, mensuły, tryglify, i między balczyce, to niedlaczego innego, tylko ze w pierwszych owych czasach, tak i teraz w drewnianych budynkach, cały gzyms gładkiemi obiiano tarcicami.

Daley ieszcze idąc i to dociec można, że ten spadek dachu, który często osobliwie przednią kościołów ozdabia ścianę fronton, i frontispitium nazywany (Fig. VII) z naturalnego dachu nachylenia iest wynaleziony. Grecy (70) pod łagodnym Niebem nie tak wielki tym frontonom dawali spadek, większy troszkę Włochy łącząc ładność z potrzebą kraiu. W Połnocnych kraiach u nas nawet, więcey od Włoch podwyższamy dachy. U Egipcianów przeciwnie, gdzie rzadko deszcz pada, i domy bez dachów, i fabryki bez frontonów są w używaniu. I nie iest że to oczywista próba ścisłego natury z ozdobami Architektury związku?

Lecz, na tym niedosyć. W pierwszych owych sztuki naszey (71) początkach, pniaki teraz pyszny kolumn imieniem nazwane, nie bardzo od siebie odległe były wbiane by łatwiey utrzymywały się wyższe balki na przykrycie domu takem opisał służące Fig. VIII. Z czasem iednak gdy z nowemi potrzebami, nowych umysł ludzki szukał wygód, i ta odległość domów porządku, tak się była rozprzestrzeniła, że prawie nie sposobne były pniaki do utrzymywania szerokich balek. W ten czas dowcip pierwszych (72) owych mieszkańców dwoma drzewami w anguł u góry pod architrawem złączonemi nie mało ciężaru ulżył. My prawdziwe przodków naszych małpy, czy w potrzebie, czy nie, Arków ztąd wypływaiących między kolumnami zazywamy, chętnie to robiąc, a czasem nadaremno, co dawnieysi z mozołem, i nie bez przyczyny robili. (Fig. IX) Podobno z przymuszenia tylko, na uwolnienie się od deszczów, złego powietrza, szkodliwych wiatrów. Odległość pniaków, dom cały (73) okrązaiących, tarcicami tak okrywano, że ieżeli pniaki nieociosane, to okrągłe, iezeli ociosane, czworograniaste między tarcicami wydawały się. I nie iest że to oczywiste zrzódło Filarów tak często używanych i kolumn obmurowanych? (Fig. X) Ale już wszak i stillobaty, powszechnie pedestalla nazywane, niedlaczego innego były użyte, tylko albo dla podwyższenia, i lepszego fabryk z dołu na gorę patrzących widoku, albo tez u bagnistey sytuacii (74) na uwolnienie od szkodliwey wilgoci.

To ia nazywam naturalną Architekturą, która nie tylko na używanie za prawidło ninieyszey, ale też na miarę szkaluiącym ią służyć powinna. Z tego zaś com dotąd obszernie wyłożył, łatwo się cel uwagi moiey odkrywa.

Dwie ia zaiste w Architekturze upatruię ładności. Jednę wcale nie podległą odmiennemu naszemu dowcipowi, drugą podległą, ale z ograniczeniem (75) i względem na pierwszą ładność. Zakładam pierwszą ładność w naśladowaniu natury, czyli to naśladując samą naturę, czyli sposób, którym sobie ona postępuie, czyli tez naturalną Architekturę. Druga ładność zakładam w wybiorze proporcyi harmonicznych, lub tez innych, zawsze iednak z natuą zgadzajacych się. Przeto tam gdzie te obydwie ładności znaydować się będą ładna także będzie Architektura. Niech bowiem to, (76) co kto chce mówi, nie może bydz ludziom milszego, iako widok natury, do którego od młodości zaraz iesteśmy przy zwyczaieni, ani ten nie dla kogo innego, tylko dla nas służy. Maią i nierozumne bestie oczy, maią takie, iakie i my organa, równie ich żyły iako i nasze od zewnętrznych są poruszone obiektów. Iakaż więc przy tym między ludzkim i bydlęcym widokiem będzie rożnica, ieżeli gust natury, z reguł proporcii wypędziemy? Iakie nad bestiami (77) przełozenie pewne i nieodmienne upodobania naszego początki wygłuzowawszy? Moim zdaniem gdyby nawet i tak się rzecz miała, wstydzić byśmy się powinni tego naszego sromotnego unizenia, kryiąc go, a nie ogłaszaiąc. Coż dopiero teraz, kiedy oczywiście widziemy, że ładność w czym innym, nie w naszym zakłada się upodobanie? Wszak i to, co proporcyą zowiemy, proporcyą bydź niemoże, ieżeli nie iest (78) rzeczą naturalną, żadney zaś nieznaydziemy rzeczy naturalney, któraby była bez proporcyi? Bo coż to innego iest proporcya, ieżeli nie stosowanie się łatwe rzeczy zewnętrznych, z organami osoby ie oglądaiącey. I możemy z wątpić, że wszech rzeczy Stworzyciel otoczył nas obietkami przeciwnemi naszym sensom, że stworzył rzeczy dla nas, z nami niezgadzaiące się, nie iest że to gruba ślepota, i śmiałość, pierwszemu świata tego (79) Architektowi taką zarzuca omyłkę, ktora skazę czyni naszym nawet nikczemnym Architektom? Radbym i to wiedzieć, co za potrzeba wymować szlachetney naszey sztuce to, co się drugim przypisuie. Po co w tym sprzeciwiać się własnemu rozumowi? Po co ci, co tak myślą, Naturę matką, opiekunką, Mistrzynią, wizerunkiem wszystkich rzeczy nazywają! Iuż nie moim, ale Cycerona zdaniem, tacy natury nieprzyiaciele mocno naśladuią (80) baiecznych owych i śmiałych olbrzymów, którzy buntuią się na Bogów własnemi ich napastowali darami.[2]

A iako każdego człowieka iest powinność, gruntownie takie pamiętać właściwey ładnośći początki, tak do Architektów należy, pogodzić z potrzebą i wygodą ładność natury, i dowcipu. Łatwiey im to zapewne przyidzie, te trzy zachowuiąc przepisy.

Naprzód nie powinni Architektowie od natury (81) oddalać się, ale też i w naśladowaniu nie bardzo przesadzać, zachowuiąc w tym należy te pomiarkowanie. Równie bowiem iest naganna kręcona kolumna, dla tego że nienaturalna, iako i inna niekręcona, ale nie równie według prostego pniaka wyryta dla tego, że nadto naturalna. Chwalebna w tym niedbałość, ale taką iaką na dawny przepisuie Krasnomowca Negligentia quaedam diligens. Bo ieżeli iest srzodek (82) w ładności, to co łacinnicy modum nazywaią, równie grzeszy, kto przechodzi, albo kto niedochodzi pożądanego srzodka. Budynek bez żadney ozdoby, niemoże bydz oczom miły. Ale iakie iest Gockie oko, któreby mogło znieść tyle pstrocin używanych w pałacach i kościołach dawnemi czasy? Nie mówię by w zebraniu tyle drobnych figur nie było dość sztuki, owszem przyznaię, że iey iest nad to, i dla tey samey wielości (83) ganię Gocką Architekturę.

Powinni powtóre Architektowie zachować sławną ową regułę, która godna iest w każdey Akademii złotemi bydz wyrytą literami. Nic nie powinien (Witruwiusz mówi) takiego robić Architekt, czego by dobrey przyczyny, dać nie mógł. Tak iasne, i wyraźne prawo obszernego nie wyciąga wykładu.

Na koniec do Architekta należy, przystoyność w fabryce pomiescić. O tey części dziwnie (84) ładnie l'Augier w swoiey ksiąszce traktuie, pokazuiąc, że nic sprawiedliwszego, iako, aby między buduiącym, i budowaniem, to iest między domem i Panem była relacya. Często bowiem zapatruiącym się na pałace prywatnych Panów przytrafia się to, co dawnemu w Egipcie Rzymianinowi, który miarkuiąc zewnętrzną kościoła facyatę, rozumiał, iż ten wielkiemu był poświęcony Bożkowi, i z tym uprzedzeniem wszedłszy wenwątrz, z wielkim podziwieniem śmieszną małpę wsrzodku (85) figuiiącą zastał. A ieżeli podobna w tym omyłka nie grzeszy przeciwko istotney ładności, to przynaymniey niezgadza się z rostropnym iey szafunkiem.

Przeto niech już więc przestaną Pirońscy Filozofowie mówić, że nic nie masz ładnego prócz upodobania, że te upodobanie żadnemu nie podpada prawu, i podpadać nie może. Niech przestaną z tym się ogłaszać, co wstyd dobremu Filozofowi skrycie myślić.

(86) Niestraszni są prawda tacy Architektury nieprzyiaciele ale śmieli i w wielkiey liczbie. Cała ich wątpliwość z tąd pochodzi, że dotąd w odmianach Architektury, wielką niestałość i odmienność uważaią. Zapominaią iednak, że ieżeli była kiedy ta niestałość, to nie dlaczego innego, tylko, że nie którzy

podobne im maiąc opinie, wszystko odmiennemu pozwalali dowcipowi. Sami więc są autorowie, sami okazy a tey winy, którą na Architekturę (87) niewinnie zkładaią. Do tego dodaią ciż sami, że lubo Architektura iest potrzebna iey ładność iednak wcale niepotrzebna. Mówią, iż równie iest kontent Tatar z mizernego pomieszkania swego iako Niemiec, Francuz, lub Włoch z wspaniałego budynku. Z tego zaś twierdzą, że każden w swoich granicach zostwać powinien. Każden cieszyć się tą Architekturą, którą mu ślepe szczęście nadało. Prawda, że tym, co tylko szczęściem rządzą (88) się, taka myśl podobać się musi, prawda, że ci, co tylko azardem zycią, taką powinni cieszyć się Architekturą. Ale i to pewna, że zdrowy rozsądek na tym nie powinien przestawać, że przeciwnie rostropny człowiek upodobanie nawet rozumem miarkowwać powinien.

Zamknieymy więc, ze wszystkiemi Architektury Filozofami, że Architektura nie zupełnie podpada niegraniczoney naszey woli, że natura iest iey (89) wizerunkiem, że ładność nie odmienna tam tylko będzie gdzie upodobaniem z rozumnym natury naśladowaniem złączone, zazyie tych wszystkich pomoc, które miec może sztuka nasza, nie tylko od Geometryi, ale i od cáłey równie potrzebney Filozofii.

(90) III. Uwaga O pozytkach z nauki Architektury wypływaiących.

Będąc cząstką Filozofii Architektura, nie od samych tylko Architektów, ale i od innych powinna bydz szacowaną. Zdaniem niektórych, (91) Krolowie owi, Którzy pierwsi miasta stawiali nieszukaiąc obcych do załozenia murów, sami na wszystko swoie podawali planty. Była ta sztuka Krolewską kiedyś zabawą, lubo i teraz ieszcze ieden z Niemieckich Książąt tak ozdabia Miasta swoje fabrykami, Wenecyi, Rzymu, i Wincencyi wizerunki naśladuiącemi, że już Stolica iego nie tylko Marsa szkołą, ale i Apollina nazwać się może. Wszakze ręka tego wielkiego Monarchy równie piora i broni Cyrklu i Linii umie zażywać? (92) [W]szakze nowa Grobowa Kaplica dokończenie Pałacu Charlottenburg, i w tym Sala wspaniała Jego są własnym wynalezieniem? Niedziw więc, ze potakich przykładach, szlachetna sztuka, szlachetnych często zabawia. Wielu w Włoszech godnie Urodzonych Ludzi, w Architekturze zawsze cwiczyło się. Szwecya rachuie Margrabię Tessyn, który naśladuiąc Oyca swego, taką wywyższył fabrykę, iakey znaleść ciężko w Połnocnych kraiach. I Angielscy Panowie (93) między któremi Penbrocke, Margrabia Notumberlandu, Burlingston, pokazuią doskonale, że szacowana iest w Ich kraiach ta wyzwolona Sztuka. Ale domowe nawet w tym znaleść można przykłady, gdy iż naszych niektórzy powszechny ten, ale chwalebny naśladuią zwyczay, co raz bardziey doskonalą Architekturę. W rzeczy zaś samey pozyteczne iest, tym, którzy mogą budować (Krolów, Szlachtę, bogatych, Duchownych, nawet nieuwalniając) nie mowię, (94) gruntowna znaiomość ale iakieżkolwiek nauki, nasze poznanie. Bo kto kiedy może wybrać dobrego Architekta, dobry Rysunek, na Architekturze, na Rysunku nieznaiąc się? Kto architektom pewne okryslić prawa, pewne wygody, przepisać pierwsze ich początki i reguły nieumieiąc.

Przeciwnie zaś przy iakiey kolwiek tego wszsystkiego wiadomości, nie tylko same budowanie, ale i inne Sztuki, które iakieś maią z Ryzunkiem (95) złączenie, poprawiłyby się. Ominąwszy bowiem innych, Snycerze teraz według swoiey woli, co chcą z nami wyrabiaią, w Meblach, w Boazeriach, śmieszne Ozdoby, a co gorsza kosztowne, bez naymnieyszey na naturalność uwagi wyrczyniaiąc. Omyłki często iak na złość pozłocone drogo sobie płacić kazą.

Ale daley ieszcze rozciągaią się, skutki pochodzące z nieumieiętności Architektury. Patrzmy, już nie na buduiącego, lub zdobiącego (96) domostwa, ale na tego, który dla wygody tylko nowey, w stolikach, szafkach, biurkach szuka formy. Codzienne nam zaraz doświadczenie pokazuie, że taki w boiaźni niezapomnienia, co słabo w myśli trzyma, iak nayprędzey do Rzemieśnika się kwapi, i w puł zmordowany nie statecznemi Konceptami, co krok prawie odnowionemi, przychodzi nakoniec do naznaczonego mieysca, gdzie dopiero nasza zaczyna się Komedya. Rozmawia bowiem nowy gość (97) z robotnikiem, ale ieden drugiego nierozumi. Kazden cudzą myśl na swoią nakręca, cudzo wygody do swego stosuie zdania. Ztąd Babilońskie zamieszanie. I kilka nadaremnie przechodzi godzin. Więcey pracy Rzemieśnik na rozmowę, niz na robotę zażywa, mniey czasu na nią więcey daleko na dorozumienie się traci. Przeto niechcąc dłużey męczyć się, próżno, a może gotowy zysk gubić, iuż upewniać zaczyna, że wszystko doskonale (98) zrozumiał, że wykona rozkazuiącego wolą naznaczaiąc do tego dzień godzinę, ieżeli nie minutę. W ten czas wynosić się zaczyna moy gość nie przestaie iednak bełgotać w drz-wiach na wschodach, i iezeli potrzeba, na ulicy nawet. Nie wie iednak z tym wszystkim Rzemieśnik, do czego ma się brać, składa poprzedaiących rozka-zów części, ale w nich przeciwności tylko i niepodobne do skutku, układy znaydu ie. Wpada zatym w niecierpliwość. (99) Niewiele myśląc bierze się do roboty, całe na tym zakłada staranie, by rzecz swoią iak nayprędzey według danego dokończył słowa. Wraca się tym czasem niezbyty ów i przykry gość wpada znowu raptem do Rzemieśnika, wyrywa, może niedokończoną ieszcze robotę. Opatruie ią, ale sam nie wie, czy taka iest, iakiey niegdyś pragnął.

Zamieszany troszkę, nie śmie nic mówić. Zyska zawsze z tego wstydu, i milczenie Rzemieśnik (100) wychwala gust Pański (o którym nigdy niemyslał) swoią wślepym naśladowaniu cudzey myśli pilność (którey nigdy niezazył) słowem zabałamuconego bardziey bałamuci: Nie tak by zapewne rzecz uchodziła Rzemieśnikom, gdyby szlachetni cokolwiek na rysunku znaiąc się własnemu bardziey dowierzali dowcipowi.

Lecz i na tym niedosyć. Zwidywamy cudze kraie, od Państwa do Państwa, od Miasta do Miasta (101) ieżdząc. Naypierwsze rzeczy, które biią w oczy, są Fabryki. Te więc widziec musiemy, byle niepowierzchownie. Tym bowiem sposobem, zamiast obiasnienia, pomieszanie iakieś i fałszywa rzeczy znaiomość w umyśle naszym rośnie. A ztąd zaś pochodzi, że często quid pro quo (iak mowią) biorąc, trafiłby się taki który z własną swoią ochydą, powróciwszy do Oyczyzny, kolumnę, za Pilastr, kopułe za wiezę, Portyk kościoła, za sam (102) kościoł wziołby. Z takiego zaś widzenia proszę, co za pożytek?

Daymy iednak i to, że szlachetny obywatel nie wyieżdza z Oyczystego (kraiu), ze dla niego za murami własnego Miasta, świata już nie masz. Krótko mówiąc, obrócmy na tak opisanego całe nasze uwagi, zapatruiąc się iako na nieumieiącego Architektury. Od tego pewnie prócz przykrego w chwaleniu wrzasku, nieznośnego ieszcze, i ustawicznego, oczekiwać (103) potrzeba dziwowania się. Tak bowiem okryśloney w nauce osobie, naymnieysza rzecz, wspaniałą, owszem naywspanialszą zdawać się będzie, podłą inna, lubo wszelkiey uwagi godna, bo iemu nieznajoma. Rozumieiącego zaś Architekturę daleko inne, i owszem przeciwne rozmowy, prowadzone rostropnie, skutek szacowney umieiętności pokażą. Bo co się podziwienia niemiłego tyczę, wszakże te często pochodzi, z niepoięcia umysłu (104) zalepionego nieuchamowaną własnych, a czasem cudzych, rzeczy miłością.

A ponieważ z doświadzenia także dobrze wiemy, że kształt fabryk nietylko w generalności, ale i w częściach zachowany, każdemu z osobna Obywatelowi, i całemu kraiowi sławę czyni. Przeto do dobrego miast porządku należy by i Architektura publicznym podpadała rządom. Jedno bowiem iest powiedzieć, ładne Miasto, co to i ładna Architektura. Gdyby (105) więc przez ustanowienie panuiących, faciaty Pałaców, pierwey od Architektów na to naznaczonych były roztrząśnione, mniey zapewne każde Miasto nie kształtnych zamykałoby gmachów. Wiemy, że Turin we Włoszech tym pożytecznym sposobem budowany, za iedne między nayładnieyszemi, za porządnieysze od innych uchodzi Miasto ale z tey wiadomości korzystać nie umiemy.

Tu iednak już się obawiam (106) Tulliuszowego Ucznia iakiego, ktory z książką Mistrza swego, nieomieszkałbym i przeciwne troszke moim Cycerona czytać zdania. Wiadomo mi bez tego, że ten wielki Krasomowca prywatnych fabryk, między potrzebnemi nie rachuie, że nagania kościoły, nawet wspaniałe, że mówi, iż podobne gmachy zamiast honoru, niesławę miastom czynią. Ale o Cyceronie to uważam, iż tak surowe obywatelskie myśli, w ten czas (107) mu dopiero przyszły, kiedy widział, zbytkami upadaiącą, w Oyczyznie wolność i swobodę. Zalem przeto i passyą uwiedziony na naymniey ze okazye, czyli przez siebie szkodzące, czyli przez złe tylko zażywanie, skarzyłsię Cycero. Z wszelkim więc dla niego zostaiąc uszanowaniem, nieuwazam nic złego, by kray w potrzebne opatrzony, miał inne do wspaniałości i zabaw fabryki. Lubo co się tyczę w szczególności naszey (108) Oyczyzny z kazdym zgadzam się, że u nas bardziey opublicznych trzeba myślić fabrykach. Z czasem Rzecz-Pospolita powinnaby Osobom, na wyższych godnościach zostaiącym przyzwoite i do Urzędu należące wyznaczyć pomieszkanie. Takim bowiem sposobem nieosłabiałyby się prywatne Domy prawie na królewskie pałace na zamki, i na inne podobne gmachy nieprzechodząc na Następców Urzędu, ale tylko do swoiey krwi, (109) których Dziedzicom więcey częstokroć ciężaru, niz pozytku przynoszą. Bo maiąc nawet, iak często bywa, partykularni Obywatele upodobanie w budowaniu, mieliby większe i chwalebnieysze pole do zadosyć uczynienia chęci swoiey; łożąc takie sumy na kościoły, na szpitale, na Szkoły, na Kloaki, koniecznie dla czystości potrzebne, a rzadko u nas używane. Mało ma naśladowców (110) Witten pewny Burmistrz Amsterdamski, którego całe przychody na pospolite w budowaniach rozchodziły się potrzeby. A z tym wszystkim, gdyby bogaci pilniey uczyli się Sztuki dobrego pieniędzy zazycia pokazuiącey, upewniam, iż próżniactwo, ubostwo, i niecnota, w przemysły, w iako z kolwiek maiętność, w pracę i robotę, w kazdym mieyscu odmieniłyby się.

Te są prawdziwe pożytki z umieiętności Architektury wypływaiące żaden na nie (111) tylko leśny iaki rozgniewa się Filozof, przestrzegaiąc wszystkich, że Miasta więzieniem, Fortece prawdziwemi są klatkami. Ale takiemu Filozofowi namienić łatwo można, że gdyby Społeczeństwa i Miast niebyło, nieznaydowałyby się na ziemi Sprawiedliwość, Przyjaźń, Miłość i inne pierwsze cnoty, cały Naród Ludzki utrzymuiące. Nieznana także byłaby Filozofia, nie wiadome inne wyzwolone Sztuki, zarzucona, i zakopana (112) wcale nasza do nauk, do społeczności sposobność. Prawda, że często rządzącym, łatwiey iest przynaymniey co do prędkości i zakonczenia podbić w pieszczotach po Miastach żyiących ludzi ciężey zaś rozdzielonych w borach, i dzikich uśmierzyć. A i to pewna, że żelżywy iest ten i smutny dzikości przywiley, że niewszyscy są tacy nieprzyiaciele wolności by ią zawsze zupełnie zgubić usiłowali. Do tego żadney (113) rzeczy na tym świecie nieznaydziemy, zupełny pożytek przynoszącey.

Każda miewa małą iakąś niewygodę, a przynaymniey sposobność i skłonność do niey. Wybieraiąc iednak według przepisów rostropności te sztuki, które naywięcey ludziom wydaią pożytku, naymniey szkody. Ia rozumiem, że surowy nawet Filozof, Architekturze, pierwsze między innemi dałby mieysce.

(114) IV. Uwaga o ozdobach budowania.

Wszystkie naturalne rzeczy nie tylko te które rozumem poymuiemy, ale i inne, które zmysłami tylko czuiemy, podlegaią Filozoficznemu dowcipowi przeto dobremu gustowi właściwey ładności Filozofia sprzeciwiać się niemoże, owszem odkrywaiąc prawdziwe we (115) wszystkim początki, niemieszaiąc iedno z drugim, ale opatruiąc wszystko według istoty rzeczy. Wiele może dobremu nawet gustowi dopomóc ta pierwsza i powszechna umieiętność. Łatwo więc będzie i mnie (iuż w inney uwadze filozoficznie wyłożywszy właściwe ładności przymioty) odkryć w ozodobach architektury potrzebne przestrogi, tym tylko niemiłe iż często będą przeciwne wprowadzonemu zwyczaiowi, a może ugruntowanemu (116) ztąd przykładowi.

Ozdoby Architektury do tey części ładności należą, którą ia założyłem w upodobaniu ludzkim, byle naturze nieprzeciwnym. Między różnemi w architekturze ozdobami pierwsze mieysce maią ordines, to iest miary, według których różnie kolumny wyryte, różnie przezywaią się. Pięć miar powszechnie w Architekturze rachuiemy, chociasz trzy są tylko miary: (117) Dorycka, Ionska, i Koryncka. Gruntowna ładność w Doryckiey, delikatna w Korynckiey, srzednia w Iońskiey upatruie się mierze. Cokolwiek na iedną lub na drugą przechodzi stronę, mieć niemoże miłey proporcyi. Nadto naprzykład, Toskańska miara prostą, nad to delikatną Rzymska, czyli Composita, dobremu Architektowi wydawać się będzie.

Każda miara składa się z większych (118) części, które znowu z mnieyszych są złożone. Większe części zacząwszy od gzymsu są Cornia, Fryz lub Fregium Architraw, daley idąc sam pniak kolumny i iey podstawa. Styloblaty, czyli pedestalla niewchodzą w istotne wszelkich miar ułożenie.

Mnieysze części większe składaiące dla krótkości w Tablicy I odrysowane, każdą ze swoim imieniem wyznaczyłem. Łatwiey będzie przy (119) dołączoney, figurze poiąc pamiętać te kawałki, z których wszystkie prawie architektury naszey wypływaią ozdoby.

Grubość kolumny do swoiey wysokości, i też do wysokości gzymsu nie iest tak ustawiona, by od niey oddalić się nie mogliśmy. Same kolumn ułożenie często wielkiey w tym wyciąga odmiany. Ia wszelkim dla niektorych godnych i znanych Mistrzów uszanowaniem, w tym tylko (120) od nich oddalam się, że iednostaynie we wszystkich miarach czwartą część kolumny gzymsowi wyznaczam tak dalece, iż i w Doryckiey i Ionskiey mierze, cztery razy tylko kolumna moia wyższa od gzymsu będzie. Bo prawdę mówiąc kiedy Dorycka i Iońska kolumna iedney iest wysokości niewidzę, ani poymuię, czemu mnieyszy ma bydz gzyms Ioński, większy Dorycki? (121) Wszak gzyms z natury swoiey od dachu zaczynać się powinien, i dlatego tylko, że budynek naprzykład będzie Doryckiey miary, dach bez potrzeby podwyższać należy? Ale powie kto, więc wten czas Koryncka miara straci delikantość swoią względem innych? bynaymniey właściwa bowiem delikatność kolumny podlega grubości do swoiey wysokości, którą ia za powszechnym (122) zwyczaiem tak ustanowiam.

w Doryckiey   w Ionskiey

1/8   1/9

w Korynckiey

1/10

Acz właściwe kazdey miary proporcye głębiey rozstrzążnieymy. Będąc naprzod miara Dorycka do tych fabryk naznczona, które powierzchowną nawet okazuią gruntowność i prostotę iuz iest rzecz oczywista, że z nią nie (123) zgadza się. Mnogość szczupłych cząstek. Wielki człowiek, wielkie członki, wielkie drzewo, wielkie gałęzie od natury ma dane. Cała Grecka Architektura na drobne nie dzieliła się kawałki.

Więc i Dorycka podstawa ta, która powszechnie iest w używaniu daleko byłaby kształtnieyszą, gdyby w niey małe membrum literą X w Figurze I wyznaczone, podużym a wypukłym nienastępowało, (124) tak iako w Figurze II, gdzie po tey części która Torus zowie się, prosta następuie listewka. W głowicy Doryckiej miary nic naganić nie można. Wszystko w przyzwoitey, miłey, i naturalney iest mierze.

Grubość Dyametru kolumny do swoiey wysokości wu dawnych wielkiey podlegała odmianie. Grecy mało co od pięc dyametrów podwyzszali swoie Doryckie kolumny (125) więcey troszkę Rzymianie kolumna w Teatrum Marcella siedm razy w Dyokleciana, zaś Termach ośm razy dyameter swóy przechodzi. Tey ostatniey proporcyi i ia trzymam się.

Architraw Dorycki iedną tylko lisztewką od Fregium oddzielać się powinien, na kształt tego który w Figurze II widać, gdzie umyślnie ziedney strony kolumnę, z niektórymi omyłkami, drugą (126) oczyszczoną i uwolnioną od nich wyraziłem w tey nadziei, iż łatwiey tym sposobem będzie złe od dobrego oddzielać.

Fregium Doryckie ma tryglify, których odległość między balczycą ozdabia się. Wielu bez potrzeby w Doryckich kolumnach opuszczaią między balczyce, dlatego tylko, iż te im w czworograniastey nie wypadaią Figurze. Przyznaię chętnie, iż nadto (127) podługowate nie byłyby kształtne. Ale iakie iest prawo, iaki początek, by koniecznie czworograniaste ie robić, wcale niewidzę. Bardziey daleko ganię ząbki, które w ostatniey gzymsie części używaią niektórzy za przykładem Vignoli w tey mierze, w którey nad to są delikatne takie cząstki.

W Figurze II między innemi i ząbki z gzymsu Doryckiego wygluzowałem. (128) Mniey daleko znayduię omyłek w Ionskiey mierze. Głowica Iońska taka, iakiey dawni uzywali Rzymianie, wcale nie iest kształtna, lepsza nasza i dawnych Greków, których niewiem czemu w tym nie naśladowali Rzymianie. Dwie ciękie lisztewki opodal troszkę oddalone od zawiianey części głowicy daleko milszy sprawuią widok, niż kiedy zaraz pod nią są ułożone.

(129) Dzielą niektórzy Architraw Ioński na trzy części. Takiey rozdział Korynckiey mierze lepiey iest zostawić a tu dwoma tylko obeyść się lisztewkami. (Patrz na Figurę IV) Podstawa Iońska nie zgadza się z tą Architektury regułą, która przykazuie, by zawsze, cienkie na grubych, nie grube na cienkich utrzymywały się cząstkach. Lepsza daleko iest podstawa w Figurze IV wyrażona.

(130) Model naylepszy Korynckiey miary upatruie się w ruinach Rzymu na dawnym rynku Rzymskim za Kapitolem, kolumna którą ułożyłem w Figurze VI ztamtą iest wyięta. Wniey łatwą rożnicę między głowicą i podstawą teraźnieyszych czasów uzywaną każden zobaczy. Ale iuż po tak długim miar celnieyszych roztrząśnieniu nie od rzeczy i w tym uwiadomić się, czy wolno z rozmaitych miar iedną (131) złożyć miarę? Dać naprzykład kolumnie głowicę Iońską, postawę Koryncką, gzyms Dorycki? Na takie pytanie to tylko odpowiadam, iż każda miara maiąc właściwy swoy charakter przestaie bydz z Architekturze użyteczną miarą ile razy w właściwości przy zwoitey wychodzi. Moim zdaniem takie różnych cząstek złączenie, nie tylko iest niepożyteczne, niepotrzebne ale i nienaturalne i śmieszne. (132) Bo kogoby do śmiechu nieprzyprowadziła statua Herkulesa z nogą Wenery, albo widok wesołego Kupidyna z twarzą kulawego Wulkana? Nie bez przyczyny Xiąże wszystkich Architektów Witruwiusz gardził tym zwyczaiem mieszania miar iedney z drugiemi. Taki postępek nayczęściey i naytłatwiey wprowadza się przez miłość nowości, na niedostatek

umieiętności i dowcipu w wynaydywaniu (133) odmiennych rzeczy. Bo czemu już przy takim upodobaniu w nowości nie szukamy nowey iakiey i dotąd nieznaney miary? Czemu w tym iesteśmy tak niedbali? Czemu mamy się w tym za niesposobnych i przeniesiemy Grecki nad własny dowcip? Mamy zaś dwie drogi do wynalezenia nowey miary, która z nich bespiecznieysza uważamy.

Do doyścia pożądanego celu dwie są drogi, albo łącząc (134) różnie między sobą mnieysze miar cząstki, albo inne nowe wynayduiąc. Pierwszego sposobu śmiele chwycilisię Rzymianie, kiedy wziąwszy wyższą część głowicy Iońskiey, złączyli ią z Koryncką głowicą. Podobnego coś Francuzi za czasów Ludwika XIV zażyli. Każden z nich rozumiał iż do dostąpienia pożądanego wynalezienia dość było głowicę odmienić. Zaden z tych Architektów o Korynckiey niezapominał (135) głowicy. Zamiast oliwnych listków strusie piora z orderami pomieszane kolumnie dodano, w tey imaginacyi, iż ta miara przy tak małey odmianie za odmienną i nową u świata wydzie Płona imaginacya! Gdyby w tym tylko cała zakładała się nowość gdyby za odmianą głowicy, miara za nieużywaną uchodzić miała jużbyśmy w ten czas Architektów prosili, żeby wcale niestarali się o wynalezienie (136) nie miar nowych.

Lepiey iest więc daleko drugiego zazyć sposobu, nieznayome dotąd wynaiduiąc cząstki. Ile bowiem układać i przekładać będziemy dawne cząstki, to pewna że zawsze w nich wielkie podobieństwo mała i prawie żadna roznica wydawać się będzie. Wydobyć można kształt i figurę nowych cząstek z wizerunku natury. I owszem różne listków formy tysiączney (137) odmiany wiele by w tym ułatwiły pracy. Kto temu nie wierzy, kto w tym mnię ma za podeyrzanego, i moią radę za taką, po przeczytaney często odemnię chwaloney sławnego Mr. L'Augier architekturze łaskawszym na mnię będzie. Mniemam, iż pilna tey książki uwaga, złączona z wolą, i chęcią pracy, mogłaby wielu osobom wybić z głowy te fałszywe zdanie, iż nowey miary w Architekturze wynalezienie iest wcale (138) niepodobne.

Wszystkie kręcone i krzywe kolumny w budowaniu powinny bydź iak naydaley oddalone. Pierwszy krzywych kolumn model znalazłem w książce** sławnego Pozzi, lepszego malarza niz Architekta. Naprzód sam autor wyznaie, iż takie kolumny są nad to wykwintne, potwierdza iednak ie taką przyczyną, która zupełnie iest iemu, (139) i iego zdaniu przeciwna. Mówi iż dawni nawet, często osoby (Karyatydy w architekurze nazwane) siedzące, to iest według niego nachulone, i krzywe używali. Wcale iakby przykład dawnych miał przywiley potwierdzenia omyłek i nienaturalności, wcale iakoby była rzecz natu-

---

**Prospettiva di Pittori e Architetti in folio.

ralna, osoby moc, i siłę wydaiące w siedzącey figurze wydawać, wcale nakoniec, iakoby była rzecz przyzwoita, kolumny, które żadnego z (140) ludzmi podobieństwa niemaią, na model ludzi wykręcać. Nadto są takie kolumny niegruntowne, nienaturalne, niekształtne, by mogły pomiescić się, nie mówię o fabrykach, ale nawet i w tych kawałkach, w których cokolwiek więcey pozwolono iest architektom zażyć wolności. Kręconych kolumn gdzie niegdzie zażyć możemy. Ładnie się takie kolumny wydaią w Konfessyi Stego Piotra utrzymuią wspaniały (141) baldachim. Ale wcale wątpie by na utrzymanie nawet badlachimu krzywe kolumny mogły bydz uzywane. (Patrz w Fig. VII i VIII w którey umyślnie zkrzywioną wydałem kolumnę)

Każda iakieykolwiek bądź miary kolumna ma podstawę, [...]³ i naywyższą część głowicy czworograniastą więc niemoże bydz tam uszykowaną, gdzie nieprosty róg, lub iest nad to szczupły lub nad to szeroki, w tenczas (142) albo umnieyszyć, albo tak trzeba powiększyć róg, by się kolumna z mieyscem spaiała. Wielkiego dla tey przyczyny zażyć trzeba dozoru w wybieraniu figur, tam tylko zażywaiąc nieczwórógraniastych gdzie innych wybioru mieysce uczynić niedozwala. Kiedy zaś w podobney iuż znayduiemy się okoliczności, wten czas zażyć należy tych wszystkich sposobów, które nam głębsza sztuki naszey (143) odkrywa nauka.

Łatwy bowiem mamy i do unikniena takiego, niekształtu sposob. Kiedy róg figury iest nadto szczupły, tak iak rogi xx. w Fig IX tam w rogu murem nadrabia się poty, poki w podstawie dwoch kolumn razem złączonych rogi prostą figurę niewezmą. Inaczey rogi czworograniestey podstawy nie tylko wychodziłyby z mieysca, w którym zamykać się maią, ale też żadnego (144) kształtnego złączenia niemiałyby z innemi pobliskiemi kolumnami. W Figurze X podstawa czworograniasta A. w rogu nieprostym ma boki bb które nie idą równo z bokami pobliskich kolumn. Ile razy zaś róg obszerny przechodzi róg prosty, w ten czas podobną sztuką murem nadstawiaią się kolumny złączone na kształt rogów dd w Figurze IX takim spoionych sposobem. Ale by te tak potrzebne rzeczy (145) łatwo czytelnik ciekawy poioł pomnożyłem w teyże Tablicy inne mnieysze i większe rogi, na nie zapatruiąc się prętko wszystko poymie. Dodałem dla tego na końcu czworograniastą Figurę w którey ze złączenie dwoch razem kolumn nie iest potrzebne, z spoyrzenia samego wydaie się (Patrz Figu XI).

Przytrafia się często samym Architektom, iż w okrągłey figurze szykuią kolumny, a w gorsza, i w kilka rzędy, tak (146) iako widać w Figurze XII. Kto tylko na plantę patrzy, żadney w takim uszykowaniu nie znaydzie omyłki, mimo istotney prawdzie. Bo podwyzizaiąc z planty wzmiankowane kolumny pierwszy rząd przymałą będzie miał proprocyą. (Patrz Fig. XIII) Ale ostatni w teyże kolumn wysokości, iak będzie szeroki, wydaie figura XIV. I coś więc w takim przypadku Architekt robić może? Unikać powinien okrągłych, zazywać zaś iak (147) naybardziey okrągławych figur, inaczey ostatni rząd nad to szeroki mu wyidzie.

Także ile razy kolumny w iedynym rzędzie w okrągłey figurze uszykuią się, w ten czas kolumny bez arków zażywać należy. Przykład kolumn z arkami masz w Fig. XV bez arków w XVI. Przyczyna dla którey daię taki przepis, iest iasna. Tam bowiem gdzie arki maią mieysce, ark bb kropkami w figurze XVII (148) wyznaczony wychodzi z linii dd to iest z rogów kolumny na których sam ark utrzymywać się powinien. Taka omyłka sprzeciwia się gruntowności ieżeli nie właściwy, to przynaymniey widoczny. Te gzymsy, które u kolumn używamy, służą nie tylko na ozdobę tychże kolumn, ale też i w wyższey okien i drzwi części zażywaią się. Z figur, które umyślnie łączą, łatwo każdemu przyzwoite odkryć (149) proporcye.

Mamy nakoniec i inne w architekturze ozdoby, ktore od rysunku bardziey, niż od czego innego biorą cały swoy kształt i ładność. W takim rodzaiu wszystkich innych Grecy i dawni przewyższyli Rzymianie. W ich gzymsach, sufitach, podłogach nawet miłe bardzo oczom wydaią się sztuki. Grecków i Rzymian Włochy naśladuią. Moim zdaniem nicby dla naszey sztuki niebyło pożyteczneyszego, (150) iako zbiór tych ozdob, które Grecka i Rzymska zamykała Architektura. Słyszałem z wielką radością, że iedna osoba w Rzymie nazebranie podobnych ozdob całe swoie łozy staranie. Te dzieło iak wyidzie na świat, użyteczne, ciekawe, i potrzebne będzie. Dotąd zadnego nie znayduię Autora o tym obszernie piszącego, każden, którykolwiek o architekturze pisze, dotyka tylko, ala niewyłuszcza (151) tę tak potrzebną materyą. Mnie w krótkim tyle rzeczy zbiorze o pewnych w szczególności częściach obszernie rozmawiać nieowolno, osobliwie zaś o tey, która lubo wszelkiego poważenia godna, z figur bardziey, z doświadczenia, z dobrego gustu, i częstego dawnych gmachów widoku, niz z uwag lub roztrząśnienia, i pewnych przepisów, poymuie się powszechnie.

(152) V. Uwaga O wygodzie w fabrykach.

Dotąd w przeszłych uwagach bardziey Architekturę w sobie samey zamkniętą, niż do budowania stosowaną roztrząsnołem porządek wyciąga praktyczne sztuki naszey odkryć przepisy. W każdey fabryce zachować nalezy wygodę, gruntowność, ładność. (153) Więc ia o wygodzie naprzod, o gruntowności, zaś i ładności w dalszych uwagach rozmawiać będę. To co wygodą zowię od dobrego części rozłożenia i onych umieszczenia zawisło. Wielu nie tak ostro te rzeczy biorą i owszem rozumieią, że iedno wcale znaczą. Rozłożenie iednak części nic innego nie iest, tylko ilkość, to iest: przystoyna wielkość kawałków, czy to osobno, czy to z całą machiną zgadzaiących się, iako (154) i przysposobienie fabryki do pożadanego używania. Umieszczenie zas nic innego nie iest, tylko iakość, to iest: przyzwoitey wybior położenia sytuacyi, zgadzaiący się z koncem, któremu ma służyć budowanie. Także i wygoda podobnie od pożytku, w Architekturze tym się rożni, że wygoda ułatwia wszelką ciezkość w wykonywaniu tych rzeczy, które odprawiać się powinny, pożytek zaś (155) zadosyć czyni temu użycu, ktore sobie buduiący w fabryce założył. Może więc bydz budynek pożyteczny, ale niewygodny, iako przeciwne wygodny, ale nie zgadzaiący się z wolą buduiącego. Obydwie rzeczy pogodzić Architekt powinien.

Ia według tak okryśloney wygody o to starać się będę, abym celnieysze w tym przepisy iaśnie wyłożył inne ile krótkość wymaga, dotknoł (156) tylko. Naprzód uważam, że iezeli kiedy, to w założeniu miasta naybardziey starać się trzeba, by żyzną ziemię a przynaymniey opatrzoną, rzeką, do sprowadzenia łatwieyszego żywności wybierać. Wszyscy w tym zgadzaią się, iż dobroć powietrza, będąc pierwszym zdrowia naszego początkiem, bydz także powinna nie ostatnim buduiącego względem; dobroć zaś iego zależy od mieyscowego (157) wszystkich miast gruntu, od exhalacii i pary, iako tez i od wiatrów, które złą i zepsutą z sobą z pobliskich mieysc wpędzaią Atmosferę. Pospolicie z piaszczystego gruntu mało waporów wypływa, wiele zaś grubych mineralnych partykuł z żyżney i tłustey ziemi. Przeto pierwsza za dobrą druga iest miara za szkodliwą.

Do poznania iednak dobrey, lub szkodzącey aury, mamy pewne i nie zawodne (158) znaki. Z Chimicznego zaraz doświadczenia miarkować można z rosy słoney partykuły z atmosferą pomieszane. A że grube i mineralne wapory odmieniaią metalom i iedwabiom właściwy kolor, na żelazie zaś rdzę wydaią, tam więc, gdzie takie odmiany uważać się będą i podeyrzana powinna bydz aura. Powszechnie gdzie woda dobra, tam i aura nie zła. Lecz na tym przestawać nie trzeba. Pilny i rostropny Architekt (159) wywiadywać się będzie o stanie zdrowia, dawnieyszych mieszkańców a przynaymniey w okolicy pobliskich iako też i bydłąt chorobach. Tego osobliwie dozoru dawni zazywali: kiedy buduiąc miasta, bydłąt na ofiarę zabitych pilnie rozważali wnętrzności z ich koloru i zepsucia nie bez przyczyny do mieszkania sposobność aury miarkuiąc.

Z taką dopiero ostroznością wybior aury uczyniwszy, mozna dopiero miasta buduiąc (160) o ulicach pomyśleć. W ulicach wystrzegać się trzeba niezdrowych i przeciwnych wiatrów. Łatwo dobre każdego kraju poznanie odkryie, któremu ten nayczęściey podlega wiatrowi, któren dla niego iest nayszkodliwszy. Sławny Palladiusz o ulicach mówiąc i to wyciąga aby w ciepłych kraiach domy wysokie, ulice zaś szczupłe były, tym bowiem sposobem rozumie, iż w lecie niemało uiełoby się upału. I owszem potwierdza te swoje (161) zdanie Tacyta słowami, który upewnia, iż daleko w Rzymie szkodliwsza była aura za Nerona, kiedy ten Cesarz dla kształtu miasta, ścisłe rozprzestrzenił ulice. Z tym wszystkim lepiey iest zawsze szerokie ulicom dawać mieysce. Niewygoda bowiem gorąca samym wolnieyszym wiatru przewiewaniem nadgradza się.

Widok zaś prywatnych domów w każdym mieście tym iest szacownieyszy, im otwarcia (162) na wprowadzenie aury i światła, bardziey zgadzaią się z użyciem każdey części domostwa. Tak naprzykład szafarnie, szpichlerze, i wszystkie inne mieysca służące na utrzymanie rzeczy podległych zepsuciu, powinny bydz na pułnóc obracone. Biblioteki zaś i Gabinety do sprawunków na wschód, tak dla prędszego światła, iako też dla pewnego, i długiego ksiąg utrzymywania. Podobnie zimowe pomieszkania (163) na południe, letnie na pułnoc mogą bydz ułozone.

Często odemnie wzmiankowany Witruwiusz to osobliwie w pismach swoich zaleca, aby wszystkie fabryki przyzwoite miały światło. Bez aury żyć, bez światła pracować nie można. Gdzie fabryka nie iest okrążona innemi budynkami, tam początkowy nawet Architekt niewiele sobie zada pracy, ale inaczey będzie w mieyscu innym fabrykom (164) pobliskim. Dla unikniena wszelkiey w podobnych okolicznościach trudności, o to starac się trzeba. 1° aby niewięcey w fabryce było okien nad potrzebę, bo zawsze otwarcia osłabiaią fabrykę; 2° aby iedne okno drugiemu nie było bardzo bliskie, lub bardzo dalekie. 3° aby okna równie od siebie odstawały, i iezeli domostwa z wielu piątr składaią się, aby okno nad oknem było uszykowane. Takie okien rozporządzenie (165) nie tylko iest oczom miłe, ale też z wszelką domostwu gruntownością zgadza się.

Rożna bydz może okien forma. Gdzie tego potrzeba, okrągłe używaią się okna, często okrągławe, albo u wyższey części wygięte, ale naypospoliciey czworograniaste bywaią, i w rzeczy samey ta figura iest w tym naywygodnieysza i nayozdobnieysza. Dla łatwieyszego światła po pokoiach rozchodu, nie od rzeczy wewnętrzną okien część (166) szerszą od zewnętrzney robić, iako wydaie się w Figurze I gdzie otwarcie a,b szersze iest od c,d.

Do tego, ile można, i o to starać się, trzeba, aby okno w budynku ni szersze od 4 części proporcyonalnego pokoiu, ni wąższe od piątey nie były. Wzaiemnie szerokość okna do wysokości naznacza się, iak 12 albo iak 13, a kiedy fabryka z wielu części składa się im bardziey w górę idziemy, tym wąższe okna wydawać się powinny. Osobiliwie w tym Palladiusza (167) zdanie, który drugiego piątra okno szostą częścią zmniesza od pierwszego, i inne wciąż w teyże proporcyi układa.

Na koniec i to w oknach zachować potrzeba, aby ta część która Lorica po naszemu ostrzeżenie mianuie się, niebyła ni nizszą ni wyższą dla wygody patrzących nad 3 Rzymskie stopy (Fig XI). Wszak dla tey samey przyczyny te ostrzezenie ściśleysze zawsze od muru robi się. W figurze B Lorica b. daleko iest (168) wazsza od muru domostwa litera x. naznaczonego. Ale to są pierwsze reguły, którym wielką dodać trzeba pilność w uważaniu natury kraiów. Do nich bowiem wszczegulności to wszystko stosować nalezy, co tu w powszechności wykładam.

W budowaniu, i wybiór figur sposobnieyszych do zadosyć uczynienia buduiącego końcom, niemałey iest wagi. A lubo w Geometryi ze wszystkich Geometrycznych figur, to (169) iest tych, których linia w koło krążąca iedney iest długości, nayzdolnieszya do uszykowania osob, iest cyrkularna figura, z tym wszystkim zażywać się niepowinna, ile że dobremu pokoiów rozporządzeniu, i rozłożeniu iest w cale przeciwna. Wniey albo wiele nieregularnych pokojów, albo mury nadto często niepotrzebnie grube cierpieć trzeba. Z kąd to wypływa, że im bardziey do cyrkułu figury zbliza ią się, tym daley powinny (170) bydz od fabryk do pomieszkania oddalonemi. Mowię o wielokątnych figurach, których używanie od pierwszych nauki naszey Mistrzów iest naganione. Sławny w Kapraroli pałac pięciograniasty nie tak dla wygody, iako dla osobliwości swoiey iest szacowny. Tam zaś Wignola, który na niego dał swoy abrys, to niby na przestrogę, wszystkim, w iednym napisie umyślnie na to uczynionym wyznaie, że wiele nałożył czasu nie tylko na (171) niknienie dziur, i mieysc proznych ale tez i na przyzwoite okien rozporządzenie.

Czworograniasta więc figura nad wszystkie inne powinna bydz potrzebna. Romby, trapezia, w ten czas tylko zażywać wolno, kiedy wygonieyszych sytuacya wybrać niepozwala. Można iednak okrągłą nawet figurę u fabrykach pomieścić, ile razy te nie na pomieszkanie, ale na gromadę ludzi służą. Iako to wszystkie (172) prawie publiczne fabryki.

Ciężko, i owszem nie podobna, na każden z osobna budynek, ile okoliczność wymaga partykularne dawać przepisy, chociasz to rzecz pewna, iz rozłożenie i rozporządzenie fabryk tysiącznym podpada odmianom. Powszechnie o to starać się należy, aby mnieysze części większym służyły, aby galerie miały pobliskie pokoie. Mierzyć powinna rozległość fabryki wielkość (173) pokoiów. Mały pałac niewielkie stancye, wielki niepowinien mieć szczupłe. Kto bowiem niewidzi, że nicby nie było niewygodnieyszego, iako aby wielki gmach małe sale, w małych zaś pałacach obszerne cztery pokoie całe zabierały mieysce? Zgadzać się potrzeba, około porządnego złączenia pokoiów z wolą i wygodą buduiącego byleby to właściwey niesprzeciwiało się ładności. Prawdę mówiąc (174) Włochy wspaniale ale niewygodnie mieszkaią. Apartamenta ich w długim i prostym pokoiów ciągu zakładaią się. Wymawia słusznie Włoskim Architektom ten sposób ułożenia Witton. Wszyscy cudzoziemcy naganiaią ten zwyczay. Sami nawet kraiowi na to zalą się, ale to wszystko nieodmieni zwyczay tak długim używaniem wprowadzony i potwierdzony.

(175) Są także w każdey fabryce pewne mieysca, które wyciągaią innych pobliskich, nie tylko dla wygody, ale i dla potrzeby. Sala do iadania, kuchnia, spiżarnie &c. takie architekt razem pomieścić powinien. Ma do tego i inne części, które muszą mieć swoie mieysce, by drugie znowu z wygodą były użyte mówię o drzwiach, wschodach, kominach tak bardzo w budynkach potrzebnych. Co się naprzod drzwi tyczę, z temi (176) architekt oszczędnie, a nie szczodsze obchodząc się, będzie ie od rogu domostw, iako naybardziey oddalał, łatwo ale rostropnie do nich stosuiąc to wszystko, co oknach wyłożyłem, z tą tylko odmianą, że drzwi w prywatnych budynkach, ni wyższe, ni niższe od 6 stóp Rzymskich, w publicznych zaś osobliwie w bramach miasta, nie ~~szersze~~[4] od 10 stóp bydz maią. Iaka zaś w wielkich pałacach bram powinna bydz wielkość, na to żadney nie masz (177) reguły. W nich z rozległości fabryk, i wyznaczonego ich używania zgadzać się nalezy.

Zważywszy wysokość domów i częstą potrzebę tey wysokości iaka ze wschodów wygoda wypływa łatwo każdy zrozumieć może; iakiego iednak dozoru iakiey pilności i uwagi w ich ułożeniu, zażyć należy, nie iest łatwo poiąć. Bo kto roztrząśnie, że wschody naprzód oświecone bydz przywoicie powinny i (178) otwarcie wolne, że same wschodów gradusy, dla wolnego przechodu, szerokie, a nie wysokie robić trzeba, kto to wszystko mowię, roztrząśnie, ieszcze nie zmiarkuie ciężkości cáłey wybioru przyzwoitych do budynku wschodów. Jedyne zaświadczenie iasnie to nam otwiera. Naywięcey i nayczęściey biegli nawet błądzą Architektowie.

Długo Watykan w Rzymie stał bez wschodów godnych tak wielkiego pałacu. Ładna w Neapolu fabryka di Capo (179) di monte, nazwana dla nieprzyzwoitych wschodów między innemi iest opuszczona.

Miara na stopnie wschodów tak iest wyznaczona, że prawie wszędzie stopień, wysokości siedem calów, szerokości zaś naymniey pietnaście lub szesnaście robi się. Dawni Rzymaianie za świadectwem Witruwiusza o to nawet starali się, by stopy w wschodach nie do pary były. Bo kto prawą nogą wchodząc do kościoła na wschody wstąpił (180) i tąż ostatni stopień skończył ten iuż mogł szczęśliwego coś sobie nie bez przyczyny wrózyć.

Od różnego ułożenie róznie przezywaią się wschody. Proste mianuią się kiedy prosto kręcone, kiedy wokrąg idą. Ieżeli dusza wschodów literą x w Fig. III naznaczona iest czworograniasta, wschody czworograniaste, ieżeli dusza wschodów troygraniasta podobnie i wschody zwać się będą. (Patrz Fig. IV i V)

Kiedy dusza, około którey (181) stopnie krążą się iest zupełnie okrągła, cyrkularne kiedy okrągława eliptyczne nazywaią się wschody. Słowem, inne częścią kręcone, często zaś proste imie biorą od rożnych figur złączonych, z których składaią się. Takiego rodzaiu wschodów mamy przykład w fig: VI. lubo ie w potrzebie tylko, i gdzie drugich sytuacya niedozwala żażywać powinniśmy.

Pospolicie iest rzecz rozgłoszona, że dawni kominów (182) nie znali, i że kominy płodem są dowcipu poźnieyszych Architektów. Ia chociasz temu niesprzeciwiam się, że dawniey mieli rożne sposoby do rozgrzewania domostw, trzymam iednak za pewnę, że używali coś podobniego do naszych kominów. Bo nie o czym innym, ale o nich wykłada się owe Wirgiliusza wyraznie: „Et iam summa procul[villar—sic! villarum] culmina fuma[sic! fumant]" Wszak i Apian w iednym swoim (183) opisaniu, kominy Fumaria sub tecto posita, zowie Aristofanes nawet w iedney swoiey Komedyi wprowadza starego Polikleonta, który silnieyszy wnogach, niż u rękach, z izby kominem uciekać myślał Oczywiste, ieżeli nie mylę się potwierdzenie błądzącego, a pospolicie rozsianego o tym zdania.

Wielkość kominów wielkości pokoiów, szerokość zas komina, wysokości tegoż w proporcyi 3 do 2 odpowiedać powinna. (184) Cięższe są daleko inne o kominach przepisy, które tyczą się kanałów, dym na górę wyprowadzaiących. Ciekawy czytelnik chcąc bydz doskonale o tym uwiadomionym, niech czyta: La meccanique du feu par Mr. Gauger. Po przeczytaniu książki ciekawość iego uspokoiona będzie.

Ia to tylko ostrzegam, że te wszystkie reguły, które kanałom w kominach służą, służyć mogą piecom pospolicie u nas używanym. Uczy nas (185) Palladiusz że dawniey zamiast pieców, kanały w murach wewnętrznych taką robili sztuką, iż te wszystkie do iedney zbiegały się dolney stacyi, gdzie ognie rozpalano. Taki ekonomiczny palenia sposób, wątpie, by w pułnocnych kraiach, był dostatecznym do obronienia od zimna.

Ale iuż gdyby nieprzełozona krótkość, i ten cel uwag na którén zawsze obzieraiąc się [. . .] i przypominam potrzebnieysze tylko a pierwsze (186) Architektury przepisy, wiele by mi ieszcze zostawało do pisania, o podwórzach, studniach, i ogrodach. Nad to iednak są długie te materye bym ie mógł wszystkie doskonale wyłuszczyć. A choćby nawet i to nie z wielkim mi przyszło wykonać mozołem, kto wie czy by ta sama wielość czytelnikom albo wcale niesprzykrzyła się, albo przynaymniey zamieszanie nie sprawiła. Lepiey podobno w tym krótkość (187) z pozytkiem złączyć. Co iest wiadomości godnego i pożytecznego, dostatecznie, iak rozumiem wyraziłem, inne rzeczy głębsze nauk naszey, książki odkryią. Tym zaś którzy tylko dla zabawy i chwalebney ciekawości, poznanie iakieszkolwiek chcą mieć Architektury dosyć będzie przeczytać wzmienione przestrogi, i przeczytane pamiętać.

(188) VI. Uwaga O tych naukach, które są potrzebne dla Architekta.

Niemoże mieć lepsze mieysce ta moia uwaga iako na końcu tey książeczki, w którey całą krótko opisałem Architekturę. A lubo z tyłu rzeczy dość iasnie odemnię roztrząśnionych, iaka iest sztuki naszey ciężkość, iak (189) wielkiego wymaga przyłożenia się tak iest szacowną łatwo poiąć można, ia iednak na tym nieprzestaiąc niektóre także nauki, do umieiętności Architektury potrzebne, uważam.

Upatruię zaś zaraz na początku, iż dla Architektów między innemi pożyteczna iest znaiomośc tych sztuk, które kształt w sobie maią, i miły pozor. Plutark powiada, iż w Atenach, gdy dwa Architekci stawili się, przed (190) pospolstwem do dostąpienia pewnego nad farbryką dozoru, ieden z nich tak mową swoią zobowiązał pospolstwo, iż te wcale iemu przychylne, drugiemu przeciwne było. Chociasz zaś w tych czasach niepotrzebuiemy tak biegłych w wymowie Architektów, dobrze by iednak było by terazneysi iasny przynaymniey i łatwy styl mieli w wyłuszczeniu tych rzeczy, które albo robią, albo robić z ułożonych plant maią. (191) Często i to przytrafia się osobliwie w Włoszech, iz Sędziowie w sprawach do budynków ściągaiących się uwiadomie nia z iedney i drugiey strony od Architektów biorą. Wten czas ieżeli Architekt niepotrafi doskonale swoie wyłożyć racye, zbić przeciwne, iuż i Pana i swoią powinność zdradzi.

Ale daleko od wymowy potrzebnieysza iest dla każdego Architekta umieiętność historyi, z którey nie tylko bierze (192) znaiomość początków, srzodka, powstania, i przyczyn upadku sztuki swoiey, ale razem uwiadomia się o dawnych, wspaniałych i kosztownych fabrykach o sposobach do ich budowania zażytych, słowem o samch Architektach, których w dobrych rzeczach naśladować powinien. Więcey troszkę wymaga surowy Witruwiusz, chce by Architekt wiedział prawo nawet, osobliwie te, które spadku wód, otwarcia okien, i tym podobnych (193) rzeczy tyczą się. Gdyby zaiste tey nauki nasi niezaniedbywali Architekci, wszelkim przed budowaniem zapobiegaiąc omyłkom, niemało umnieyszyłoby się w sądach ztąd wypływaiących zwadek.

Osobliwie iednak czy do rysowania, czy do budowania iest potrzebna Architektowi arytmetyka. Ani dosyć iest umiec pierwsze 4 arytmetyki operacye. Starać (194) się trzeba o gruntowne tey sztuki poięcie, ieżeli niechcemy w rachunkach mylić się, z których i to pochodzi, że czasem fabryki sześć i siedm razy nad dane kosztuią słowo. Rożumne niegdyś w Efezie było prawo gdzie kiedy szło o publiczne fabryki, architekt był obowiążanym uwiadomić Magistrat o koszcie, i wszystkich expensach, którekolwiek mogły bydz na nie uczynione. Po dokończoney (195) fabryce, ieżeli koszt nieprzewyższał wyznaczoną summę, miał swoią Architekt nagrodę, ieżeli zaś przewyższał czwartą nawet częścią, do niego należał wydatek.

Geometria istotnie Architektowi służy na wyrażenie łatwe figur, na ich zmniey szenie, lub powiększenie, na dociecenie różnych przymiotów, które krzywe linie mieć mogą w arkach i suffitach, (196) na koniec na zrozumienie reguł proporcyi, od których cała zawisła Architektura.

Mechanika uczy także architekta iakim sposobem ma zgodzić w budowaniu rózne mocy wzaiemnie sobie przeciwne, iak zmiarkować grubość murów które opisać się mogą arkom i sklepieniom. Słowem, iaką sztuką i to dokazać by fabryka nie tylko istotną, ale powierzchowną (197) nawet miała gruntowność.

Po mechanice następuie wodna nauka, to iest Idraulika, służy ona do budowania mostów, portów, akweduktów, młynów, tam służy do wykopywania kanałów, ułatwienia handlu, i do innych, ciężkich prawda ale godnych uwagi potrzeb.

Dla dobrego umieszczenia fabryk, Optyka i Perspektywa bardzo iest architektowi potrzebna. Gdyby (198) sławny Bernini ie nie znał nigdy by Watykańskie wschody tego niemiały kształtu, ktory w nich upatruie się. Optyka do widoku należąca wielki ma z architekturą związek. Dziwna iednak rzecz, że po Newtonie i tylu innych nikt ieszcze praktycznie optyki do Architektury nie stosował.

Pilnie uważali dawni osobliwie Rzymianie w budynkach grunt i położenie mieysca. (199) My w tym nietak iesteśmy pilni, łatwo spuszczamy się na samą miłą mieysca sytuacyą. Dozór ten przynaymniey powinniby sami Architekci zazywać, applikuiąc się i do Fizyki experymentalney w tych osobliwie czasach, gdzie ta nauka powszechną iuz iest, i wszędzie znaiomą.

Łączyć do tego wszystkiego trzeba rysunek osob. Tey ostatniey sztuki tak niektórzy (200) wymagaią, iż rozumieią, że nie można bydz dobry[m] architektem, biegłym niebędąc malarzem. Ia temu zdaniu wcale iestem przeciwny. Wiem, że inne są rysunku i architektury przepisy, że lubo wspomagaią się wzaiemnie są iednak w wielu rzeczach sobie przeciwne. Ani dziwię się, że wielcy Malarze niezłemi byli architektami, maiąc bowiem w malowaniu potrzebę częstą tey sztuki, w niey wielkie nieznacznie (201) czynią kroki.

Z tym wszystkim Architekt nigdy dobrym nie będzie, ieżli mu zbywa na geniuszu, to iest wspaniałym i wielkim dowcipie. W każdey bowiem sztuce natura i rozum pewne nam daie przepisy, które dowcip do okoliczności stosuie, i rozprzestrzenia. Ślepe naśladowanie dalekie wcale od tego dowcipu ten tylko sprawuie skutek, że nauka zamiast iakiego postępku w jednym (202) zawsze zostaie stopniu. Między innemi przyczynami, dla których od dawnego czasu w Chinach górę nie biorą wyzwolone sztuki, iest nierozumne uszanowanie chińczyków na to wszystko, co od przodków swoich biorą.

Lecz te i inne rzeczy, które potrzebne są Architektowi, szlachetnym nawet osobom do tey sztuki upodobanie maiącym służyć powinny tym łatwiey, im te w szkołach (203) nawet Filozofią słuchaiąc, wykładaią się. Bo i Architekt nawet nie iest obowiązany gruntowną mieć wszystkich wzmienionych umieiętność. Niewymagam tego, by był biegłym wcale Fizykiem, wiadomym obszernie Historykiem, Matematykiem przednim, ale chcę, by dobre miał tego wszystkiego początki, by z nich w potrzebie, co mu iest pożytecznego, mogł (204) łatwo wydobyć i zrozumieć.

Na tym zapewne przestaćby mi nalezało, atoli ia we wszystkim szukaiąc Oyczyzny pożytku, krótko ieszcze uważam, iakimby sposobem u nas rozprzestrzenić się mogła Architektura. Miłość zaiste sławy i emulacya między uczącemi się niemały by w tym sprawiła skutek. Nie dość bowiem iest zapatrywać się na dawne gmachy, iść w nich ślady (205) starać się trzeba przewyższyć przodków nawet naszych. Nigdy by do tey doskonałości nie przyszli ani Rafael ani Bonaroti gdyby inney trzymali się drogi. Nienaśladowanie same, ale cnota i miłość chwały iest ta, która podwyzsza i rozprzestrzenia wszystkie nauki. Przeto kiedy u nas uczący się o to starać się będa, by mordowali imieniem swoim sławę, w ten czas powstaną (206) nauki, w ten czas kwitnąć będą z pospolitym dla wszystkich pożytkiem.

Ale iaka między uczącemi się może bydź emulacya, iaka pobudka bez nagrod, które naznaczać powinni Monarchowie, Magistraty, Panowie. Bo iuż prawdę iaśnie mówiąc, coż innego ieżeli nie ta chwalebna szczodrobliwość wszystkich pobudza ludzi do pilnowania swoiey powinnosci? (207) Nagroda złych dobremi, dobrych lepszemi czyni. Rzućmy oko tylko na Grecyą w nadgrody obfitą a obaczemy zaraz, Stezikratesa, Praxitelesa, Apellesa. Ieżeli więc chcemy i Oyczyznę naszą opatrzyć w Architekturę, nie żałuymy cokolwiek odłożyć na tych, którzy krwawo około niey pracuią; szanuymy tych wszystkich co do niey aplikuią się. Naśladuymy Franciszka I i Karola (208) V ktorzy z takim dla nauk byli przywiązaniem iż pierwszy przy śmierci swemu Malarzowi służył, drugi pendzel z góry upadły Tycianowi podał. Więcey czasem nad pieniężną zapłatę waży ta estymacia naymilszy sprawuiąca skutek. Daie nam świeży w tym przykład Niemiecki Cesarz JOZEF II szczęśliwie panuiący, który pod bytność moią w Rzymie, nietylko często nawiedzał biegłego Malarza <u>Pompeo</u> (209) <u>Battoni</u>, ale go potym po wielu nadgrodach Szlachcicem kreował, w wątpliwości podobno, co bardziey, czy te iego, czy on Szlachectwo zdobi.

Preface

1. From 1569 until 1795 "Poland" was more correctly referred to as the Commonwealth of the Two Nations, the Polish and the Lithuanian (Rzeczpospolita Obojga Narodów, Polskiego i Litewskiego). The dynastic union of Poland and Lithuania was accomplished in 1386 by the marriage of Jadwiga, daughter of Louis of Anjou (r. 1370–82), to Władisław II Jagiełło of Lithuania, though the Polish Crown and the Grand Duchy of Lithuania were still technically autonomous states until the constitutional Union of Lublin in 1569. This union the Crown and the vast territory of the grand duchy. The ensuing Commonwealth shared a parliament, among other government institutions, as well as a very ethnically diverse population that included Poles, Jews, Ukrainian Cossacks, Tartars, Armenians, Scots, Germans, Byelorussians, Lithuanians, Greeks, and even descendants of Dutch Mennonites. In the fifteenth century the Jagiellonian dynasty—which, during the sixteenth century, would come to rival the Austrian Habsburgs as a significant European power—expanded the territory considerably. The system of territorial expansion practiced by the Jagiellonian kings included Władisław III Jagiełło's election to the Hungarian throne in 1440 and the acquisition of the Bohemian crown by Vladislav II (1456–1516; son of Casimir IV Jagiełło, r. as king of Poland-Lithuania 1447–92) in 1471, as well as the Hungarian throne in 1490. The election of the Catholic Swedish Vasa king Zygmunt III (r. 1587–1632) brought Poland-Lithuania to its territorial apex, reaching 435,547 square miles, with Polish victories on Russian soil (e.g., the capture of Smolensk in 1611) during the "Time of Troubles" accounting for the latest gains. With the Treaty of Polanów, in 1634, the Commonwealth then contracted in size to 386,719 square miles, still twice the size of France. During the first partition, of 1772, by Russia and Prussia, the Commonwealth lost a third of its territory. In 1795, it was eliminated from the map. In other words, the largest country in Europe disappeared as a political entity.

2. Halecki, *Borderlands of Western Civilization,* 9.

3. Murawska-Muthesius, "Geography of Art," 11.

4. In Polish scholarship, the "Orient" in Polish culture is understood as Ottoman and Caucasian elements and influences. See, for example, Biedronska-Słotowa, *Orient in Polish Art;* Bardach, "Ormianie na ziemiach dawnej polski"; Reychman, *Orient w kulturze polskiego oświecenia;* and Cynarski, "Shape of Sarmatian Ideology in Poland." Polish-Turkish cultural exchange is the subject of the exhibition *Distant Neighbor, Close Memories: 600 Years of Turkish-Polish Relations,* Sakıp Sabancı Museum, Istanbul, 6 March–15 June 2014.

5. See Vidler, *Writing of the Walls*, 7–22; for a recent translation and commentary, see Vitruvius, *Ten Books on Architecture*. For the most comprehensive recent study of the Vitruvian exegetical tradition among early modern architectural theoreticians, see Payne, *Architectural Treatise in the Italian Renaissance*.

6. I first explored these ideas in a seminar taught by Thomas DaCosta Kaufmann on Central European art at Princeton University in the spring of 1997. See, by Białostocki, *Art of the Renaissance in Eastern Europe*, "Borrowing and Originality in the East-Central European Renaissance," "'Mannerism' and 'Vernacular' in Polish Art," and "Renaissance Sculpture in Poland in Its European Context." For an analysis of Białostocki's arguments, see DaCosta Kaufmann, "Italian Sculptors and Sculpture Outside Italy."

7. See, for example, Burke, *European Renaissance* and, by the same author, *Fortunes of the Courtier*.

8. See, by DaCosta Kaufmann, *Court, Cloister, and City* and *Toward a Geography of Art*, with extensive bibliography pertinent to "artistic geography."

9. See, for example, the discussion by Muthesius, "Kunstgeographie Revamped?" 19.

10. The question of the French influence on Polish architecture has been addressed, albeit not by way of architectural theory, by Miłobędzki, "Polish Country Houses in the Age of the Baroque."

11. Scholarship emerging over the last decade, including the "Crossing Borders" sessions of the 2008 International Congress of the History of Art, is leading this inquiry. See variously Elkins, *Is Art History Global?*; Carrier, *World Art History and Its Objects*; Brzyski, *Partisan Canons;* Summers, *Real Spaces;* and DaCosta Kaufmann, Dossin, and Joyeux-Prunel, *Global Artistic Circulations* (in press), which includes Guile, "Circulations: Early Modern Architecture in the Polish-Lithuanian Borderlands."

12. An accessible summary of developments in eighteenth-century Polish arts and architecture discussed according to period style and formal trends is Rottermund and Lorentz, *Neoclassicism in Poland*. For a survey of Polish arts and architecture in English, see Muthesius, *Art, Architecture and Design in Poland, 966–1990*. For a historical work that incorporates discussions about arts and architecture in the Poniatowski era, see Butterwick, *Poland's Last King and English Culture*.

13. Carpo, *Architecture in the Age of Printing*, 10.

14. These Polish-language monographs include Jaroszewski, *Chrystian Piotr Aigner, architekt warszawskiego klasycyzmu;* Batowska, Batowski, and Kwiatkowski, *Jan Chrystian Kamsetzer architekt Stanisława Augusta;* Kwiatkowski, *Szymon Bogumił Zug, architekt polskiego oświecenia;* Tatarkiewicz, *Dominik Merlini;* and Lorentz, *Efraim Szreger architekt polski XVIII wieku*. For an ongoing inventory of sacral monuments in the eastern regions of early Poland-Lithuania, see the indispensable multivolume work edited by Ostrowski, Kuczman, Kałamajska, and Betlej, *Materiały do dziejów sztuki sakralnej na ziemiach wschodnich dawnej Rzeczypospolitej*.

15. Carpo, *Architecture in the Age of Printing*, 12–13.

Introduction

1. Laugier, *Essai sur l'architecture*. Durand, *Recueil et parallèle des édifices de tout genre, anciens et modernes*. See Rottermund, *Jean-Nicolas-Louis Durand a polska architektura pierwszej połowy XIX wieku*. For the influence of André Le Nôtre on Polish garden design in the early eighteenth century, see Szafrańska, "Réception d'André le Nôtre en Pologne."

2. The pastelist Anna Gault de Saint Germain, née Rajecka (Warsaw ca. 1760–Paris 1832), completed a number of portraits of the Polish *szlachta* before departing for Paris

under the patronage of Stanisław August Poniatowski. It is possible that many of her works survive under misattributions (e.g., Batoni). She fled Paris for Clermont-Ferrand during the Revolution. See Jeffares, *Dictionary of Pastellists Before 1800,* s.v. "Gault de Saint-Germain, Mme, née Anna Rajecka."

3. See, in particular, Payne, *Architectural Treatise in the Italian Renaissance;* Hart and Hicks, *Paper Palaces;* and Kruft, *History of Architectural Theory.* For the influence of Vitruvian ideas on Polish architecture, see Kowalczyk, *Sebastiano Serlio a sztuka polska.* For a brief overview of Polish architectural treatises from the mid-sixteenth through the beginning of the nineteenth centuries, see Mieszkowski, *Podstawowe problemy architektury w polskich traktatach,* whose author seems unaware of Potocki's treatise.

4. Krystyna Gutowska-Dudek describes the manuscript as being extant in a form intended for publication. See Gutowska-Dudek, *Rysunki z wilanowskiej kolekcji Potockich,* 2:151.

5. See Rudnicka, *Biblioteka Ignacego Potockiego,* 67, and Michalik, *Działalność oświatowa Ignacego Potockiego,* 209.

6. Staszic, *Przestrogi dla Polski.* Staszic is best known for his political and scientific writings. He served as tutor to Andrzej Zamoyski's sons and, during the time of the Four-Year Sejm, was in the reform camp and promoted burgher mercantile interests. He was a member of the Towarzystwo Przyjaciół Nauk from its inception in 1800.

7. Rogaliński, *O sztuce budowniczey na swoie porządki podzieloney zabawa ciekawa miana w szkołach poznańskich Soc. Iesu roku 1764,* and Rogaliński et al., *Sztuka budownicza na swoie porządki podzielona.* Delorme, *Premier tome de l'architecture.* Blondel, *Cours d'Architecture.* Perrault, *Dix livres d'architecture.* Laugier, *Essai sur l'architecture.* Penther, *Bau-Kunst.* Goldmann, *Vollständige Anweisung zu der Civil-Baukunst.* Sturm, *Vollständige Anweisung allerhand öffentliche Zucht- und Liebesgebäude.* See Mieszkowski, *Podstawowe problemy architektury w polskich traktatach,* 110 and 113 n. 17, and Kowalczyk, *Sebastiano Serlio a sztuka polska,* 26.

8. Stanisław Konarski as cited by Mrozowska, "Educational Reform in Poland During the Enlightenment," 114. See also Konarski, *Pisma wybrane,* and Kołłątaj, *Stan oświecenia w Polsce.*

9. For an important study of the national education curriculum and culture, see Jobert, *Commission d'éducation nationale en Pologne.*

10. *Polski słownik biograficzny,* 28:1. On the history of the project for the Załuski Library, see Bobrowski, "Budynki użyteczności publicznej."

11. *Polski słownik biograficzny,* 28:3–4.

12. See Skierkowska, "Księgozbiór z dziedziny sztuki Stanisława Kostki Potockiego," 199.

13. Destroyed in 1944 and subsequently reconstructed. For Tylman van Gameren, see especially Mossakowski, *Tylman van Gameren: Leben und Werk,* and Ottenheym, *Tilman van Gameren, 1632–1706.*

14. Secondary sources include Bernhard, "'O sztuce u dawnych, czyli Winkelman polski' Stanisław Kostki Potockiego," and Guile, "Winckelmann in Poland," which includes bibliography on related literature.

15. "Katalog rzeczowy biblioteki."

16. See "Katalog rzeczowy biblioteki." The most comprehensive overall study of the inventory of Stanisław Kostka Potocki's library remains that by Skierkowska, "Księgozbiór z dziedziny sztuki Stanisława Kostki Potockiego." On Stanisław's artistic and architectural interests, see Polanowska, *Stanisław Kostka Potocki, 1755–1821.*

17. Kowalczyk, *Sebastiano Serlio a sztuka polska,* 12.

18. Burke, *Fortunes of the Courtier,* 90–94.

19. Miłobędzki dates the design to the period of Zbaraski's travels to Venice, either ca. 1604 or, more likely, ca. 1612, when Scamozzi's name appeared in Zbaraski's writings. Construction on the building itself was probably begun around 1626, under the direction of Krzysztof's brother, Jerzy, who was the castellan of Cracow at the time. The design was most similar to Scamozzi's 1574 design for the Villa Verlato in Villaverla. See Miłobędzki, "Tajemnica zamku w Zbarażu," with extensive bibliography of nineteenth-century Polish sources.

20. Payne, *Architectural Treatise in the Italian Renaissance,* 216 and 303 n. 8. Payne also notes that Scamozzi's treatise stood somewhere between builder's manual and philosophical discourse (215). On Scamozzi's travels, see also Breiner, "Vincenzo Scamozzi, 1548–1616," 200, who refers to the palace at Zbaraż anachronistically as having been built in Polish Galicia.

21. "Witruviusza tu nie odrzucamy tylko w tym, co zwyczaj pospolity odrzucił, przystępujemy zaś do Wincentego Scamozzyusza sposobu jako tego, który się dobrze przysłużył architekturze." As cited in Kowalczyk, *Sebastiano Serlio a sztuka polska,* 24.

22. Carpo, *Architecture in the Age of Printing,* 12.

23. Kowalczyk, *Sebastiano Serlio a sztuka polska,* 291, 302. See also Miłobędzki, *Architektura polska XVII wieku.*

24. Kowalczyk, *Sebastiano Serlio a sztuka polska,* 291.

25. Vautrin, *Pologne du XVIIIe siècle.* In my essay "Sebastian Sierakowski and the Language of Architecture," I discuss Vautrin's opinions in relation to the state of architecture in eighteenth-century Poland.

26. Wraxall, *Memoirs of the Courts,* 2:11–12, 30.

27. Stanisław Staszic, Ignacy Potocki, and Hugo Kołłątaj were three notable persons of this latter disposition, and the work they did during the Four-Year Sejm, which produced the Polish Constitution of 1791, was the most articulate and deliberate in the area of land reform. The bibliography for the Four-Year Sejm is substantial. Widely cited and recognized Polish secondary sources remain Leśnodorski, *Dzieło Sejmu Czteroletniego 1788–1792,* and Kalinka, *Sejm Czteroletni.* For patriotic literature and poetry during the period of the Four-Year Sejm, see Maksimowicz, *Wiersze polityczne Sejmu Czteroletniego,* vol. 1. In English, see Fiszman, *Constitution and Reform.*

28. See Fabré, *Stanislas-Auguste Poniatowski et l'Europe des lumières,* 266–94, as well as Rostworowski, *Polska w świecie.*

29. I. Potocki, "Uwagi o architekturze," 208–9.

30. After the losses of the 1830s, the collection was reconstituted in 1923, following the 1921 Treaty of Riga. For the Cabinet of Prints losses during the Second World War, see Sawicka and Sulerzyska, *Straty w rysunkach z Gabinetu Rycin.*

31. Stanisław Zawadzki to Ignacy Potocki, 13 II 1782. Also published in Michalik, *Korespondencja Ignacego Potockiego,* 107.

32. See Malinowska, *Stanisław Zawadzki 1743–1806,* 21–22.

33. See Gutowska-Dudek, *Rysunki z wilanowskiej kolekcji Potockich,* 1:50–51. The Potocki brothers and Aigner frequently collaborated on architectural projects; Stanisław commissioned Aigner to design Ignacy's grave monument for the cemetery at their palace in Wilanów, the former residence of King Jan III Sobieski just south of Warsaw proper.

34. Rousseau's text was most likely written in 1770 or 1771, that is, before the first partition. Michał Wielhorski contributed materials, and it is likely that Rousseau was directly or indirectly aware of the reform-minded writings of Konarski. See Hoensch, "Citizen, Nation, Constitution," 445 n. 11. For an in-depth discussion of Rousseau's *Considérations* and European perception of Poland, see also Wolff, *Inventing Eastern Europe,* 235–83.

35. Jobert, *Magnats polonais et physiocrats français 1767–1774*, 59–60. Some schools did remain religious but were supervised by the commission. This point is also made in Butterwick, "Catholicism and Enlightenment in Poland-Lithuania," 330–31 and 331 n. 118.

36. Butterwick, "Catholicism and Enlightenment in Poland-Lithuania," 331.

37. Kamieński, *Edukacja obywatelska*, 139.

38. Mrozowska, "Educational Reform in Poland During the Enlightenment," 128. Mrozowska notes that "[e]ditorial work on all the textbooks progressed very slowly because of the high standards of the Society's members, the need for translations into Polish, and diversion of the Society's attention by other matters. . . . Overall, from 1775 to 1792 seventeen textbooks and six exercise and reference books (selections from Latin authors, dictionaries, logarithmic tables), and six teachers' manuals appeared as the result of the Society's work" (132). Mrozowska also notes that the idea of civic education in Poland "preceded the appearance of the expression in French thought of La Chalotais and Rolland d'Erceville by more than ten years" (116). See also Konarski, *Pisma wybrane*, 2:317–79, and Butterwick, "Catholicism and Enlightenment in Poland-Lithuania," who observes that the Jesuits in the commission numbered 293 in 1773.

39. Piramowicz died on 14 November 1801. Ignacy Potocki to Stanisław Kostka Potocki, 28 XII 1801 and 21 I 1802, pp. 1183–84, 1185–88, 1179–81. Published in Michalik, *Korespondencja Ignacego Potockiego*, 224–31.

40. I. Potocki, "Uwagi o architekturze," 107–10.

41. Michel, *Compte général de la dépense*.

42. Héré, *Recueil des plans, élévations et coupes*.

43. Rykwert, *On Adam's House in Paradise*, 48.

44. I. Potocki, "Uwagi o architekturze," 110–13.

45. Most notable is Konarski's influential monograph *O skutecznym rad sposobie*, in which he rejects the *liberum veto* and advocates the restriction of monarchical powers.

46. See Sucheni-Grabowska and Dybkowska, *Tradycje polityczne dawnej Polski*.

47. According to Janusz Tazbir, Polonization was a priority among the *szlachta* that ensured inclusion, rendering the nobility relatively homogeneous, which was not true of other estates within the Commonwealth. Tazbir, "Polish National Consciousness in the Sixteenth to Eighteenth Century," 317. However, there was no official policy of "Polonization," and the adoption of the Polish language was not synonymous with such a policy.

48. Tazbir, "Polish National Consciousness in the Sixteenth to Eighteenth Century," 321.

49. I. Potocki, "Uwagi o architekturze," 7–8.

50. See Rostworowski, *Legendy i fakty XVIII w.*, 319–28.

51. The literature on the 3 May 1791 Constitution and Enlightenment-era reform is extensive. In English, see Lukowski, *Liberty's Folly*; Gierowski, "Reforms in Poland"; and Walicki, *Enlightenment and the Birth of Modern Nationhood*. On Polish political writing in the eighteenth century, see Konopczyński, *Polscy pisarze polityczni XVIIIw.* Potocki's political activities are described in Janeczek, *Ignacy Potocki* and, by the same author, *Polityczna rola marszałka litewskiego Ignacego Potockiego*.

52. Bożenna Michalik suggested in 1979 that Potocki had probably written the *Remarks on Architecture* sometime around 1806, during a period when he had written a variety of essays as well as poetry. Michalik, *Działalność oświatowa Ignacego Potockiego*, 209.

53. Kurów is east of Olesin, near Puławy; today the area is simply referred to as Olesin. See Jaroszewski, "Olesin."

54. Niemcewicz, *Pamiętniki czasów moich*, 164: "Powróciliśmy . . . do Puław, gdzie już książę z całym swym domem letnią rezydencję założył. Jak same Puławy, tak i sąsiedztwo wielce były przyjemnymi. O małe dwie mile mieszkał w Kurowie marszałek Potocki, ad

unguem factus homo, tuż w Olesinie państwo Stanisławostwo Potoccy, którzy mnie przez lat tyle zaszczycali przyjaźnią swoją." Niemcewicz (1758–1841) was a poet, writer, and close friend of the Czartoryski family. He served as an envoy to the Four-Year Sejm and was a vociferous opponent of the Confederation of Targowica, which plotted to dethrone the king. After the failed Kościuszko Uprising, he emigrated to America (Elizabethtown, N.J.), where he remained until 1807.

55. See *Recueil de pièces relatives au procès*. For a colorful relation of the anecdotes pertaining to the scandal, see Zamoyski, *Last King of Poland,* 284–87.

56. Mrozowska, "Educational Reform in Poland During the Enlightenment," 119. On the Cadet Corps, see also Fabré, "Propagande des idées philosophiques."

57. For a study of Puławy closely based on the Czartoryski archives in Cracow, see Dębicki, *Puławy (1762–1830).* See also Kretowicz, *Puławy.* A useful secondary source is Aleksandrowicz, *Izabela Czartoryska: Polskość i europejskość,* which deliberately casts Izabela Czartoryska as a Pole and a European and contains a study of the cultural milieu at Puławy based on Czartoryska's correspondence with the French abbé and poet Jacques Delille (1738–1813).

58. See Czartoryska, *Myśli różne o sposobie zakładania ogrodów,* a catalog of botany, identified in Latin and Polish (with indications of national origin), and a meditation on the theory of garden design. Izabela Czartoryska later assembled a catalog of the museum contents of Gothic House. For the original 1828 publication, see Czartoryska, *Poczet pamiątek zachowanych w Domu Gotyckim w Puławach.* Though the collection remains assembled in the Gothic House today, it is possible that in Czartoryska's time part of the display was located in the Temple of the Sybil on the same property.

59. Bobrowski, "Budynki użyteczności publicznej," 100.

60. Skowronek, "Zainteresowania historyczne."

61. Haskell, *History and Its Images,* 280.

62. Wraxall, *Memoirs of the Courts,* 2:5–6.

63. Czartoryski, "Dla Pana Adama do Anglii, 1788–89," cited by Skowronek, "Zainteresowania historyczne," 127.

64. Skowronek, "Zainteresowania historyczne," 127.

65. Bieliński, *Sposób edukacji w xv listach,* also cited by Skowronek, "Zainteresowania historyczne," 127 n. 3.

66. Skowronek, "Zainteresowania historyczne," 128.

67. See S. K. Potocki, "Notes et observations"; Lorentz, "List V. Brenny do Stanisława Kostki Potockiego"; and du Prey, *Villas of Pliny from Antiquity to Posterity,* 148–66.

68. See Gutowska-Dudek, *Rysunki z wilanowskiej kolekcji Potockich,* 2:158–59.

69. Nax, "Tabela terminów architektonicznych."

70. The original manuscript is located in the Biblioteka Jagiellońskiej syg. 5376/1.

71. *Krótka nauka,* xxii–xxv.

72. See Frost, *After the Deluge.*

73. I. Potocki, "Uwagi o architekturze," 163.

74. The assassination attempt was carried out by the Confederation of Bar, members of the *szlachta* estate who sought to expel Muscovy's influence from Polish politics.

75. I. Potocki, "Uwagi o architekturze," 4.

76. I. Potocki, "Uwagi o architekturze," 5–6. The Rome-based historian and critic Francesco Milizia (1725–1798), who had described himself as a "mosaicist," "defined architecture as the 'bond of civilised society,' and . . . consider[ed] human progress and its critical expression in functional building types." McQuillan, "From Blondel to Blondel: On the Decline of the Vitruvian Treatise," 356–57. See Milizia, *Principj di architettura civile.*

77. I. Potocki, "Uwagi o architekturze," 163; he mentions Vitruvius by name eleven times. He mentions Vignola by name three times. Laugier is mentioned by name once, but

his ideas appear throughout; Potocki never mentions Cordemoy, to whom Laugier was responding.

78. "I. Uwaga o Odmianach Architektury." Here, I take *odmiany* to mean not merely "type or genre" but something transformed. As such, a consciousness of the historical cycle of development is implied. "II. Uwaga w czym ładność Architektury zakładać się powinna"; "III. Uwaga O pozytkach z nauki Architektury wypływaiących"; "IV. Uwaga o ozdobach budowania"; "V. Uwaga O wygodzie w fabrykach"; "VI. Uwaga O tych naukach, które są potrzebne dla Architekta."

79. I. Potocki, "Uwagi o architekturze," 208–9.

80. I. Potocki, "Uwagi o architekturze," 1.

81. I. Potocki, "Uwagi o architekturze," 63–64.

82. Vidler, *Writing of the Walls*, 3.

83. Rykwert, *On Adam's House in Paradise*, 48.

84. See Jobert, *Commission d'éducation nationale en Pologne*, 111–13. See letters from Condillac to Potocki citing the *Logique* project, 4 April 1780 (Archiwum Główne Akt Dawnych, Archiwum Publiczne Potockich, MS 279a/59, pp. 1–3) and 8 July 1780 (Archiwum Główne Akt Dawnych, Archiwum Publiczne Potockich, MS 179a/59, pp. 4–6).

85. Vidler, *Writing of the Walls*, 3, 19.

86. McQuillan, "From Blondel to Blondel," 338.

87. McQuillan, "From Blondel to Blondel," 354.

88. McQuillan, "From Blondel to Blondel," 345.

89. Vidler, *Writing of the Walls*, 88.

90. Vidler, *Writing of the Walls*, 83–102. For a comprehensive historical treatment of Freemasonry in Eastern Europe, see Haas, *Wolnomularstwo w Europie środkowo-wschodniej*.

91. *Polski słownik biograficzny*, 28:3.

92. Haas, *Wolnomularstwo w Europie środkowo-wschodniej*, 169–70.

93. Haas, *Wolnomularstwo w Europie środkowo-wschodniej*, 170.

94. Kulecka, Osiecka, and Zamojska, ". . . *który nauki, cnotę, Ojczyznę kochają*," 212.

95. Potts, "Political Attitudes," 191.

96. It is worth mentioning that in 1754 the *Piarist Ordonnances pour la province de Pologne* (1753), which recommended the study of Bacon, Descartes, Locke, Wolff, and others, were officially approved. The *Ordonnances* made space in the curriculum for national history and introduced an idea of "civic spirit" into the study of rhetoric. Importantly, those pupils studying philosophy also had access to courses in civil and military architecture, as well as drawing. See Jobert, *Commission d'éducation nationale en Pologne*, 94–99.

97. I. Potocki, "Uwagi o architekturze," 24.

98. I. Potocki, "Uwagi o architekturze," 16.

99. See Blondel, *Cours d'Architecture*, 1:377, cited in Kruft, *History of Architectural Theory*, 149.

100. I. Potocki, "Uwagi o architekturze," 17.

101. The Potocki library inventory includes "D'architecture de Vitruve par Perrault a Paris 1684." "Katalog rzeczowy biblioteki," 191.

102. See Kruft, *History of Architectural Theory*, 143–45, and Boffrand, *Livre d'architecture: Contenant les principes generaux de cet art*.

103. I. Potocki, "Uwagi o architekturze," 53.

104. I. Potocki, "Uwagi o architekturze," 42–43.

105. I. Potocki, "Uwagi o architekturze," 87.

106. I. Potocki, "Uwagi o architekturze," 88.

107. I. Potocki, "Uwagi o architekturze," 18.

108. I. Potocki, "Uwagi o architekturze," 204–5.

109. I. Potocki, "Uwagi o architekturze," 45.

110. I. Potocki, "Uwagi o architekturze," 45–46.

111. I. Potocki, "Uwagi o architekturze," 46.

112. Laugier, *Essay on Architecture*, 10.

113. I. Potocki, "Uwagi o architekturze," 17–18.

114. I. Potocki, "Uwagi o architekturze," 18.

115. I. Potocki, "Uwagi o architekturze," 19.

116. Laugier, *Essay on Architecture*, 9.

117. I. Potocki, "Uwagi o architekturze," 30.

118. See Glacken, *Traces on the Rhodian Shore,* 538. Herder, *Ideen zur Philosophie der Geschichte der Menschheit.*

119. S. K. Potocki, "Listy do Małżonki."

120. Stanisław criticized Heyne sharply in *The Polish Winckelmann.* See Guile, "Winckelmann in Poland."

121. See Ostrowski and Śliwa's introduction to Potocki's *O sztuce u dawnych,* 1:25 n. 6.

122. I. Potocki, "Uwagi o architekturze," 70.

123. See DaCosta Kaufmann, *Toward a Geography of Art,* 23–24, and Glacken, *Traces on the Rhodian Shore,* 551–622.

124. Aigner, *Projekt do urządzenia budowniczych policji,* 1.

125. "Prawdziwie Sama tylko Polska (mówi pewny Autor w Dziele Budownictwa) iest owym cudownym fenixem, który z popiołów swoich na nowo powstaiąc, na to prawie nieustannie buduie się, aby się co raz rozległéy paliła." Aigner, *Budownictwo wieyskie z cegły glino-suszoney z plantami chałup wieyskich.*

126. "Namieniłem iuż powyżey w ogólności, iak dalece troskliwym bydź powinien budowniczy zwiedzaiący swą. Prowincyą względem materyałów do budowania należących: mówiąc o miastach, dokładniey zastanowić się nam nad tym potrzeba. Jak w zagranicznych kraiach iest chwalebnym zwyczaiem tak też i u nas iest rządu starannością wprowadzanie zwyczaiu wystawiania miast murowanych po całym kraiu, a wytępianie przeciwnie drewnianych. Usilnie przeto budowniczy baczyć na to powinien, aby ułatwił sposoby do tego zmierzaiące celu: a mianowice aby podawał różne sposoby dogazaiące łatwości w murowaniu trwałych budów z oszczędzeniem lasów, co z łatwością, w naszym kraiu przychodzi dla obfitości kamieni i innych materyałów wybornych do murowania." Aigner, *Projekt do urządzenia budowniczych policji,* 3.

127. DaCosta Kaufmann, "Early Modern Ideas," 272.

128. I. Potocki, "Uwagi o architekturze," 71–72.

129. I. Potocki, "Uwagi o architekturze," 73.

130. I. Potocki, "Uwagi o architekturze," 156. Laugier's section "On Convenience," article II, is an apparent source:

> Buildings are made to be lived in and only inasmuch as they are convenient can they be habitable. Three things contribute to the convenience of a dwelling: the situation, the planning, and the internal communications [*dégagements*].
>
> The situation is either open or closed. If it is open, a place must be chosen having good air and a fine view. Health is always affected by bad air; a dull view deepens or causes melancholy. It is therefore of great consequence to decide on a situation—provided one is free to choose—which combines healthy air with a pleasant view. Air is really only healthy when it is neither too dry nor too humid. Too much dryness is bad for the chest, too much humidity is the cause of a thousand misfortunes.

Laugier, *Essay on Architecture,* 82.

131. I. Potocki, "Uwagi o architekturze," 156–57.

132. See Moszyński, "Observations générales sur les eaux souterraines," which treats the problems of climate faced in the Warsaw environs, making particular reference to dampness and humidity. The treatise has been published in Polish translation; see Morawińska, *Augusta Fryderyka Moszyńskiego rozprawa o ogrodownictwie angielskim.*

133. I. Potocki, "Uwagi o architekturze," 157–59.

134. I. Potocki, "Uwagi o architekturze," 160–61.

135. I. Potocki, "Uwagi o architekturze," 161.

136. I. Potocki, "Uwagi o architekturze," 161–62.

137. Laugier, *Essay on Architecture,* 83–84.

138. I. Potocki, "Uwagi o architekturze," 168.

139. I. Potocki, "Uwagi o architekturze," 90.

140. I. Potocki, "Uwagi o architekturze," 91.

141. I. Potocki, "Uwagi o architekturze," 91. See DaCosta Kaufmann, *Court, Cloister, and City,* 298. For Frederick II and architecture, see Giersberg, "Friedrich II. und die Architektur."

142. I. Potocki, "Uwagi o architekturze," 92.

143. See DaCosta Kaufmann, "Early Modern Ideas," 270–71; Ottenheym, "Classicism in the Northern Netherlands"; and Josephson, *Tessin: Nicodemus Tessin d. y.*

144. I. Potocki, "Uwagi o architekturze," 93. For a discussion on the relationship of English culture to late eighteenth-century Polish royal patronage, see Butterwick, *Poland's Last King and English Culture.*

145. I. Potocki, "Uwagi o architekturze," 93.

146. I. Potocki, "Uwagi o architekturze," 94.

147. I. Potocki, "Uwagi o architekturze," 104–5.

148. I. Potocki, "Uwagi o architekturze," 105.

149. I. Potocki, "Uwagi o architekturze," 106–7.

150. S. K. Potocki, from an untitled and undated manuscript in "Zbiór manuskryptów własnoręcznie pisanych."

151. S. K. Potocki, from an untitled manuscript in "Zbiór manuskryptów własnoręcznie pisanych."

152. S. K. Potocki, from an untitled manuscript in "Zbiór manuskryptów własnoręcznie pisanych."

153. S. K. Potocki, from an untitled manuscript in "Zbiór manuskryptów własnoręcznie pisanych."

154. I. Potocki, "Uwagi o architekturze," 199–200.

155. S. K. Potocki, from an untitled manuscript in "Zbiór manuskryptów własnoręcznie pisanych."

156. The only significant studies on the architectural activity of Stanisław Kostka Potocki are Lorentz, "Działalność Stanisława Kostki Potockiego w dziedzinie architektury," and Polanowska, *Stanisław Kostka Potocki, 1755–1821.*

157. See Mossakowski, "Potocki, Palladio, e la facciata."

158. See S. K. Potocki, "Notes et observations." For the Potocki-Brenna collaboration, see, in addition to du Prey, *Villas of Pliny from Antiquity to Posterity,* Lorentz, "List V. Brenny do Stanisława Kostki Potockiego."

159. See Lorentz, "Działalność Stanisława Kostki Potockiego w dziedzinie architektury."

160. S. K. Potocki, "Architekturze wiejskie."

161. S. K. Potocki, *O sztuce u dawnych,* 1:332.

162. Aigner, *Projekt do urządzenia budowniczych policji,* 2.

163. I. Potocki, "Uwagi o architekturze," 104–5.

164. Aigner, *Projekt do urządzenia budowniczych policji*, 7.

165. See, by DaCosta Kaufmann, "Early Modern Ideas" and *Toward a Geography of Art*.

166. See Lukowski, *Liberty's Folly* and, by the same author, *Partitions of Poland*; see also Tazbir, "Polish National Consciousness in the 16th–18th Centuries."

167. See Grześkowiak-Krwawicz, "Political and Social Literature," 195.

Remarks on Architecture

1. Numbers in parentheses correspond to the original manuscript page numbers, with the caveat that sensible English syntax renders the insertion of the numbers imprecise in places. Figure numbers appearing in parentheses are Potocki's own references to the drawings or prints he originally included in the treatise. Those images are now lost.

2. Grzegorz Piramowicz, ex-Jesuit and parish priest at Kurów, site of the Potocki estate; professor of philosophy at the Jesuit college in Lwów; close collaborator and friend of Ignacy Potocki; cofounder of the National Commission for Education and secretary of its Society for Elementary Textbooks, of which Ignacy Potocki was the head.

3. Potocki's subject headings are preserved here.

4. Meaning "Middle Easterners" here.

5. He reasons that the Barbarians could not have brought those styles themselves, that they must have been drawing upon what they found *in situ*. The aesthetic genealogy he describes could not have come from Barbarian territory; Potocki insists it came from Italy itself and ultimately Rome.

6. Potocki's own footnote shows an estimate of one hundred.

7. "Let this be your brazen wall of defense." Horace, *Epistulae* 1.60.

8. Illegible. Presumably he continues his amazement that anyone can think Nature gives no examples to architecture.

9. "Dla większego kształtu"—meaning obscure. This can also mean "to make it more impressive" or "to make it more clear" (possibly by juxtaposing two things in a more shocking manner).

10. "There is such a thing as careful negligence." He refers to Cicero, *Orator* 23.

11. That is, "source."

12. Likely Frederick II of Prussia.

13. Ironic meaning. The uglier the object, the more expensive it is.

14. Meaning that someone who knows nothing will have a sense of wonderment about everything.

15. The scotia.

16. Potocki's footnote cites "Prospettiva di Pittori e Architetti in folio." Here he is referring to the Jesuit architect Andrea Pozzo (1642–1709), whose two-volume *Perspectiva Pictorum et Architectorum* (1693, 1700) was dedicated to Leopold I.

17. That is, too florid.

18. Most likely meaning the lines must be parallel or perpendicular.

19. See Palladio, *Four Books on Architecture*, 166.

20. Palladio, *Four Books on Architecture*, 60–61.

21. Palladio, *Four Books on Architecture*, 60.

22. Palladio, *Four Books on Architecture*, 61.

23. Enfilade.

24. Unknown; he may be referring to Sir Richard Grenville of Wotton House, Buckinghamshire, who employed the landscape architect Lancelot "Capability" Brown (1716–1783).

25. "Even now the housetops yonder are smoking." Virgil, *Eclogues*, 1.82.

26. The text in places corresponds to the entry on chimneys in the seventh edition of *Encyclopedia Britannica* (1842), itself doubtlessly based on the entries in earlier editions; the first edition appeared in three volumes, 1768–71; the second edition in ten volumes, 1777–84. I am presuming Potocki's familiarity with one of these earlier entries.

27. That is, architecture.

Transcription of the Manuscript

"Uwagi o Architekturze Przez Ignacego Potockiego," Archiwum Główne Akt Dawnych, Archiwum Publiczne Potokich, zespół 235 (no. 278).

1. Illegible.
2. The word *darami* appears to have been added in another hand.
3. Illegible.
4. The word *szersze* is crossed out and *szczupleysze* penciled in.

BIBLIOGRAPHY

Aigner, Chrystian Piotr. *Budownictwo wieyskie z cegły glino-suszoney z plantami chałup wieyskich, stosownie do gospodarstwa Narodowego.* Warsaw: Drukarnia Piotra Zawadzkiego, 1791.

———. *Projekt do urządzenia budowniczych policji z umieszczeniem sposobów zagradzających upadkowi miast a wzrost im nadal zapewniających podany Prześwietnej Komisji Policji Obojga Narodów przez Piotra Aignera Budowniczego Wojsk Rzeczypospolitej.* Warsaw, 1792.

Aleksandrowicz, Alina. *Izabela Czartoryska: Polskość i europejskość.* Lublin: Wydawnictwo Uniwersytetu Marii Curie-Skłodowskiej, 1998.

André, Yves. *Essai sur le Beau, ou l'on Examine en quoi consiste précisément le Beau dans le Physique, dans le Moral, dans les Ouvrages d'Esprit, et dans la Musique.* Paris: Hippolyte-Louis Guérin et Jacques Guérin, 1741.

Baranowski, Andrzej. "The Baroque Geography of the Polish Commonwealth: Centres and Peripheries." In *Borders in Art: Revisiting Kunstgeographie,* edited by Katarzyna Murawska-Muthesius, 77–86. Warsaw: Institute of Art, 2000.

Bardach, Juliusz. "Ormianie na ziemiach dawnej polski." *Kwartalnik historyczny* 90, no. 1 (1983): 109–18.

Barnard, F. M. *Herder's Social and Political Thought: From Enlightenment to Nationalism.* Oxford: Clarendon Press, 1965.

Batowska, Natalia, Zygmunt Batowski, and Marek Kwiatkowski. *Jan Chrystian Kamsetzer architekt Stanisława Augusta.* Warsaw: Państwowe Wydawnictwo Naukowe, 1978.

Bernhard, Maria Ludwika. "'O sztuce u dawnych, czyli Winkelman polski' Stanisław Kostki Potockiego." *Rocznik historii sztuki* 1 (1956): 514–21.

Białostocki, Jan. *The Art of the Renaissance in Eastern Europe: Hungary, Bohemia, Poland.* Ithaca: Cornell University Press, 1976.

———. "Borrowing and Originality in the East-Central European Renaissance." In *East-Central Europe in Transition: From the Fourth to the Seventeenth Century,* edited by Antoni Mączak, Henryk Samsonowicz, and Peter Burke, 153–66. New York: Cambridge University Press, 1985.

———. "'Mannerism' and 'Vernacular' in Polish Art." In *Walter Friedlaender zum 90. Geburtstag,* edited by Georg Kauffmann and Willibald Sauerlaënder, 47–57. Berlin: Walter de Gruyter, 1965.

———. "Renaissance Sculpture in Poland in Its European Context: Some Selected Problems." In *The Polish Renaissance in Its European Context,* edited by Samuel Fiszman, 281–90. Bloomington: Indiana University Press, 1988.

Biedronska-Słotowa, Beata, ed. *The Orient in Polish Art*. Exhibition catalog. Cracow: Muzeum Narodowe, 1992.

Bieliński, Franciszek. *Sposób edukacji w xv listach pisany, które do Komissyi Edukacji Narodowej od bezimiennego autora były przesłane*. Warsaw: Drukarnia Mitzlerowska, 1775.

Blondel, Jacques-François. *Cours d'Architecture, ou Traité de la Décoration, Distribution & Construction des Bâtiments*. 6 vols., plus 3 vols. of plates. Paris: Desaint, 1771–77.

Bobrowski, Zbigniew. "Budynki użyteczności publicznej w Polsce wieku Oświecenia." *Studia i materiały do teorii i historii architektury i urbanystiki* 3 (1961): 94–101.

Boffrand, Germain. *Livre d'architecture: Contenant les principes generaux de cet art et les plans, elevations et profils de quelques-uns des batimens faits en France & dans les pays etrangers*. Paris: Guillaume Cavelier, 1745.

Bogucka, Maria. "Polish Towns Between the Sixteenth and Eighteenth Centuries." In *A Republic of Nobles: Studies in Polish History to 1864*, translated by J. K. Federowicz and edited by Maria Bogucka, J. K. Federowicz, and Henryk Samsonowicz, 135–52. Cambridge: Cambridge University Press, 1982.

Breiner, David. "Vincenzo Scamozzi, 1548–1616: A Catalogue Raisonné." Ph.D. diss., Cornell University, 1994.

Brzyski, Anna, ed. *Partisan Canons*. Durham: Duke University Press, 2007.

Burke, Peter. *The European Renaissance: Centres and Peripheries*. Oxford: Blackwell Publishers, 1998.

———. *The Fortunes of the Courtier: The European Reception of Castiglione's "Cortegiano."* London: Polity Press, 1995.

Butterwick, Richard. "Catholicism and Enlightenment in Poland-Lithuania." In *A Companion to the Catholic Enlightenment in Europe*, edited by Ulrich Lehner and Michael Printy, 297–358. Brill's Companions to the Christian Tradition 20. Boston: Brill, 2010.

———. *Poland's Last King and English Culture: Stanisław August Poniatowski, 1732–1798*. Oxford: Clarendon Press; New York: Oxford University Press, 1998.

Carpo, Mario. *Architecture in the Age of Printing: Orality, Writing, Typography, and Printed Images in the History of Architectural Theory*. Translated by Sarah Benson. Cambridge: MIT Press, 2001.

Carrier, David. *A World Art History and Its Objects*. University Park: Pennsylvania State University Press, 2008.

Casanova, Pascale. *The World Republic of Letters*. Translated by M. B. DeBevoise. Cambridge: Harvard University Press, 2004.

Cynarski, Stanisław. "The Shape of Sarmatian Ideology in Poland." *Acta Poloniae Historica* 19 (1968): 5–17.

Czartoryska, Izabela. *Myśli różne o sposobie zakładania ogrodów*. Wrocław: Drukiem Wilhelma Bogumila Korna, 1808.

———. *Poczet pamiątek zachowanych w Domu Gotyckim w Puławach*. Warsaw: Drukarni Banku Polskiego, 1828.

Czartoryski, Adam. "Dla Pana Adama do Anglii, 1788–89." Biblioteka Czartoryskich w Krakowie, MS 1046:17. Cracow.

DaCosta Kaufmann, Thomas. *Court, Cloister, and City: The Art and Culture of Central Europe, 1450–1800*. Chicago: University of Chicago Press, 1995.

———. "Early Modern Ideas About Artistic Geography Related to the Baltic Region." *Scandinavian Journal of History* 28 (2003): 263–72.

———. "Italian Sculptors and Sculpture Outside Italy (Chiefly in Central Europe): Problems of Approach, Possibilities of Reception." In *Reframing the Renaissance: Visual*

Culture in Europe and Latin America, 1450–1650, edited by Claire Farago, 47–67. New Haven: Yale University Press, 1995.

———. *Toward a Geography of Art.* Chicago: University of Chicago Press, 2004.

DaCosta Kaufmann, Thomas, Catherine Dossin, and Beatrice Joyeux-Prunel, eds. *Global Artistic Circulations.* Burlington, Vt.: Ashgate, forthcoming 2015.

Dębicki, Ludwik. *Puławy (1762–1830): Monografia z życia towarzyskiego, politycznego i literackiego na podstawie archiwum ks. Czartoryskich w Krakowie.* 4 vols. Lwów: Nakład Księgarni Gubrynowicza i Schmidta, 1887.

Delorme, Philibert. *Le premier tome de l'architecture.* Paris: Fédéric Morel, 1567.

du Prey, Pierre de la Ruffinière. *The Villas of Pliny from Antiquity to Posterity.* Chicago: University of Chicago Press, 1994.

Durand, Jean-Nicolas-Louis. *Recueil et parallèle des édifices de tout genre, anciens et modernes.* Paris: École polytechnique, 1800.

Elkins, James, ed. *Is Art History Global?* New York: Routledge, 2007.

Fabré, Jean. "La propagande des idées philosophiques en Pologne sous Stanislas-Auguste et l'École varsovienne des Cadets." *Revue de littérature comparée* (1935): 643–93.

———. *Stanislas-Auguste Poniatowski et l'Europe des lumières.* Paris: Institut d'études slaves, 1952.

Fiszman, Samuel, ed. *Constitution and Reform in Eighteenth-Century Poland: The Constitution of 3 May 1791.* Bloomington: Indiana University Press, 1997.

Frost, Robert I. *After the Deluge: Poland-Lithuania and the Second Northern War, 1655–1660.* Cambridge: Cambridge University Press, 1993.

Gauger, Nicolas. *La mécanique de feu, ou L'art d'en augmenter les effets, & d'en diminuer la dépense contenant le traité de nouvelles cheminées. . . .* Paris, 1713.

Gierowski, Józef Andrzej. "The International Position of Poland in the Seventeenth and Eighteenth Centuries." In *A Republic of Nobles: Studies in Polish History to 1864,* translated by J. K. Federowicz and edited by Maria Bogucka, J. K. Federowicz, and Henryk Samsonowicz, 218–38. Cambridge: Cambridge University Press, 1982.

———. "Reforms in Poland After the 'Dumb Diet' (1717)." In *Constitution and Reform in Eighteenth-Century Poland: The Constitution of 3 May 1791,* edited by Samuel Fiszman, 65–86. Bloomington: Indiana University Press, 1997.

Giersberg, Hans-Joachim. "Friedrich II. und die Architektur." In *Friedrich II. und die Kunst: Ausstellung zum 200. Todestag; 19. Juli bis 12. Oktober 1986, Neues Palais in Sanssouci,* 2:192ff. Potsdam: Generaldirektion der Staatlichen Schlösser und Gärten Potsdam-Sanssouci, 1986.

Glacken, Clarence J. *Traces on the Rhodian Shore: Nature and Culture in Western Thought from Ancient Times to the End of the Eighteenth Century.* Berkeley: University of California Press, 1967.

Goldmann, Nikolaus. *Vollständige Anweisung zu der Civil-Baukunst.* Wolfenbüttel: Caspar Johann Bismarck Witwe, 1696.

Grześkowiak-Krwawicz, Anna. "Political and Social Literature During the Four-Year Diet." In *Constitution and Reform in Eighteenth-Century Poland: The Constitution of 3 May 1791,* edited by Samuel Fiszman, 175–202. Bloomington: Indiana University Press, 1997.

Guile, Carolyn. "Sebastian Sierakowski, S.J. and the Language of Architecture: A Jesuit Life During the Era of Suppression and Restoration." In *Jesuit Survival and Restoration: 200th Anniversary Perspectives,* edited by Robert Maryks and Jonathan Wright. Boston: Brill, 2014.

————. "Winckelmann in Poland: An Eighteenth-Century Response to the *History of the Art of Antiquity.*" *Journal of Art Historiography* 9 (December 2013): 1–24. http://arthistoriography.files.wordpress.com/2013/12/guile.pdf, accessed 15 July 2014.

Gutowska-Dudek, Krystyna. *Rysunki z wilanowskiej kolekcji Potockich w zbiorach Biblioteki Narodowej.* 4 vols. Warsaw: Biblioteka Narodowa, 1997–2004.

Haas, Ludwik. *Wolnomularstwo w Europie środkowo-wschodniej w XVIII i XIX wieku.* Wrocław: Zakład Narodowy im. Ossolińskich, 1982.

Halecki, Oscar. *Borderlands of Western Civilization: A History of East Central Europe.* 2nd ed. Safety Harbor, Fla.: Simon Publications, 1980.

Hart, Vaughan, and Peter Hicks, eds. *Paper Palaces: The Rise of the Renaissance Architectural Treatise.* New Haven: Yale University Press, 1998.

Haskell, Francis. *History and Its Images: Art and the Interpretation of the Past.* New Haven: Yale University Press, 1993.

Herder, Johann Gottfried von. *Ideen zur Philosophie der Geschichte der Menschheit.* Edited by Martin Bollacher. Vol. 6 of *Johann Gottfried Herder Werke.* Frankfurt am Main: Deutscher Klassiker Verlag, 1989.

Héré, Emmanuel. *Recueil des plans, élévations et coupes tant géométrales qu'en perspective des châteaux, jardins et dépendances que le roy de Pologne occupe en Lorraine.* Paris: François, 1756.

Hoensch, Jörg K. "Citizen, Nation, Constitution: The Realization and Failure of the Constitution of 3 May 1791 in Light of Mutual Polish-French Influence." In *Constitution and Reform in Eighteenth-Century Poland: The Constitution of 3 May 1791,* edited by Samuel Fiszman, 423–52. Bloomington: Indiana University Press, 1997.

Janeczek, Zdzisław. *Ignacy Potocki: Marszałek Wielki Litewski (1750–1809).* Katowice: n.p., 1992.

————. *Polityczna rola marszałka litewskiego Ignacego Potockiego w okresie Sejmu Wielkiego 1788–1792.* Katowice: Wydawnictwo Akademii Ekonomicznej im. Karola Adamieckiego, 2005.

Jaroszewski, Tadeusz Stefan. *Chrystian Piotr Aigner, architekt warszawskiego klasycyzmu.* Warsaw: Państwowe Wydawnictwo Naukowe, 1970.

————. "Olesin." *Biuletyn historii sztuki* 24, no. 1 (1962): 96–111.

Jeffares, Neil. *Dictionary of Pastellists Before 1800.* Norwich, U.K.: Unicorn Press, 2006. http://www.pastellists.com/.

Jobert, Ambroise. *La Commission d'éducation nationale en Pologne, 1773–1794, son oeuvre d'instruction civique.* Paris: Société d'édition Les belles lettres, 1941.

————. *Magnats polonais et physiocrates français 1767–1774.* Paris: Société d'édition Les belles lettres, 1941.

Josephson, Ragnar. *Tessin: Nicodemus Tessin d.y.; Tiden, mannen, verket.* 2 vols. Stockholm: P. A. Norstedt, 1930–31.

Kalinka, Walerian. *Sejm Czteroletni.* 4th ed. 2 vols. Warsaw: Volumen, 1991.

Kamieński, Adolf. *Edukacja obywatelska.* Warsaw: Gröll, 1774.

"Katalog rzeczowy biblioteki i zbioru sztychów Lubomirskich, St., i Ign. Potockich, XIX w." Archiwum Główne Akt Dawnych, Archiwum Publiczne Potockich, no. 141. Warsaw.

Kołłątaj, Hugo. *Stan oświecenia w Polsce w ostatnich latach panowania Augusta III (1750–1764).* Edited by Jan Hulewicz. Wrocław: Ossolineum, 1953.

Konarski, Stanisław. *Pisma wybrane.* 2 vols. Edited by Juliusz Nowak-Dłużewski. Warsaw: Państwowy Instytut Wydawniczy, 1955.

————. *O skutecznym rad sposobie, albo O utrzymywaniu ordynarnych seymów.* 4 vols. Warsaw: W Drukarni J. K. Mci y Rzpltey u XX. Scholarum Piarum, 1760–63.

Konopczyński, Władysław. *Polscy pisarze polityczni XVIII w. (do Sejmu Czteroletniego)*. Warsaw: Państwowe Wydawnictwo Naukowe, 1966.

Kowalczyk, Jerzy. *Sebastiano Serlio a sztuka polska: O roli włoskich traktatów architektonicznych w dobie nowożytnej*. Studia z historii sztuki, 16. Edited by Władysław Jaworska and Jerzy Pietrusiński. Wrocław: Zakład Narodowy im. Ossolińskich Wydawnictwo Polskiej Akademii Nauk, 1973.

Kretowicz, August. *Puławy*. Lwów: Drukiem Piotra Pillera, 1831.

Krótka nauka budownicza dworów, pałaców, zamków podług nieba i zwyczaju polskiego. Edited by Adam Miłobędzki. Wrocław: Zakład Ossolińskich, 1957.

Kruft, Hanno-Walter. *A History of Architectural Theory from Vitruvius to the Present*. Translated by Ronald Taylor, Elsie Callander, and Antony Wood. New York: Princeton Architectural Press, 1994.

Kulecka, Alicja, Małgorzata Osiecka, and Dorota Zamojska, eds. *". . . który nauki, cnotę, Ojczyznę kochają": Znani i nieznani członkowie Towarzystwa Królewskiego Warszawskiego Przyjaciół Nauk*. Warsaw: Archiwum Polskiej Akademii Nauk, Archiwum Główne Akt Dawnych, 2000.

Kwiatkowski, Marek. *Szymon Bogumił Zug, architekt polskiego oświecenia*. Warsaw: Państwowe Wydawnictwo Naukowe, 1971.

Laugier, Marc-Antoine. *Essai sur l'architecture*. Paris: Chez Duchesne, 1755.

———. *An Essay on Architecture*. Translated by Wolfgang Hermann and Anni Hermann. Documents and Sources in Architecture 1. Los Angeles: Hennessey & Ingalls, 1977.

Leśnodorski, Bogusław. *Dzieło Sejmu Czteroletniego 1788–1792: Studium historycznoprawne*. Wrocław: Wydawnictwo Zakładu Narodowego im. Ossolińskich, 1951.

Lorentz, Stanisław. "Działalność Stanisława Kostki Potockiego w dziedzinie architektury." *Rocznik historii sztuki* 1 (1956): 450–501.

———. *Efraim Szreger architekt polski XVIII wieku*. Warsaw: Państwowe Wydawnictwo Naukowe, 1986.

———. "List V. Brenny do Stanisława Kostki Potockiego z r. 1789." *Biuletyn historii sztuki* 12, nos. 1–4 (1950): 324–29.

Lukowski, Jerzy. *Liberty's Folly: The Polish-Lithuanian Commonwealth in the Eighteenth Century, 1697–1795*. London: Routledge, 1991.

———. *The Partitions of Poland: 1772, 1793, 1795*. London: Longman, 1999.

Maksimowicz, Krystyna, ed. *Wiersze polityczne Sejmu Czteroletniego*. Vol. 1, *1788–1789*. Warsaw: Wydawnictwo Sejmowe, 1998.

Malinowska, Irena. *Stanisław Zawadzki 1743–1806*. Warsaw: Państwowe Wydawnictwa Techniczne, 1953.

McQuillan, James. "From Blondel to Blondel: On the Decline of the Vitruvian Treatise." In *Paper Palaces: The Rise of the Renaissance Architectural Treatise*, edited by Vaughan Hart and Peter Hicks, 338–57. New Haven: Yale University Press, 1998.

Michalik, Bożenna. *Działalność oświatowa Ignacego Potockiego*. Wrocław: Zakład Narodowy im. Ossolińskich, 1979.

———. *Korespondencja Ignacego Potockiego w sprawach edukacyjnych (1774–1809)*. Wrocław: Zakład Narodowy im. Ossolińskich, 1978.

Michel, Nicolas Léopold. *Compte général de la dépense des edifices et batimens que le roi de Pologne, duc de Lorraine et de Bar: A fait construire pour l'embelissement de la ville de Nancy, depuis 1751, jusqu'en 1759*. Lunéville: Claude François Messuy, 1761.

Mieszkowski, Zygmunt. *Podstawowe problemy architektury w polskich traktatach od połowy XVI do początku XIX w*. Warsaw: Państwowe Wydawnictwo Naukowe, 1970.

Milizia, Francesco. *Principj di architettura civile*. Finale: Jacopo de' Rossi, 1781.

Miłobędzki, Adam. *Architektura polska XVII wieku*. 2 vols. Warsaw: Państwowe Wydawnictwo Naukowe, 1980.

———. "Polish Country Houses in the Age of the Baroque: The French Connection." In *Polish and English Reponses to French Art and Architecture: Contrasts and Similarities; Papers Delivered at the University of London / University of Warsaw History of Art Conference, January and September 1993*, edited by Francis Ames-Lewis, 49–58. London: Birkbeck College, University of London, 1995.

———. "Tajemnica zamku w Zbarażu." *Kwartalnik architektury i urbanistyki: Teoria i historia* 1, no. 4 (1956): 371–82.

Morawińska, Agnieszka. *Augusta Fryderyka Moszyńskiego rozprawa o ogrodownictwie angielskim, 1774*. Wrocław: Zakład Narodowy im. Ossolińskich, 1977.

Mossakowski, Stanisław. "Potocki, Palladio, e la facciata della chiesa di Sant'Anna a Varsavia." *Napoli nobilissima* 37, nos. 1–6 (1998): 57–62.

———. *Tylman van Gameren: Leben und Werk*. Munich: Deutscher Kunstverlag, 1994.

Moszyński, August. "Observations générales sur les eaux souterraines avec quelques remarques sur les eaux de Łazienki." Archiwum Główne Akt Dawnych, Zbiór Popielów, 368. Warsaw.

Mrozowska, Kamilla. "Educational Reform in Poland During the Enlightenment." In *Constitution and Reform in Eighteenth-Century Poland: The Constitution of 3 May 1791*, edited by Samuel Fiszman, 113–54. Bloomington: Indiana University Press, 1997.

Murawska-Muthesius, Katarzyna. "Introduction: Geography of Art, or Bordering the Other?" In *Borders in Art: Revisiting Kunstgeographie*, edited by Katarzyna Murawska-Muthesius, 9–18. Warsaw: Institute of Art, 2000.

Muthesius, Stefan. *Art, Architecture, and Design in Poland, 966–1990: An Introduction*. Königstein im Taunus: K. R. Langewiesche Nachfolger H. Köster Verlagsbuchhandlung, 1994.

———. "Kunstgeographie Revamped?" In *Borders in Art: Revisiting Kunstgeographie*, edited by Katarzyna Murawska-Muthesius, 19–26. Warsaw: Institute of Art, 2000.

Nax, Ferdynand. "Tabela terminów architektonicznych." Biblioteka Uniwersytetu Warszawskie, Gabinet Rycin, Zbiór Krol, T.186, no. 2. Warsaw.

Niemcewicz, Julian Ursyn. *Pamiętniki czasów moich: Pierwsze wydanie według obszerniejszej wersji rękopiśmiennej*. Vol. 1. Edited by Jan Dihm. Warsaw: Państwowy Instytut Wydawniczy, 1957.

Ostrowski, Jan K., Kazimierz Kuczman, Maria Kałamajska, and Andrzej Betlej, eds. *Materiały do dziejów sztuki sakralnej na ziemiach wschodnich dawnej Rzeczypospolitej*. 20 vols. Cracow: Secesja; Wydawnictwa Antykwa; Międzynarodowe Centrum Kultury w Krakowie, 1993.

Ottenheym, Konrad. "Classicism in the Northern Netherlands in the Seventeenth Century." In *Palladio and Northern Europe: Books, Travellers, Architects*, edited by Claudio Nasso and Serena Parini, 150–56. Exhibition catalog. Milan: Skira, 1999.

———. *Tilman van Gameren, 1632–1706: A Dutch Architect to the Polish Court*. Amsterdam: Royal Palace Foundation, 2002.

Palladio, Andrea. *The Four Books on Architecture*. Translated by Robert Tavernor and Richard Schofield. Cambridge: MIT Press, 1997.

Payne, Alina A. *The Architectural Treatise in the Italian Renaissance: Architectural Invention, Ornament, and Literary Culture*. Cambridge: Cambridge University Press, 1999.

Penther, Johann Friedrich. *Eine ausführliche Anleitung zur bürgerlichen Bau-Kunst*. 4 vols. Augsburg: Pfeffel, 1744–48.

Perrault, Claude. *Les dix livres d'Architecture de Vitruve corrigez et traduits nouvellement en François, avec des Notes & des Figures*. Paris: Jean Baptiste Coignard, 1673.

Piarist Ordonnances pour la province de Pologne. 1753.

Polanowska, Jolanta. *Stanisław Kostka Potocki, 1755–1821: Twórczość architekta amatora, przedstawiciela neoklasycyzmu i nurtu picturesque.* Warsaw: Instytut Sztuki Polskiej Akademii Nauk, 2009.

Polski słownik biograficzny. 48 vols. Warsaw: Zakład Narodowy im. Ossolińskich, Wydawnictwo Polskiej Akademii Nauk, 1984.

Potocki, Ignacy. Letter of Ignacy Potocki to Stanisław Kostka Potocki, 28 XII 1801. Archiwum Główne Akt Dawnych, Archiwum Publiczne Potockich, MS 279b/I, p. 1177. Warsaw.

———. Letter of Ignacy Potocki to Stanisław Kostka Potocki, 21 I 1802. Archiwum Główne Akt Dawnych, Archiwum Publiczne Potockich, MS 279b/I, pp. 1179–81. Warsaw.

———. Letter of Ignacy Potocki to Stanisław Kostka Potocki, 21 I 1802. Archiwum Główne Akt Dawnych, Archiwum Publiczne Potockich, MS 279b/I, pp. 1183–84. Warsaw.

———. Letter of Ignacy Potocki to Stanisław Kostka Potocki, 21 I 1802. Archiwum Główne Akt Dawnych, Archiwum Publiczne Potockich, MS 279b/I, pp. 1185–88. Warsaw.

———. "Uwagi o architekturze." Archiwum Główne Akt Dawnych, Archiwum Publiczne Potockich, zespół 235, no. 278. Warsaw.

Potocki, Stanisław Kostka. "Architekturze wiejskie." Archiwum Główne Akt Dawnych, Archiwum Publiczne Potockich, 255. Warsaw.

———. "Listy do małżonki." Archiwum Główne Akt Dawnych, Archiwum Publiczne Potockich, 262. Warsaw.

———. "Notes et observations sur la lettre XVIII du II livre de Pline le Jeune." Archiwum Główne Akt Dawnych, Archiwum Publiczne Potockich, 244. Warsaw.

———. *O sztuce u dawnych, czyli Winkelman polski.* 4 vols. Edited by Janusz Ostrowki and Joachim Śliwa. Warsaw: Państwowe Wydawnictwo Naukowe, 1992. (Originally published by Drukarni Xięży Piiarów in Warsaw, 1815.)

———. "Zbiór manuskryptów własnoręcznie pisanych przez Sta. Hrabie Potockiego prezesa Senatu i kopiiowanych przez sekratarzy." Archiwum Główne Akt Dawnych, Archiwum Publiczne Potockich, 243:128. Warsaw.

Potts, Alex. "Political Attitudes and the Rise of Historicism in Art Theory." *Art History* 1, no. 2 (June 1978): 190–213.

Pozzo, Andrea. *Perspectiva Pictorum et Architectorum.* 2 vols. Rome: J. J. Komarek, 1693, 1700.

Recueil de pièces relatives au procès entre S.A. le Prince Adam Czartoryski, accusateur, & MM. Komarzewski & Ryx, accusés du crime d'empoisonnement. Warsaw, 1785.

Reychman, Jan. *Orient w kulturze polskiego oświecenia.* Wrocław: Zakład Narodowy im. Ossolińskich, 1964.

Rogaliński, Józef. *O sztuce budowniczey na swoie porządki podzieloney zabawa ciekawa miana w szkołach poznańskich Soc. Iesu roku 1764.* Poznań: Drukarni Jezuitów, 1764.

Rogaliński, Józef, Michał Gröll, Zofia Krasińska, and Franciszek Degen. *Sztuka budownicza na swoie porządki podzielona.* Warsaw: Michała Groella, 1775.

Rostworowski, Emanuel. *Legendy i fakty XVIII w.* Warsaw: Państwowe Wydawnictwo Naukowe, 1963.

———. *Polska w świecie: Szkice z dziejów kultury polskiej.* Warsaw: Państwowe Wydawnictwo Naukowe, 1972.

Rottermund, Andrzej. *Jean-Nicolas-Louis Durand a polska architektura pierwszej połowy XIX wieku.* Wrocław: Zakład Narodowy im. Ossolińskich, 1990.

Rottermund, Andrzej, and Stanisław Lorentz. *Neoclassicism in Poland.* Translated by Jerzy Bałdyga. Warsaw: Arkady, 1986.

Rudnicka, Jadwiga. *Biblioteka Ignacego Potockiego.* Wrocław: Zakład Narodowy im. Ossolińskich, 1953.

Rykwert, Joseph. *On Adam's House in Paradise: The Idea of the Primitive Hut in Architectural History.* 2nd ed. Cambridge: MIT Press, 1981. (First edition published by the Museum of Modern Art, New York, in association with the Graham Foundation for Advanced Studies in the Fine Arts, Chicago, 1972.)

Sawicka, Stanisław, and Teresa Sulerzyska. *Straty w rysunkach z Gabinetu Rycin Biblioteki Uniwersyteckiej 1939–1945.* Prace Biblioteki Uniwersyteckiej w Warszawie 3. Warsaw: Uniwersytet Warszawski Dział Wydawnictwa, 1960.

Sierakowski, Sebastian. *Architektura obejmująca wszelki gatunek murowania i budowania.* 2 vols. Cracow, 1812.

Skierkowska, Elżbieta. "Księgozbiór z dziedziny sztuki Stanisława Kostki Potockiego na tle polskich bibliotek XVIII wieku." *Rocznik historii sztuki* 13 (1981): 171–202.

Skowronek, Jerzy. "Zainteresowania historyczne środowiska puławskiego na przełomie XVIII/XIX w. i ich związki z ideologią i życiem politycznym." In *Edukacja historyczna społeczeństwa polskiego w XIX w.,* edited by Jerzy Maternicki, 125–55. Warsaw: Państwowe Wydawnictwo Naukowe, 1981.

Staszic, Stanisław. *Przestrogi dla Polski.* Edited by Stefan Czarnowski. Cracow: Nakładem Krakowskiej Spółki Wydawniczej, 1926.

Sturm, Leonhardt. *Vollständige Anweisung allerhand öffentliche Zucht- und Liebesgebäude.* Augsburg, 1717.

Sucheni-Grabowska, Anna, and Alicja Dybkowska, eds. *Tradycje polityczne dawnej Polski.* Warsaw: Editions Spotkania, 1993.

Summers, David. *Real Spaces: World Art History and the Rise of Western Modernism.* London: Phaidon, 2003.

Szafrańska, Małgorzata. "La réception d'André le Nôtre en Pologne." In *Le Nôtre, un inconnu illustre?* 216–33. Paris: Centre des Monuments Nationaux; Monum, Éditions du Patrimoine, 2003.

Tatarkiewicz, Władysław. *Dominik Merlini.* Warsaw: Budownictwo i Architektura, 1955.

Tazbir, Janusz. "Polish National Consciousness in the 16th–18th Centuries." *Acta Polonia Historica* 46 (1982): 47–72.

———. "Polish National Consciousness in the Sixteenth to Eighteenth Century." *Harvard Ukrainian Studies* 10, nos. 3–4 (1986): 316–35.

Vautrin, Hubert. *La Pologne du XVIIIe siècle: Vue par un précepteur français.* Edited by Maria Cholewo-Flandrin. Paris: Calmann-Lévy, 1966.

Vidler, Anthony. *The Writing of the Walls: Architectural Theory in the Late Enlightenment.* Princeton: Princeton Architectural Press, 1987.

Vitruvius. *Ten Books on Architecture.* Edited by Ingrid Rowland and Thomas Noble Howe. Cambridge: Cambridge University Press, 2001.

Walicki, Andrzej. *The Enlightenment and the Birth of Modern Nationhood: Polish Political Thought from Noble Republicanism to Tadeusz Kościuszko.* Notre Dame: University of Notre Dame Press, 1990.

Winckelmann, Johann Joachim. *History of the Art of Antiquity.* Translated by Harry Francis Mallgrave, with an introduction by Alex Potts. Texts & Documents. Los Angeles: Getty Research Institute, 2006.

Wojna i pokój: Skarby sztuki tureckiej ze zbiorów polskich od XV do XIX wieku; Wystawa zorganizowana przez Muzeum Narodowe w Warszawie, Warszawa, 25 lutego–3 maja 2000 roku. Exhibition catalog. Warsaw: Muzeum Narodowe, 2000.

Wolff, Larry. *Inventing Eastern Europe: The Map of Civilization on the Mind of the Enlightenment.* Stanford: Stanford University Press, 1994.

Wraxall, N. William, Esq. *Memoirs of the Courts of Berlin, Dresden, Warsaw, and Vienna in the Years 1777, 1778, and 1779.* 2 vols. London: T. Cadell & W. Davies, 1799.

Zamoyski, Adam. *The Last King of Poland.* London: Phoenix, 1992.

Zawadzki, Stanisław. Letter of Stanisław Zawadzki to Ignacy Potocki, 13 II 1782. Archiwum Główne Akt Dawnych, Archiwum Publiczne Potockich, MS 279a/470. Warsaw.

INDEX

Page numbers in *italics* indicate illustrations.